HAYEK'S BASTARDS

ALSO IN THE *NEAR FUTURES* SERIES

Portfolio Society: On the Capitalist Mode of Prediction
IVAN ASCHER

Undoing the Demos: Neoliberalism's Stealth Revolution
WENDY BROWN

Markets in the Making:
Rethinking Competition, Goods, and Innovation
MICHEL CALLON

Counterrevolution:
Extravagance and Austerity in Public Finance
MELINDA COOPER

Family Values:
Between Neoliberalism and the New Social Conservatism
MELINDA COOPER

Discounting the Future:
The Ascendancy of a Political Technology
LILIANA DOGANOVA

Rated Agency: Investee Politics in a Speculative Age
MICHEL FEHER

Market Civilizations: Neoliberals East and South
QUINN SLOBODIAN & DIETER PLEHWE

Hayek's Bastards: Race, Gold, IQ, and the Capitalism of the Far Right

Quinn Slobodian

ZONE BOOKS
633 Vanderbilt Street, Brooklyn, New York 11218

Printed in the United States of America.
Distributed by Princeton University Press, Princeton, New Jersey

Library of Congress Cataloging-in-Publication Data
Names: Slobodian, Quinn, 1978– , author.
Title: Hayek's bastards : race, gold, IQ, and the capitalism of the far right / Quinn Slobodian.
Description: Brooklyn, New York : Zone Books, [2025] | Series: Near futures | Includes bibliographical references and index. | Summary: "The story of the American Right is often told as the fusion of the free market and religion. Yet recent decades have seen the rise of a new fusionism which turns to nature and science to defend naturalized inequality and the Social Darwinist virtues of competition" —Provided by publisher.
Identifiers: LCCN 2024036155 (print) | LCCN 2024036156 (ebook) | ISBN 9781890951917 (hardcover) | ISBN 9781890951931 (ebook)
Subjects: LCSH: Hayek, Friedrich A. von (Friedrich August), 1899–1992—Influence. | Economics—Political aspects. | Scientific racism. | Equality. | Right-wing extremists. | BISAC: HISTORY / United States / 21st Century | BUSINESS & ECONOMICS / Economics / Theory
Classification: LCC HB74.P65 S5795 2025 (print) | LCC HB74.P65 (ebook) | DDC 330—dc23/eng/20241120
LC record available at https://lccn.loc.gov/2024036155
LC ebook record available at https://lccn.loc.gov/2024036156

CONTENTS

INTRODUCTION

Volk Capital

> Together, we are promoting a new fusionism that argues that there are—as Mises knew—iron links between culture, economics, and politics.
> —Lew Rockwell

In 2006, Charles Murray, the longtime think-tanker and tireless advocate of a revived race science, gave the keynote address at a "Freedom Dinner" marking the twenty-fifth anniversary of the international hub for neoliberal think tanks, the Atlas Economic Research Foundation. A member of the Mont Pelerin Society (MPS) since 2000, Murray used his time to rehearse the well-worn story of how Ronald Reagan and Margaret Thatcher provided the opportunity for the ideas of Friedrich Hayek, Ludwig von Mises, and Milton Friedman to break through, aided by "Cato and Heritage and Hoover and the dozens of think tanks around the world that Atlas has fostered."[1] Projecting forward, Murray asked what they would be discussing at an Atlas meeting on its fiftieth anniversary in 2031. It would not be economic liberty, free trade, the genius of the entrepreneur, or any of the other standbys of the neoliberal script. He predicted they would be talking about science.

"For the last forty years," he said, "the battle cry of the Left has been 'equality.'" Science would deal the death blow to this demand. "The explosive growth of genetic knowledge," he said, "means that within a few years science will definitively demonstrate precisely how it is that women are different from men, blacks from whites, poor from rich, or, for that matter, the ways in which the Dutch are different from Italians." If the enemy, at its root, was the claim of human equality, science would deliver the coup de grace. The confirmation of ineradicable group differences would leave a void "in the moral universe of the Left," Murray predicted. "If social policy cannot be built on the premise that group differences must be eliminated, what can it be built upon?"[2] The same year that he gave the talk, he argued in one of his rare peer-reviewed articles that the persistence of Black/white intelligence differences made affirmative action untenable.[3]

A few years later, Murray expanded on the theme at a meeting of the Mont Pelerin Society in an exotic location: the Galápagos Islands. The name of the meeting was "Evolution, the Human Sciences, and Liberty" and his talk was titled "the rediscovery of human nature and human diversity," a process that he claimed was going to happen because of new discoveries in genetics. These would induce "reversions to age-old understandings about the human animal." This would lead to the reconfirmation of discredited prejudices as scientific truths. He dwelled on the question of racial difference. "Throughout the 19th century and first half of the 20th century," he wrote, "physical anthropologists accepted the concept of race with little dissension." Carleton Coon's magnum opus, *The Origin of Races* (1962) "provoked no outrage when it appeared," he claimed. (Not true; in fact, it "sparked enormous controversy in the anthropological community.")[4] Two events led to what he called "the intellectual eclipse of human nature and human diversity in the United States": the civil rights movement and the feminist movement.[5] Political developments had since obscured the primal origins of difference between not only the races but the sexes. Appealing to the sociobiology and evolutionary psychology developed at Harvard University by E. O. Wilson, Robert L. Trivers, and his students, Leda Cosmides and John Tooby (the latter two who were in attendance in the Galapagos), Murray claimed that we still bore binary gender differences as an inheritance of the savanna. "Men who could process trajectories in three dimensions—the trajectory, say, of a spear thrown at an edible mammal—had a survival advantage," he said in Ecuador. "Women did the gathering. Those who could distinguish among complex arrays of vegetation, remembering which were the poisonous plants and which the nourishing ones, also had a survival advantage." This is why, he claimed, "elevated three-dimensional visuospatial skills" for men and "an elevated ability to remember objects and their relative locations" for women "show up on tests of these abilities today." Going back to nature was necessary to reaffirm hierarchies hardwired into genetics challenged by insurgent social movements and progressive ideologies. Shattering taboos around race and gender differences was necessary not only to fight the pernicious effects of what Murray called the "Equality Premise" but to better recognize and organize patterns of aptitude in a changing economy.[6]

This book argues that the appeal to nature was a central part of the neoliberal solution to a problem they faced in the decades after the Cold War. This was an era in which communism was dead but, as they put it, Leviathan lived on. Public spending continued to expand even as capitalism became the only surviving economic system. Behind this was a political problem. The social movements of the 1960s and 1970s had injected the poison of civil rights, feminism, affirmative action, and ecological consciousness into the veins of the body politic. An atmosphere of political correctness and "victimology" stultified free discourse and nurtured a culture of government dependency and special pleading. Neoliberals needed an antidote.

Confounded by persistent demands for the redress of inequality at the expense of efficiency, stability, and order, neoliberals turned to nature in matters of race, intelligence, territory, and money as a way to erect a bulwark against the encroaching demands of progressives and hopefully roll back social changes to return to a hierarchy of gender, race, and cultural difference they imagined to be rooted in genetics as well as tradition.

Neoliberals had always been concerned with the extra-economic conditions for capitalism's survival, but they had usually focused on law, religion, and morality. The growing influence of Friedrich Hayek's ideas of cultural evolution and the mainstream popularity of neuroscience and evolutionary psychology led many to turn to the harder sciences. Changing demographics—an aging white population matched by an expanding nonwhite population—made some right-wing neoliberals and libertarians rethink the conditions necessary for capitalism. Perhaps some cultures, and even some races, might be predisposed to market success while others were not? Perhaps cultural homogeneity was a precondition for social stability, and thus the peaceful conduct of market exchange and enjoyment of private property?

I call the new strain of the neoliberal movement that crystallized in the 1990s the "new fusionism." While the original fusionism of the 1950s and 1960s and the New Right melded libertarianism and religious traditionalism in the style of William F. Buckley and the *National Review*, the new fusionism defended neoliberal policies through arguments borrowed from cognitive, behavioral, and evolutionary psychology and in some cases genetics, genomics, and biological anthropology.[7] As early as 1987 the conservative historian Paul Gottfried, who coined the term "alternative right" with Richard Spencer, identified that new fusionism on the Right. Whereas older conservatives may have used a language of religion to back up claims about human differences, Gottfried noted that they had begun to use disciplines like sociobiology, the discipline created by ecologist E.O. Wilson to, in Wilson's words, "biologicize" questions of human ethics.[8] New fusionism uses the language of science to justify the extension of competitive dynamics ever deeper into social life.

FRONTLASH, NOT BACKLASH

Identifying the rise of new fusionism offers a new story about the resurgence of the Far Right in recent years. While it has become popular to describe a "backlash" against forces of neoliberal globalization, attention to the unlikely coalitions described in this book offer a different picture.[9] As we will see, new fusionists formed alliances with advocates of traditionalism, nationalism, and cultural homogeneity. Among the new fusionists we find self-described "paleolibertarians" who sought to build their claims on the bedrock of biology and immutable differences. The right-wing neoliberals who joined, and in some cases founded, new populist parties did not reject the dynamic of market competition; they deepened it. "Closed borders" libertarians continued to demand free movement for capital and goods; they simply drew a hard line against certain kinds of people. As I argue in chapter 3, the demand for an ethnostate was better understood as the demand for an "ethno-economy."

New fusionism gathered steam in the disorienting era that followed the end of the Cold War. Existing studies of neoliberalism account poorly for the period that neoliberals were supposedly at their peak: the 1990s and 2000s. It was then, we are told, that the neoliberals had routed their enemies, won the battle against communism, and conscripted international financial institutions to carry out their world-changing project. One could be excused for assuming there was not much left to explain. Neoliberals must have spent the decade polishing busts of Mises and Hayek to be placed in libraries and squares across Eastern Europe and gloating over their victories.[10] But this was not the case at all. In fact, looking back at the meetings of the neoliberals in the wake of Berlin Wall's fall and the Soviet collapse, one discovers something startling. They seemed to fear the Cold War had been lost.

"It is fitting that the Mont Pelerin Society, the world's leading group of free market scholars, was meeting the week that communism collapsed in the Soviet Union," the *Wall Street Journal* reported in September 1991, but those gathered saw that as "Communism exits history's stage, the main threat to liberty may come from a utopian environmental movement that, like socialism, views the welfare of human beings as subordinate to 'higher' values."[11] Communism was a chameleon. It was changing shades from red to green. "Having fought back a red tide, we are now in danger of being engulfed by a green one," warned Fred Smith of the Competitive Enterprise Institute at a Mont Pelerin Society meeting a decade later. "The forces that once marched under the banner of economic progressivism have regrouped under a new environmental banner."[12]

Interviewed by the journalist and later restrictionist firebrand Peter Brimelow in 1992, Milton Friedman expressed a similar sentiment. Asked about the Cold War's end, he responded: "Look at the reaction in the U.S. to the collapse of the Berlin Wall.... There weren't any summit meetings in Washington about how to cut down the size of government. What was there a summit meeting about? How to increase government spending. What was the supposedly rightwing President, Mr. Bush, doing? Presiding over enormous increases in paternalism—the Clean Air Act and the Americans with Disabilities Act, the so-called Civil Rights quota bill."[13] Friedman saw ecological protection and the "special interests" of disabled people and minorities as the growth areas for postcommunist statism.

LEVIATHAN LIVES

"The enemy has mutated," wrote the economist Victoria Curzon-Price, one of the Mont Pelerin Society's only three female presidents. "In 1947 the founders of our Society battled with outright communism, planning and hard Keynesianism. Today our opponents are more elusive."[14] At the very first meeting of the MPS after the wall fell in Berlin, held a train ride away in Munich, the president and Italian economist Antonio Martino declared that "socialism is dead, statism is not."[15] The three biggest threats were environmentalism, state spending, and European integration. On the first, those in attendance heard that the depletion of ozone layer could just as well be due to kelp beds, ocean currents, and volcanoes as human activity.[16] More pressing was the problem of Europe. The supranational institutions that had once promised to be engines of what Curzon-Price called "the Ferrari model of integration"—speeding up competition between labor, product, and finance markets—had proved to be socialist Trojan horses.[17] The parallel of the unification of Europe to the dissolution of the Soviet bloc struck many libertarians as uncanny and frightening. "It would be an irony of history," German historian of science Gerard Radnitzky said at the MPS meeting in Munich, "if, at the time when the 'postsocialist' countries attempt to de-socialize, to make the transition to freedom, a European super-state should embark on the road to more government and more bureaucracy, to creeping socialism and hence to less freedom and less growth."[18]

Europe was only part of the problem. "Leviathan not only lives," Radnitzky wrote, "but has been growing."[19] At the next year's meeting, the new president, University of Chicago economist Gary Becker, repeated the refrain: "The mission of the MPS may appear to have been largely accomplished with the collapse of communism in most of Eastern Europe.... But unfortunately much remains to be done. The vast majority of the world's populations still live in countries that sharply curtail both economic and political freedoms. And even in the democratic countries of Western Europe, the U.S., and elsewhere, government control and regulation of economic activities is expanding, not contracting."[20]

Part of the problem for neoliberals was that they had been so concentrated on their opponent that they had not spent enough time reflecting on what day one in their utopia would look like. The neoliberal quandary at the Cold War's end was that decades of "collectivism" and state dependency—even in the capitalist world—had eroded the virtues of self-reliance that would allow for the reproduction of social life. Speaking at the fiftieth anniversary meeting of the MPS at the Hoover Institution in 1997, the president of the Bradley Foundation, MPS member Michael S. Joyce, said that "attention has consistently failed to focus on a very important and very sobering reality. Were we tomorrow to have the political forces to dismantle the welfare state, and should we set about dismantling it, we would face a frightening but unavoidable fact: behind the welfare state, there is almost nothing."[21]

Neoliberals' own logic dictated that the dependency produced by the nanny state had left thin roots where the dense connective tissue of community and family should be. "The mechanisms which existed prior to the welfare state and in some measure served to fulfill its functions are gone," Joyce observed. This posed a problem: "the fuzzy and attractive promise that the private sector and the free market will fill the gap instantly—like Athena sprung fully born from Zeus—thus replacing the welfare state and making the new order acceptable to our citizens is an utter chimera."[22] Here we find something remarkable. It was not just that neoliberals denied they had won the Cold War. They were afraid of the reality that would result if they actually *had*.

SOCIAL OPIUM AND THE HUMAN ANIMAL

Charles Murray expanded on this theme in a paper circulated for a Mont Pelerin Society meeting in Cancún, Mexico in 1996. Because "a radical liberal reform... now seems potentially within reach in the United States," neoliberals needed to think about "how a liberal state may be expected to deal with the human suffering that persists after liberal policies are in place." Murray, no doubt mindful of the enormously disruptive process being unleashed by economic shock therapy in post-Soviet Russia as he wrote, approvingly quoted Herbert Spencer's analogy of society to a drug-addicted human: "the transition from state beneficence to a healthy condition of self-help and private beneficence must be like the transition from an opium-eating life to a normal life—painful but remedial."[23]

The paragraph from which the quote came was brutal in its negative eugenic judgment. "Having, by unwise institutions, brought into existence large numbers who are unadapted to the requirements of social life, and are consequently sources of misery to themselves and others," Spencer wrote in 1898, "we cannot repress and gradually diminish this body of relatively worthless people without inflicting much pain. Evil has been done and the penalty must be paid."[24] Here he cites the "social opium-eating" of welfare and state assistance as only a delay of the inevitable withdrawal and "misery." One could hope that the addict would recover. As Murray pointed out, many neoliberals claimed that "the last thirty years represent an aberration which goes against human nature, and all that is required for health is to stop the poison and let the healing process begin." Yet these remained hypotheses, and "scholars have yet to flesh them out with data."[25] It was precisely because neoliberals were so close to success that they needed to look with clear eyes at the painful transition out of the world of the social state. Would recovery of the masses be possible or, as in Spencer's calculus, was the very existence of the dependent population a problem in need of solution?

In the 1990s, neoliberals and libertarians argued that the future society had to be constructed from ground zero. It was necessary to return to first principles, to open a wide-ranging discussion on the human condition and the prerequisites for market order. This meant a shift in focus. "It is of the utmost importance that we get away from the tendency to give too much weight to purely economic issues," Mont Pelerinians Pascal Salin and Henri Lepage wrote. "We must diversify our intellectual outlook by calling more on academics from other disciplines: historians, philosophers, political scientists, lawyers, anthropologists. Our choice of topics should be enlarged to more philosophical, political or sociological issues."[26]

Enter science and the return to nature. "Much of liberal thought has assumed that the human animal is fitted for liberalism everywhere and under all circumstances," Murray wrote. "If liberal institutions are in place, right behavior will follow. Perhaps it will be more difficult to install those institutions in some cultures in others but, once installed, they will work their magic. Is this really the case? I am cautiously optimistic. I think that, over the very long run—centuries perhaps—the assumption is in fact true. But it is much less obviously true in the short run. Can Russia become a prosperous liberal state in the foreseeable future no matter what laws are put on the books? Can

Iran? Can Tanzania? Can Peru? Just listing the countries serves to emphasize how different are the cultural obstacles that each must surmount." Murray wrote that "it is now beyond serious scientific dispute that a great many of the most individual human capacities are fixed before a person reaches an age at which they have any control over the matter.... Of the variation attributable to the environment after birth, much is determined within the first few years of life—probably within the first months of life. This combination of genetic and early environmental influences is so powerful that IQ scores stabilize around the age of six, before anyone can be called an independent moral actor."[27] The advantages that led to long-term prosperity were implanted deeply in particular cultures and could not be extracted or replicated easily.

EVOLUTIONARY LIBERTARIANISM

Gerard Radnitzky elaborated this approach when he said of the "evolutionary libertarianism" of Hayek and the Austrian school was that "its central tenet is the claim that *there is a human nature*, and it is part of our phylogenetic inheritance." Against this he posed the socialist belief that the human was "a blank slate whose phylogenetic inheritance is negligible in comparison with the influence upon him of the social environment."[28] If this was a market fundamentalism, it was one firmly anchored in a belief in the science of nature and human difference.

Like Radnitzky, many new fusionists took inspiration from Hayek's immersion in themes of evolution, morality, and demography by the end of his life. As the first chapter argues, we cannot understand the enduring status of these themes in neoliberal discussions or the anointing of Charles Murray as the Friedrich Hayek Emeritus Chair in Cultural Studies at the American Enterprise Institute without diving into areas with which few noninitiates are familiar.[29] Yet I question the legitimacy of intellectual parentage claimed by these thinkers. In 1993, the Canadian intellectual John Ralston Saul recounted the tortuous history of reason and rationality in Western philosophy and politics in a book called *Voltaire's Bastards.*[30] In partial homage to this book that meant so much to me as a teenager scouring the shelves of used bookstores on an island off the Western edge of North America, I dub my cast of characters *Hayek's bastards* because so many lapse into the very intellectual errors that Hayek himself diagnosed. Above all is the danger of what Hayek called "scientism" and the "pretense of knowledge." Both intentionally and not, these thinkers paid poor tribute to their master. As later chapters show, those who turned to Hayek's own teacher, Ludwig von Mises, as their intellectual center of gravity also often misread and stretched the writings of their mentor to fit their politics. The point is not to salvage the honor of the Austrian school sages but to show how ideas are instrumentalized, adapted, and weaponized, taking different form in different contexts, while pedigrees hide mutations from generation to generation.

The scientization of neoliberal thought in the new fusionism is a further twist of the screw in the argument dominant since the 1930s that neoliberalism is not a doctrine of the market as much as what some of them call the *metamarket.* The flight to nature is an attempt to ground neoliberalism in something beyond the social. A key figure in the new fusionism of race theory and libertarianism was Murray himself, an MPS member and self-avowed libertarian, who has melded genetic pronouncements with bootstrapping family-values talk for over two decades and become beloved to the racialist Right. More directly engaged in politics was the self-described Austrian economist and libertarian Murray Rothbard, also an MPS member, who advised Republican presidential candidate Patrick J. Buchanan and outlined a strategy of "paleo-populism" in the early 1990s as a way of using electoral democracy as a transition to the libertarian goal of a stateless society. He pushed a hard line on racial difference and saw the dissolution of Yugoslavia, for example, as evidence that culturally homogeneous secession was the only viable form of organization.

Rothbard's intellectual heir Hans-Hermann Hoppe, a speaker at

MPS meetings, radicalized his mentor's program further, vilifying democracy as "the god that failed," proposing racial explanations for patterns of economic behavior, and creating forums for exchange between theorists of eugenics, ethnic secessionism, and Austrian economics. Hoppe was active in both the United States and Central Europe, acting as a bridge to dissident MPS members in Germany and Austria who sought to create their own alliances to the Right of the mainstream parties to counteract both European integration and the demographic threat of nonwhite immigration.

In Germany, the racialist Right position crystallized in the unlikely figure of a card-carrying Social Democrat and central bank board member in 2010. Thilo Sarrazin's book *Germany Abolishes Itself* has sold more than 1.5 million copies and draws on the same body of research as Murray, Rothbard, and Hoppe to make the case for race differences in cognitive capacity. Sarrazin's synthesis of free trade, independent monetary policy, and biological racism is the intellectual core of the insurgent Alternative for Germany (AfD) and Austrian Freedom Party. Hoppe's rhetoric of violent suppression of difference and program of racialized secession has been embraced by the alt-right.

Attention to the new fusionism and Hayek's bastards helps clear up some of the confused framing of politics in the last several years. Since the political surprises of the Brexit vote and Trump's victory in 2016, there has been a stubborn story that explains so-called right-wing populism as a grassroots rejection of neoliberalism, often described as market fundamentalism, or the belief that everything on the planet has a price tag, borders are obsolete, the world economy should replace nation-states, and human life is reducible to a cycle of earn, spend, borrow, die. This "New" Right, by contrast, claims to believe in the people, national sovereignty and the importance of culture. As mainstream parties lose support, the elites who promoted neoliberalism out of self-interest seem to be reaping the fruits of the inequality and democratic disempowerment they sowed.

But as this book helps make clear, this story does not capture the whole truth. By looking more closely, we can see that important factions of the emerging Right were, in fact, mutant strains of neoliberalism. The parties dubbed as right-wing populist, from the United States to Britain and Austria, have rarely been avenging angels sent to smite economic globalization. They offer few plans to rein in finance, restore a Golden Age of job security, or end world trade. By and large, the so-called populists' calls to privatize, deregulate, and slash taxes come straight from the playbook shared by the world's leaders for the past thirty years.[31]

Even more fundamentally, to understand neoliberalism as an apocalyptic hypermarketization of everything is both vague and misleading. As many histories now show, far from conjuring up a vision of capitalism without states, the neoliberals gathered around the Mont Pelerin Society founded by Hayek (who used the term "neoliberalism" as self-description into the 1950s) have reflected for nearly a century about how the state needs to be rethought to restrict democracy without eliminating it and how national and supranational institutions can be used to protect competition and exchange.[32] When we see neoliberalism as a project of retooling the state to save capitalism, then its supposed opposition to the populism of the Right begins to dissolve.

Both neoliberals and the New Right scorn egalitarianism, global economic equality, and solidarity beyond the nation. Both see capitalism as inevitable and judge citizens by the standards of productivity and efficiency. Perhaps most strikingly, both draw from the same pantheon of heroes. A case in point is Hayek himself, who is an icon on both sides of the neoliberal/populist divide. Speaking alongside Marine Le Pen at the party congress of the French National Front in 2018, self-described populist Steve Bannon condemned the "establishment" and the "globalists," yet built his speech around Hayek's own metaphor of the road to serfdom and invoked the authority of the master's name. "The central government, the central banks, the central crony capitalist technology companies control you and have taken you to a Road to Serfdom in three ways," he said. "The central banks are in the business of debasing your currency, the central government is in the business of debasing your citizenship, and the crony capitalist technological powers are in the business of debasing your own personhood. Hayek told us: the Road to Serfdom will come through these three."[33]

Less important than the barely discernible link to Hayek's actual writing was Bannon's reflexive appeal to the Austrian thinker for authority. In Zurich the week before, Bannon also summoned Hayek. There he was hosted by a newspaper publisher, right-wing Swiss People's Party politician, and member of the Friedrich Hayek Society, Roger Köppel, who presented Bannon with the first issue of their newspaper, *WirtschaftsWoche,* while whispering *sotto voce* that it was "from 1933"—a time when that very newspaper was supportive of the Nazi seizure of power. "Let them call you racists," Bannon said in his stump speech, "let them call you xenophobes. Let them call you nativists. Wear it as a badge of honor." The goal of the populists, he said, was not to maximize shareholder value but "maximize citizenship value."[34] This sounded less like a rejection of neoliberalism than a deepening of the economic logic into the heart of collective identity.

While in Europe, Bannon also met with Alice Weidel, former Goldman Sachs consultant and one of two heads of the right-wing populist Alternative for Germany (AfD) party, and a member of Germany's Friedrich A. Hayek Society until early 2021.[35] Another AfD member, a former libertarian blogger and gold consultant, Peter Boehringer, whose story is told at length in chapter 5, is also a Hayek Society member, Bundestag delegate from Amberg in Bavaria, and chair of the parliamentary budget committee. In September 2017, Bannon's former outlet, Breitbart.com, ran an interview with Beatrix von Storch, the AfD's deputy party leader and another Hayek Society member. She explained how Hayek had inspired her commitment to "rehabilitate the family."[36] In neighboring Austria, the negotiator on the right-wing Austrian Freedom Party's short-lived coalition with the

Austrian People's Party was the director of Vienna's Hayek Institute, Barbara Kolm.[37]

THE THREE HARDS OF THE NEW FUSIONISTS AND PALEOS

Naomi Klein memorably described neoliberalism as a "shock doctrine": swoop in at times of disaster, gut and sell off public services, and transfer control from states to corporations.[38] The Washington consensus described by the economist John Williamson in 1989 is perhaps the most famous example of neoliberal solutionism: a list of ten must-dos for developing countries from tax reform to trade liberalization to privatization.[39] From this perspective, neoliberalism can look like a recipe book, a panacea, and a one-size-fits-all nostrum. But the writings of neoliberals themselves offer a different picture—and this is where we must go to make sense of the apparently contradictory political manifestations. When we do, we discover that neoliberal thought is not filled with solutions but with problems. Can judges, dictators, bankers, or businesspeople be reliable guardians of economic order? Can institutions be made, or must they grow? How can markets be accepted by people in the face of their frequent cruelty?[40] Radnitzky captured the puzzle well in the epigraph to his paper from the MPS meeting in Munich. It was from Anthony de Jasay: "Democracy's last dilemma is that the state must, but cannot, roll itself back."[41]

Neoliberals disagreed about which institutions would safeguard capitalism from democracy. Some defended a return to the gold standard, while others argued that currencies should be free to float. Some fought for strong antitrust policies, others accepted some forms of monopolies. Some thought ideas should circulate freely, others made the case for strong intellectual property rights. Some thought religion was a necessary condition for a liberal society, others saw it as dispensable. Most saw the traditional family as the basic economic and social unit, but others disagreed. Some saw neoliberalism as a matter of designing the right constitution, others saw a constitution in a democracy as—in a memorably gendered metaphor from de Jasay—"a chastity belt whose key is always within the wearer's reach."[42]

Compared to other political and intellectual movements, however, it was the *absence* of serious sectarian splits within the neoliberal movement that was most remarkable. From the 1940s to the 1980s, the center more or less held. The sole major internal conflict came in the early 1960s with the estrangement of one of the movement's leading thinkers and so-called intellectual father of the social market economy, the German economist Wilhelm Röpke.[43] It foreshadowed later conflicts that Röpke's split with the other neoliberals happened amid his strident advocacy for apartheid South Africa and his adoption of theories of biological racism, which posited shared Western culture and shared heredity as the precondition for a functioning capitalist society.[44] While the open embrace of whiteness was an outlier position in the 1960s, this book shows that it would return to divide the neoliberals in the decades to come.

By the early 1980s Hayek had begun to speak of tradition as a necessary ingredient for the "good society." The question of the borders of groups defined by tradition became high stakes. In front of the Heritage Foundation, he spoke in 1982 of "our moral heritage" as the foundation for healthy market societies.[45] In 1984, he wrote that "we must return to a world in which not only reason, but reason and morals, as equal partners, must govern our lives, where the truth of morals is simply one moral tradition, *that of the Christian West,* which has created morals in modern civilization."[46] The implication was clear. Some societies had developed the cultural traits of personal responsibility, ingenuity, rational action, and low time preference over long periods; others had not. Because these traits were also not easily imported or transplanted, those less culturally evolved societies—in other words, the developing world—would need to experience a long period of diffusion before catching up to the West—an endpoint he was not guaranteeing would ever arrive.

The crises that followed 2008 created the conditions for new mutations of neoliberal thought—as well as new schisms. The arrival of more than one million refugees to Europe in the course of 2015 created the opportunity for a new winning political hybrid that combined xenophobia with free-market values. The new fix found in race, culture, and nation is the most recent strain of a promarket philosophy based not on the idea that we are all the same but that we are in a fundamental, and perhaps permanent way, different. An article about the rise of the Far Right in Germany was titled "between capital and Volk."[47] But it might make more sense to combine them, as their proponents do themselves. We could call it a language of *Volk capital.* New fusionists assign intelligence averages to countries in a way that collectivizes and renders innate the concept of "human capital." They add overtones of values and traditions that cannot be captured statistically, shading into a language of national essences and national character.

The turn to nature by the new fusionists and "paleos" is marked by *three hards*: hardwired human nature, hard borders, and hard money. It implied a search for origins in the savanna for both a universal humanity and one riven by group differences. It manifested in the focus on the extra-economic cultural prerequisites for a functioning market society given rise to an idea of what I call the *ethnoeconomy* alongside the more common term of the ethnostate. It involved the recasting of humanity into "cognitive classes," or what I call *neurocastes,* as intelligence was asserted as the new sorting mechanism for a postindustrial society. The return to nature also manifested in a faith in the superiority of gold as a medium of exchange and store of value in times of uncertainty, a form of money validated by not only history and economics but also anthropology, psychology, and its effect on morality. The last chapter in the book describes the rise of the goldbugs in the 1970s, when coin dealers, including U.S. politician Ron Paul, became influential ideological entrepreneurs. The 1990s saw a resurgence of interest in gold in a decade of often racialized fears of urban unrest and global civil war. After the global financial crisis in 2008, gold returned again as a hedge against the devaluation of currency and right-wing fears of President Barack Obama's putative socialism. Gold was hawked on the television shows of right-wing ideologues like Glenn Beck, who took a cut from the bars and shares sold to his viewers.[48] Driven by geopolitical and economic uncertainty, the value of gold rose above $2,000 an ounce in 2011 before falling, only to surge again during the Covid-19 pandemic in 2020 and in the years afterward to a historic high. Money never remained money even when it was minted in gold. Especially since 2008, figures in hard Right parties like the AfD have made gold into a new kind of morality, a marker of qualitative value with analogues in culture and race. Goldbugs offered a fiscal eschatology, a future read backward from the moment of a coming economic collapse.

This book shows that many contemporary iterations of the Far Right emerged *within* neoliberalism, not in opposition to it. They did not propose the wholesale rejection of globalism but a variety of it, one that accepts an international division of labor with robust cross-border flows of goods and even multilateral trade agreements while tightening controls on certain kinds of migration. As repellent as their politics may be, these radical thinkers are not barbarians at the gates of neoliberal globalism but the bastard offspring of that line of thought itself. The reported clash of opposites is a family feud.

CHAPTER ONE

Of Savannas and Satellites

> If we wish to free ourselves from the all-pervasive influence of the intellectual presumption that man in his wisdom has designed, or ever could have designed, the whole system of legal or moral rules, we should begin with a look at the primitive and even pre-human beginnings of social life.
> —Friedrich Hayek

> All life, beginning from the bacteria, exhibits "entrepreneurial spirit."
> —Gerard Radnitzky

In the Hotel Majestic in Cannes on the French Riviera in 1994, neoliberals gathered for one funeral and to decide if they should plan another. The first was for the Mont Pelerin Society (MPS)'s founder, F.A. Hayek, whose wake was organized in a way only intellectuals would do: as a debate about the validity and relevance of the ideas of the deceased. The second was for the society itself. Should it still exist? The secretary of the society circulated the question to its members. From 1964 to 1994 the overall membership had grown from 249 to 475, with ever more members drawn from the business and think-tank community. Across thirty years, the ratio of Americans had remained steady but there were fewer Brits and Germans while Latin American membership had tripled and Japanese membership more than quadrupled.[1]

Milton Friedman had famously proposed dissolving the society in the early 1980s after the victories of Reagan and Thatcher suggested that the big battles had been fought and won.[2] But at Cannes the members contended that the fight was not over. Threats to liberty persisted even after the end of communism. Chief among those were environmentalism, feminism, and the civil rights movement. More to the point was a question of what new intellectual tools would be best suited for these new challenges. The society's self-understood goal was "to facilitate an exchange of ideas between like-minded scholars in the hope of strengthening the principles and practice of a free society and to study the workings, virtues and defects of market oriented economic systems."[3] Among the suggestions were that they should diversify even further from economics and toward other disciplines. This is where the reconsideration of Hayek came in—and the question of natural humanity, instincts, and the tribe.

BETWEEN THE CHIMPANZEE TROOP AND THE WORLD

Someone who only knew Hayek as the author of *The Road to Serfdom* (1944) and *The Constitution of Liberty* (1960) might be surprised to find that one of the categories most discussed in Cannes was evolution. Although active in the field of economics in the 1930s, when he was himself a young man in his thirties, Hayek all but departed his native field with the publication of his best-known book, *The Road to Serfdom*. For the next half century Hayek could be described as a political philosopher, but one with the wandering and eclectic interests that he carried from the omnivorous culture of the conjoined seminar-coffeehouse complex of his interwar Vienna.

In the 1960s, Hayek began dabbling with the inclusion of evolution into his theories of social order. He absorbed insights from general system theory and cybernetics, freely creating analogies between the "order" found in animate and inanimate objects, the human and the nonhuman. He encouraged attention to ethology, the science of human behavior, and cultural anthropology.[4] Evolution became a means to think about the emergence of order and patterns over time.

He proposed that more functionally efficacious traits developed in groups through patterns of natural selection.[5]

For Hayek, the payoff in deploying evolution was how it helped explain the way that habits and actions happened regardless of human intention. Into the 1970s, he became especially preoccupied with what he called the "mirage of social justice" as the Kryptonite of human progress.[6] To give shape to his worldview, he told a story that would be highly influential among his followers. In what we could call the "savanna story," Hayek proposed a timeline whereby early humans lived first in small groups in tribal situations characterized by group interests and low levels of individuation. Over time, certain groups developed practices through spontaneous acts of trial and error that permitted them to exchange with other groups different from themselves, allowing for an extension of the division of labor and an ever more efficient use of the world's resources.

As what Hayek called the "extended order" expanded its reach, a perhaps lamentable but also necessary development took place, by which it became ever more necessary to be indifferent to those with whom one traded and ultimately, on whose efforts one's life depended. The solidarity of the village was inappropriate and impracticable in a modern age of long-distance trade. Attempting an overhead view of its complex machinations beggared human intelligence. The advantage gained was not only access to the products of an ever more highly developed and complex order but also a sense of individuality beyond the small group.

To seek a return to the original tiny collective was natural—it was hardwired into humans—but also potentially hugely destructive. Groups like the New Left activists of the 1960s tapped into the dormant primitive drive to their advantage. In a 1976 lecture in Australia that he would reprise two years later in apartheid South Africa, titled, "the atavism of social justice," Hayek said, "Socialists have the support of inherited instincts, while maintenance of the new wealth which creates the new ambitions requires an acquired discipline which the non-domesticated barbarians in our midst, who call themselves 'alienated,' refuse to accept although they still claim all its benefits."[7] The urgency for Hayek was his concern that the pursuit of such a program could ultimately lead to mass death. It was only by adhering to a "game" that "pays so little attention to justice but does so much to increase output" that a growing world population could sustain itself.[8] Mass mutual indifference was the secret to sustaining human civilization.

The mechanism Hayek identified for the progressive discovery of new techniques and practices to expand the ambit of production and exchange was what he called the "competitive selection of cultural institutions." Hoping to preempt accusations that he was resurrecting social Darwinism, he insisted that he was describing "not genetic evolution of innate qualities, but cultural evolution through learning—which indeed leads sometimes to conflicts with near-animal natural instincts."[9] Hayek's foregrounding of cultural rather than genetic evolution in his 1970s writings set the tone for many of his followers in the self-described Austrian movement in the United States. The effect was to lead Hayek to think ever more about the conditions of cultural imitation and development, through the lens of ethology, sociobiology, and system theory, but also cognitive psychology and political philosophy.

A consequence of Hayek's shift from genes to culture was to grant his followers a blank check for their own interpretations. What standards of veracity or empirical rigor might govern it were unclear. They had created a new subfield by analogy—a sandbox where they made their own rules, anticipating some of the atmosphere of the intellectual free-for-all that would reign in message boards and YouTube comment sections by the next millennium. The question of what to do with Hayek's idea of evolution outlasted Hayek himself. Those gathered in Cannes sought to understand the consequences of Hayek's theories. Talk of animal behavior, variation, and natural selection intersected with that of political organization and secession as neoliberals dowsed for a new space and a new form between the chimpanzee troop and the world.

Hayek once famously declared that he was "not a conservative."[10] In Cannes, Uruguayan economist Ramón Díaz set the tone by arguing that Hayek was indeed a conservative because he "believed that the key to understanding the world of spontaneous order lies in the theory of evolution, dealing with an age-long process of trial and error."[11] But the British political philosopher Norman Barry pointed out the tension in Hayek's version of evolution. Hayek rejected "the idea that human behavior is predictable through information coded in the genes" in favor of a Lamarckian evolutionary theory by which "acquired characteristics (successful adaptations to the environment) are stored in some kind of collective mind and inherited by succeeding generations." "Evolution," according to Hayek, "is a competitive struggle between groups and the phrase 'survival of the fittest' is perfectly descriptive of the process." Barry made the sharp point that "however much Hayek might wish to deny that he is a social Darwinist, his theory owes more than a little to that doctrine."[12]

Part of what made Hayek's theory resemble social Darwinism was his preoccupation with the group rather than the individual—which the average economist (and indeed the average population scientist) would be expected to prefer. Barry homed in on a tension in the evolutionary Hayek. While Hayek saw groups as the vessels of traditions that help determine economic success, he disdained groups as the principle of social and political organization. The group was the apparent protagonist of this theory but really they were supposed to be part of a global ensemble or chorus.

The group itself, or what Hayek called the "troop" in an echo of primatology, was bound by a common moral purpose but was handicapped by failing to grasp its own dependence on the macro order. Hayek's late work was, as Victoria Curzon-Prize noted in Cannes, defined by the opposition between the larger order and the "small horde or tribe."[13] Because Hayek's horizon was ultimately the world's "extended order," the group was never an end but a means, a subunit designed to plug into something larger. Groups made or broke the order, but seeing the group as the telos was the root of destructive socialism. Hayek seemed to demand something elusive: a small group without the group feeling that might move in the direction of sharing, a society absent of demands for social justice, a troop with no impulse toward redistribution: communal cohesion without a sense of community.

Neoliberals searched the animal kingdom for clues. In Cannes the philosopher of science Gerard Radnitzky proposed a solution by arguing that it was selfishness rather than solidarity that was the most primal instinct. "From ethology," he argued, "we know that respect for property is a human constant, and a counterpart of it is found in the behavior of our simian ancestors and in the form of territoriality even in many lower animals." Property had "a genetic basis," he insisted, and it was "respected in chimpanzee hordes."[14] Going even further, he suggested elsewhere that "all life, beginning from the bacteria, exhibits 'entrepreneurial spirit.'"[15]

"The litmus test," Radnitzky said, "is whether a principle that is useful or indispensable for the small group can be transposed to the anonymous society, without ruining the society."[16] What he called elsewhere "Stone Age metaphysics" developed "as a successful adaptation to the ecology of the late Pleistocene," so "it was "no wonder that this 'solidarity' norm system is deeply ingrained in our emotion."[17] It was a balancing act to make use of the centripetal forces of instinct and hardwired human nature without it tampering excessively with the centrifugal thrust that defined material progress and global division of labor. Even some of Hayek's sympathetic readers found that by the time of his later work his arguments had developed a circularity. Especially in *The Fatal Conceit*, published in 1988, the superior order was deemed to be that which produced the most human lives. As the philosopher of science Jean Dupuy said in Cannes, "If the greatest number becomes the criterion of truth and efficiency, then whatever evolution may do, it will always be right."[18]

THE MULTIPLICATION OF MANKIND

The assertion that all human development was tending toward the market order did other things too. As the Australian political theorist Kenneth Minogue pointed out, it smuggled in a telos even though Hayek professed to follow open-ended nomocratic principles without predetermined outcomes rather than teleocratic principles that declared the endpoint in advance.[19] It also took for granted that evolution could never develop in ways other than those Hayek approved of. There was a careful balance in Hayek's thought between that which happened regardless of human intention and the moments when humans needed to consciously intervene. This, as Minogue noted, was reminiscent of the Marxist distinction between determinism and voluntarism.

But if one granted that humans could intervene consciously then who was to say they would make choices consistent with the final outcome of the greatest lives? "Why ought we to cooperate with nature?" Minogue asked at a Mont Pelerin Society meeting in Sydney. "It is, after all, frequently both nasty and wasteful and human beings belong to a moral world in which mere survival is not enough. Even if the market process were to be recognized as the unique generator of prosperity, we retain the option of preferring other things to prosperity."[20]

Postmaterial values, religion in its nonacquisitive form, solidarity, and sacrifice were all qualities that Hayek's model assumed away. Perhaps most troublesome for Minogue was the style of argument sanctioned by the appeal to nature as ultima ratio. Rather than try to persuade others of your version of the good life, the tendency of Hayek's mode "is not to argue against competing ways of arranging society, but actually to rule them out of court as misunderstandings of reality." The problem as Minogue saw it was that this was not actually a political way of thinking. Rather, it created a "cordon sanitaire between the activity of politics on the one hand and the principle of the new social order on the other" and suggested that the new world would arise parallel to the scrum of interests, alliances, and persuasion. In some not-so-distant future, "mankind will have discovered the right way for human beings to live" and will do so "beyond the sphere of politics."[21]

For conservatives like Minogue there was also the concern that Hayek was instrumentalizing religion and tradition. Beginning in the early 1980s, Hayek made ever more reference to the need for morality as an anchor for market order. As Wendy Brown and Jessica Whyte have written, it was "markets and morality," not markets in the place of morality, that became his central theme.[22] Yet the way he talked about religion was enough to give a conservative pause. It was hard to shake the impression that Hayek saw morality as having little meaning for its own sake. He conceded this himself when he said that "we have to recognize that we owe our civilization to beliefs which I sometimes have offended some people by calling 'superstitions' and which I now prefer to call 'symbolic truths.'"[23] Why were these symbolic truths important and how had they prevailed in long-term processes of cultural "selection"? They facilitated the competitive order. "Our morals," he wrote, "the morals which have prevailed, the morals of private property and honesty, are simply those that favor the practices that assist the multiplication of mankind."[24]

To conservatives this functional reduction of religion was galling. They remained skeptical of new fusionists like Hayek, who seemed happy to conscript religion into the advancement of their project but only as a junior partner subordinate to a larger process (i.e., evolution) derived from scientific reasoning. As Minogue pointed out, conservatives did not desire the return to a "fancied golden age of the past"—which is how he saw them as distinguished from reactionaries—but they did "take their bearings from the past" and took inherited tradition and morality as repositories of "concrete identity" that "reveal to us what we are" rather than a means of getting to a catallaxy itself yet to be revealed.[25]

FINDING COMMON GROUND

Many of the conversations within neoliberal circles in the 1980s and 1990s entailed conservatives and economic liberals sniffing around each other trying to see to what extent they could discover enough common ground to form a common front against what John Davenport called "the barbarian collectivist at the gate" without sacrificing too many of their principles.[26] For those more inclined to liberalism, the reason to connect themselves to tradition linked directly to the dynamics of the savanna story. As Mont Pelerinian Spanish economist Pedro Schwartz said, Hayek and Karl Popper put "the African savanna [operating] through tribal solidarity, cooperative hunting behavior and defense of territory" at one end of the spectrum and "the faceless, competitive society created by capitalism" at the other. This meant that "the capitalist society, with its cosmopolitanism, its judgement of worth by results, and its acceptance of consumer choice, is in some ways unnatural and therefore always precarious."[27] An alliance with conservatives over religion and tradition made sense, even strategically, as an insurance policy against the atomizing and disrupting effects of untampered market competition. In addition to these more abstract concerns, Melinda Cooper has outlined in detail the many ways that neoliberals intent on offloading the costs of social reproduction from the state would advocate socially conservative values that substituted the "private Keynesianism" of the intergenerational and extended family for the welfare state.[28]

The American conservative Ernest van den Haag laid out the logic at a 1984 MPS meeting: "When it fosters too much diversity, freedom also threatens to erode the viability of society. Societies are formed by custom and tradition; they subsist on the sentiments generated, and by the internalization thereof. No society can survive without a fairly wide range of shared fundamental values beyond freedom itself." "Because we are able to analyze social organization rationally," he wrote, "we too easily forget the nonrational sentiments of identification and solidarity which are indispensable to human association and must be nourished by tradition."[29] One could say that Hayek was persuaded by these arguments. The standard line in neoliberal discussions by the end of the 1980s was that it was not a question of whether tradition and morality were necessary for healthy market order but how much was necessary. Finding the right balance was the quest.

SETTLED SATELLITES, NOT SPACESHIP EARTH

The economist and president of the Mont Pelerin Society from 1984 to 1986, James M. Buchanan, explored this problem of calibration and design in 1997 when he turned the metaphor of the savanna into one of satellites. The earth's surface, he wrote, had "a gravitational force that embodies the genetic constraints of the species, pulling persons and groups toward behavior, one with another, that is dictated by hard wired elements in their nature." The earth wanted us to be tribes defined by race and ethnicity. He did not deny the pull of this pole. "We are, and must remain, human animals," he said. We neglected this fact at our peril. Yet to surrender to gravity would mean the earth's surface divided into "fully autonomous separate states"—a settlement he saw as destined for zero-sum war and conflict. At the other end of gravity's spectrum was the void of deep space and what he saw as the equally destructive model of a "centralized unitary polity," what we could call a globalist world government.[30] Such a model, he said, was denying gravity, dooming us to obliterate ourselves in the vacuum of space.

The task was to design satellites that would glide between these two poles, respondent to both the hard facts of human nature and the need for economic exchange. In a way the vision is quite anodyne, seemingly reminiscent of much of the reflection on global order in the twentieth century. Yet recall that the standard way of describing the world since the 1960s was as a single spaceship, or "spaceship Earth" in the metaphor of Adlai Stevenson, Barbara Ward, Buckminster

Fuller, and later so many others.[31] What does it mean to think of many satellites? Buchanan's metaphor reflects a kind of truth about how the problem of political order continues to be imagined: his satellites are *piloted, peopled, populated*; they are not communications nodes but off-earth settlements that remain mobile, spinning with the earth, and dialed in, responsive to signals from the earth's surface, sucking up resources and sending down packets of finished products, processed information, in communication with other space settlements.

Consider where the different metaphors push us. The logic of the spaceship metaphor pushes toward cooperation. However hierarchical, we are all part of a single crew. We each have our role in maintaining the craft. There is a bridge where all the signals are available at the eyeballs and fingertips of the captain. Buchanan's stratosphere of settled satellites, by his own description, is not ruled by cooperation but by competition. The rules of the cosmic avenues prevent collisions and protocols govern exchange, but intimacy is kept at arm's length. It should be clear that despite the Space Age metaphor, Buchanan's vision was less speculation than description. By the early twenty-first century this was to a great extent the way that world order worked: states were both networked and isolated, separate but global. Borders were semipermeable. Some materials were welcomed onto the settled satellites, others were not. Buchanan was adamant in his own prescriptions that though devolution was necessary—the satellites must multiply—they must not follow too closely the tug of human nature toward sameness. Building polities on ethnic or racial lines would tempt fate, risk the fiery crash of the space stations in low orbit.

In their attraction to themes of evolution, cultural affinity, and anthropological axioms, we can see late twentieth-century neoliberals in a dangerous dance, a flirtation with the pull of gravity. Hayek was more explicit than normal when he argued in 1984, as mentioned earlier, that there was "simply one moral tradition, that of the Christian West, which has created morals in modern civilization."[32] But if only one part of the world had the claim on morality, was the rest of the world destined to only passively adopt the more adaptive mutations of the "Christian West"? Were all populations equally capable of such adoption? As the next chapter shows, the neoliberals were divided in their answer to this question. What emerged was the most radical strain of new fusionism, setting off on a path that led directly to the alt-right.

CHAPTER TWO

The Rock of Biology

This is a revolution of white Euro-males.

—Murray Rothbard on Patrick Buchanan's campaign, 1995

Debates over savannas and satellites were debates over the nature of human difference. What was the basis for inclusion and exclusion from the group? How deeply were traits hardwired into human beings? In neoliberal circles, these discussions surged first in the 1960s amid challenges to the racialized hierarchy of world order.[1] Within the United States they emerged in response to the attacks of the New Left and the civil rights movement on the twin pillars of capitalist property relations and Jim Crow racial segregation. As mentioned in the preceding chapter, Friedrich Hayek saw young activists as mobilized by the atavistic demand of social justice. Pushing back at such egalitarian visions, some neoliberals appealed to what they cast as the immovable rock of biology.

One of the most high-profile right-wing mobilizations in recent years is the so-called alt-right in the United States. Using a shortened version of the "alternative Right" moniker coined in 2008 by Paul Gottfried and Richard Spencer, the alt-right gained public attention during the presidential election campaign in 2016 as a heterogeneous collection of white nationalists, neo-Nazis, male supremacists, neo-reactionaries, paleoconservatives, online trolls, and anarcho-capitalists existing to the Right of the mainstream conservative movement. Scholars have identified different origins for the alt-right. Some connect it to the European New Right associated with the French thinker Alain De Benoist, whose response to 1968 was a conscious attempt to adapt the Italian Marxist Antonio Gramsci's tactic of what he called "metapolitics" to the causes of the Right. Others find its origins in the welter of patriot groups and conspiratorial publics expanding in the United States since the 1990s. Others follow Gottfried's own cues to emphasize the "right wing critics of American conservatism" since the Cold War's end; the alt-right becomes a more overtly racist heir to the Old Right and the "populism" of Patrick Buchanan.[2] This chapter offers its own analysis by focusing on the alt-right's anarcho-capitalist or right-wing libertarian faction.

As we will see, the incorporation of right-wing libertarians into the alt-right coalition was the result of a schism in the neoliberal movement in response to the egalitarian challenge of the 1960s, a fission of the "thought collective" under the pressure of the questions of nature and group belonging described in the previous chapter. As the welfare state expanded, civil rights were institutionalized, the New Left condemned domestic and international inequality, and neoliberals attacked what they saw as the Left's faulty premises: the perfectibility of humans through state intervention and the possibility of a future equality of not only starting points but also outcomes. Taking aim at what they saw as the "collectivism" and "blank slate" ideology of both student radicals and mainstream social democrats, neoliberals emphasized the basic inequality of human capacity and the stubborn persistence of individual and group differences. Yet—crucially—neoliberals split in identifying the key variable of difference.

One group of Austrian economists, linked to Murray Rothbard and culminating in alt-right libertarianism, saw difference as rooted in biology and race as a rigid hierarchy of group traits and abilities. The other group of Austrian economists, associated with F. A. Hayek, took a cultural turn. Performing their own critique of "economism," they perceived human nature as rooted primarily in culture, adaptable over time through social learning and selective evolution. In the process of the rupture the balance between the savanna and the satellites tipped, and a vision of racial segregation was resurrected.

THE CHIMERA OF EQUALITY IN GSTAAD

We can begin the story in 1971, when the Institute for Humane Studies (IHS) under its chairman, the libertarian philanthropist and businessman Charles Koch, hosted what it called the First Symposium on Human Differentiation. The IHS, founded in 1961, was based in Menlo Park, California, a mile from the campus of Stanford University. One of the presenters at the symposium was Murray Rothbard, an economics professor then in his mid-forties, who was also active in the neoliberal think-tank world, having become a member of the Mont Pelerin Society in the 1950s and worked for the Foundation for Economic Education. Rothbard was also a key figure in the formation of the Austrian school of economics in the United States and a leading figure in what in this book I am calling the "new fusionism."

While Rothbard had entertained a brief hope that he might be able to win over the young radicals of the 1960s to the libertarian cause, by the time of his presentation in 1971, he was in full backlash mode. He upbraided the New Left for their romanticization of the simple life. Civilization, he reminded his audience, was all about specialization, and yet people were withdrawing to communes to do a little of everything. Mao Zedong was sending city youth to the countryside. Cuban intellectuals were learning to work the land. In the United States, "hundreds of thousands of herd-like, undifferentiated youth wallowed passively in the mud listening to their tribal ritual music." The trend for astrology and mysticism was a sign of a return to "primitive forms of magic." He condemned the "passivity of the New Left, its wish to live simply and in 'harmony' with 'the earth' and the alleged rhythms of nature... it is a conscious rejection of civilization and differentiated men on behalf of the primitive, the ignorant, the herd-like 'tribe.'"[3] Young radicals were shredding the lessons of Hayek's savanna story.

Rothbard conscripted the Austrian economist and his mentor Ludwig von Mises for his argument, quoting him as asserting in 1922 that "primitive man lacks all individuality in our sense. Two South Sea Islanders resemble each other far more closely than two twentieth-century Londoners. Personality was not bestowed upon man at the outset. It has been acquired in the course of evolution of society." Rothbard believed that the egalitarianism of the 1960s New Left was both "antihuman" and "evil." It sought to strip mankind of the fruits of civilizational advancement, namely, the emergence of individuality and human diversity. The economist Karl Polanyi, too, was criticized for his "worship of the primitive." Because humans were unequal, some were simply more gifted than others. Elites must be respected: "the only sensible course is to abandon the chimera of equality and accept the universal necessity of leaders and followers."[4]

While the first Symposium on Human Differentiation was held at the Institute of Paper Chemistry in Wisconsin, the second venue boosted the glamor considerably by gathering at the Swiss resort town of Gstaad. The topic of the conference was "the nature and consequences of egalitarian ideology," and it followed a meeting of the Mont Pelerin Society in Montreux, an hour's drive down the mountain. Most of those presenting were MPS members. Each held forth on their own variation of why equality was a destructive fantasy. Many appealed to genetics and race.

Gustavo Velasco, an MPS member from Mexico, saw genetic inequalities as a limit to "what can be done to equalize man's capacities and conditions."[5] Humans were equal only in the sense that they were all bipedal with opposable thumbs and relatively large crania. After that, it was difference. Louis Rougier, who had worked closely with the Vichy regime and was an MPS member after the war, argued that the idea of the human as "tabula rasa" was the legacy of Rousseau, Descartes, and Babeuf, a fairy tale that had enchanted the hippies most recently but that denied the hard constraints of the "genotype" and its variations. This extended upward to racial differences. "The belief in the natural equality of peoples is a simple corollary to the belief in the natural equality of all men," he said. In fact, traditions were "the equivalent of what the hereditary patrimony is for individuals."[6]

British academic Arthur Shenfield argued for the "fundamental right" of "discrimination in personal or business relations for racial and cultural reasons" and against universal franchise for newly decolonized nations.[7] British-Hungarian economist Peter Bauer, the future winner of the Cato Institute's Milton Friedman Award, spoke on the futility of the pursuit of economic equality at a global level considering the variation in "economic abilities and attitudes" of the world's populations.[8] Contributing to a Festschrift for Hayek a few years earlier, he wrote about the "distinct mental and physical lassitude of the majority of the local population in many underdeveloped countries, notably so in the Middle East and South Asia" and speculated that "it is not clear how far this inertia and some of the other traits and attitudes unfavorable to material progress reflect the operation of biological, cultural, climatic, or other geographical factors."[9] Two years earlier, Shenfield had defended empire and opposed franchise for Black South Africans while describing demands for development aid as part of an "ideological war against the West," crediting conversations with Bauer on the topic. Both placed questions of race centrally, seeing the white West as having capitulated to the demands of Black populations both in the decolonizing world and in the industrial North. Along with labor unions, Shenfield described "minority racial groups" as "the most powerful and assiduous interest groups and lobbyists of our time."[10]

Also presenting in Gstaad was Nathaniel Weyl, a former communist who converted to a fusion of pseudo-scientific racism and libertarianism in the 1950s, a perspective he publicized in the pages of *Mankind Quarterly* and in books coauthored with the Hoover Institution's Stefan Possony. Weyl captured the spirit of the conference in his lament that "the West has proclaimed the dogma of human equality and it has swept all else before it. The wretched masses of the Orient and the Tropics are taught that neither race nor class should serve as barriers to their advancement... that stock is nothing and that environment or habitat is all."[11] A clearer statement of the new fusionist racialized commitment to "nature" over "nurture" and its defiant inegalitarianism is hard to imagine.

The most enduring speech of the Gstaad conference, however, came from Rothbard. He expanded on his theme from the first symposium but with an even more explicit appeal to science to back his claims. Leftists rushed to replace biology with culture, he said. He cited the work of Harvard psychologist Richard J. Herrnstein to contend that there was a "genetic basis for inequality of intelligence" which undercut any attempts to create an equality of outcomes through education or redistribution. "Biology," he wrote, "stands like a rock in the face of egalitarian fantasies." Feminists pointed to patriarchy in every culture. Why don't they consider the possibility that biology dictates that men be dominant, he wondered. To Rothbard, the egalitarian challenge to the natural inequality of ability and differences of sexuality and gender would lead to "the destruction of civilization, and even of the human race itself." "The egalitarian revolt against biological reality" was "only a subset of a deeper revolt: against the ontological structure of reality itself, against the 'very organization of nature'; against the universe as such."[12] Here the slippery slope well known in neoliberal ideology was not economic planning but the unpicking of hierarchies of sex and race. Something even worse than serfdom that way lay: the denial of the universe as such.

THE AUSTRIANS WHO TOOK THE CULTURAL TURN

The appeal to race and biology amid the peaks of Gstaad coincided with the effort to implant the discipline of Austrian economics in the United States—a project that would eventually produce a lasting and significant schism among libertarians. The iconic founding conference of the Austrian school in the United States happened in June 1974 in South Royalton, Vermont, where Rothbard gave a keynote address.[13] Mises had died the year before, and Hayek was scheduled to appear but canceled. This meant that, as historian Janek Wasserman observes, "at the first official 'Austrian Economics' conference, no one from Austria attended."[14] The Americanization of the field was no anomaly. Although the founders of the Austrian school, including Carl Menger (1849–1921) and Eugen Böhm-Bawerk (1851–1914) worked out of Vienna, the "revival" of the school in the United States was led by Rothbard and British émigré Israel Kirzner (1930–). By the 1980s, the Austrians had set up institutional bases at New York University and, above all, at George Mason University (GMU) in Fairfax, Virginia, where more than $30 million in donations to the university from Charles Koch helped sustain the Center for the Study of Market Processes (renamed the Mercatus Center in 1999).[15] Afloat on the same Koch cash wave, the IHS relocated from Menlo Park to Fairfax in 1985.

The Austrian school differentiates itself from mainstream neoclassical economics, including the Chicago school, by its emphasis on subjective value and limited knowledge and on verbal rather than mathematical arguments. As Don Lavoie, the founder of the GMU center, put it, the Austrian "view of human action does not reduce it to maximizing." Austrians are interested in, among other things, "how habits might shape the process of decision making, how tacit knowledge is involved, how certain sorts of institutions such as money, property rights and organized markets orient the agent, and how disruptions of such institutions might disorient him."[16] In the 1980s, many of the Austrian economists around GMU began to take what they later called the hermeneutic or "interpretive turn."[17] An early proponent was Richard Ebeling, who set out, in his own words, to exorcise "the ghost of 'economic man'" by emphasizing processes of "inculturation" by which we "come to share a common social world," citing Austrian sociologist Alfred Schütz along with the Austrian-born Peter Berger and Thomas Luckmann on the "social construction of reality."[18]

As with their contemporaries on the Marxist Left promoting the new field of cultural studies, this group—call them the cultural Austrians—often defined themselves against what they derided as the "economism" of their opponents. When 1970s post-Marxists, feminist, and cultural studies scholars criticized economism, this meant bringing the state, race, gender, and everyday life into the frame of analysis to compensate for an overemphasis on materialistic determinism.[19] Cultural Austrians sometimes used similar language drawn from sociology. Ludwig Lachmann described the need to reintroduce the "'life-world' in which all our empirical knowledge of social matters is embedded" to the "desiccated formalism" of textbook neoclassical economics.[20] If value was subjective, then it should be sought not only in monetized transactions but in all aspects of human action.

From Hayek, cultural Austrians took the insight that not only the market but also all social institutions had a "communicative function."[21] Lavoie argued that Hayek had identified a "knowledge problem" that only private property and free exchange could solve. The problem was not to access and organize all known information about prices—which computers could theoretically accomplish—but to access the "inarticulate," tacit, or unknown knowledge that local actors held—and computers could never know.[22] The emphasis on the situatedness of the economic actor led cultural Austrians to borrow language from phenomenology and philosophy, including frequent references to Hans-Georg Gadamer, in particular. The cultural Austrians extended the market metaphor to all domains of human life by seeing "society as an interpretive process which translates meaningful utterances of the human mind into socially useful knowledge."[23]

The basically horizontal notion of society adopted by the cultural Austrians bore resemblances to the network metaphors popular in the 1980s and 1990s. Yet while many of those discussions shaded into fascination with computing, the neoliberals were adamant, in almost all cases, about distancing themselves from either the use of computers to arrive at insight into social problems or to see computers as analogous to human brains or economic markets.[24] They saw the reliance on putatively hard science in economics and the pursuit of equilibrium through formal mathematical models as foreign to the neoliberal tradition, attributing it instead to the neoclassical inspirations of market socialists like Oskar Lange and "the desire of left-wing economists to justify Keynesian interventionism and socialism."[25] Austrians saw social democrats expanding the purview of the state into private life behind the mantle of scientism and supposedly objective facts about the economy represented by indicators like GDP. In the same vein as Hayek's Nobel speech on the "pretense of knowledge," which targeted the Club of Rome's *Limits to Growth* report, Austrians sought to disenchant putative economic expertise through appeals to the limits of what could be known and the inherent relativism and subjectivity of economic value.

Hayek's definition of culture became the chief route to move beyond methodological individualism and begin to understand collectives and institutions. While some have noted the similarity between Hayek's ideas and those of contemporary sociobiology, his intervention acknowledged genetic heredity but downplayed nature in favor of nurture and against an overemphasis on biology and genetic transmission.[26] For Hayek, a culture is not a population bounded by race or heredity but one with fluid boundaries where adaptation occurs at the margins, often through interaction with (and imitation of) other cultures, and gradually becomes generalized through a process of the survival of successful traits.

Existing critiques of neoliberalism leave us ill equipped to make sense of the cultural Austrians. Neoliberals are frequently charged with the fault of economism, meaning variously a fixation on material explanations for all social change; a disciplinary claim about the superiority of economics, or, most often, a desire to distill the messy complexity of human life down to the elegance of formal models. For Hayek and the cultural Austrians, it is not mathematical proofs but complexity that is the central intellectual concern. Reducing the story to a contrast between the simplistic, one-dimensional, reductive neoliberals and their multidimensional and expansive opponents makes it too easy for neoliberalism's critics. Attention to thick description, ethnography, culture, and the elusive quality of systems has been incorporated into important streams of neoliberal thought for decades. Rather than resist the cultural turn that emerged from the 1960s, then, an important faction of the neoliberal movement absorbed it in their own way.

SCHISMS

The turn of some Austrians to culture had major repercussions, effecting a schism that led some members of the neoliberal camp to efforts at organizing a "paleolibertarian" faction and eventually to joining what became the alt-right. The institutional base for the schism was the Ludwig von Mises Institute, a clutch of buildings in beige gable and red brick across West Magnolia Avenue from Auburn University in Alabama, launched in 1982 as a counterweight to the Heritage Foundation and the Cato Institute, the latter of which Rothbard cofounded with Charles Koch and Ed Crane in the 1970s before being squeezed out.[27] The Mises Institute's director was Llewelyn Rockwell Jr., known as Lew. Born in 1944, and educated among professors' children and blue-blood WASPs at Cambridge, Massachusetts's Browne & Nichols School before attending Tufts University for a bachelor's degree in English literature, Rockwell was a formidable operator in the world of the new fusionism.[28]

One of the opening shots in the civil war of Austrian economics was fired from the institute by David Gordon in a working paper published in 1986. He singled out the "'market process' economists, mainly to be found at George Mason University in Virginia [who] believe themselves to have transcended objectivist assumptions about method." "The false idol of rationalism has now been overthrown," he wrote, "in its place stands hermeneutics."[29] At a talk at Jagiellonian University in Krakow, Poland in 1987, Rothbard condemned what he called the "hermeneutical invasion of philosophy and economics." He singled out the attempt of the "groupuscule" of "renegade Austrians" around Lavoie to found a "Society for Interpretive Economics" at GMU as an attempt to sully the school of Mises and Hayek with the theories of Foucault, Ricoeur, and Derrida. Rothbard's summary of hermeneutics sounded remarkably close to Hayek's own thought, that "with each person being bound to his own subjective views, feelings, history, and so on, there is no method of discovering objective truth." Yet he blamed Lachmann, Deirdre McCloskey, and others for importing "nihilism" into Austrianism.[30]

In the same issue of the *Review of Austrian Economics* in which Rothbard's article appeared, Hans-Hermann Hoppe also brought out the knives against the cultural Austrians, claiming that "Lachmann and the George Mason University hermeneuticians" are singing "the ancient tune of skepticism and nihilism, of epistemological and ethical relativism."[31] This was one of the first appearances on the English-language publication scene for Hoppe, who had taken a position as Rothbard's colleague at the UNLV School of Business in his mid-thirties in 1986. Hoppe was an apostate, having been educated at the heart of the hermeneutic turn. Studying in Frankfurt in the early 1970s, his dissertation adviser was Jürgen Habermas, and he also worked with Karl-Otto Apel, a philosopher and specialist in the work of Heidegger, Dilthey, and Peirce.[32] Apel and Habermas codeveloped the theory of discourse ethics that Hoppe would later seek to adapt into what he called "argumentation ethics."[33] His earlier work bore traits of both the subjectivism and anti-egalitarianism of the Austrian approach, including a study critical of economic aggregates such as GDP for measuring welfare.[34]

RACE AND THE RISE OF THE PALEOS

As symbolized by their affiliation with the Mises Institute, Murray Rothbard and Hans-Hermann Hoppe took Hayek's mentor as their lodestar rather than Hayek himself. The choice was significant. While the thinkers are usually distinguished by their relative commitment to "laissez-faire," we find a more meaningful difference for our purposes in their respective treatment of culture and race. Race theory has an ambiguous place in Mises's work. Like Hayek, he takes the diversity of human capacity as a starting point or a given. Unlike Hayek, however, he explicitly associated certain traits with racial groups, writing that "it may be assumed that races do differ in intelligence and will power, and that, this being so, they are very unequal in their ability to form society, and further that the better races distinguish themselves precisely by their special aptitude for strengthening social cooperation." "This hypothesis," he continued, "throws light on various aspects of social evolution not otherwise easily comprehensible." He left the door open for the scientific study of race for new understandings of the human condition and for explaining "the development and regression of the social division of labor and the flowering and decline of civilizations." What conclusions such a study of race might discover in advance, he did not speculate, observing "we are solely concerned to show that the race theory is easily compatible with our theory of social cooperation."[35]

The ambiguous part is that Mises repeatedly expressed cautious optimism for a potential science of race even as he explicitly condemned the race theory that existed. In his earliest work, Mises laughed off the nineteenth-century theories of French ethnologist Joseph Arthur de Gobineau that linked cranial size to intelligence.[36] He also began his magnum opus, *Human Action*, with a condemnation of what he called "racial polylogism" or the belief that different races follow different rationalities. Against this, Mises—whose Jewish background can be noted here—argued that all humans are governed by the same rationality, the same motivations, and the same drive to purposive action. "Society is not a stud-farm," he wrote, "operated for the production of a definite type of men. There is no 'natural' standard to establish what is desirable and what is undesirable in the biological evolution of man."[37] At the same time, in his 1944 work, Mises conceded the difficulties of racial integration, writing about immigration barriers that "there are few white men who would not shudder at the picture of many millions of black or yellow people living in their own countries."[38]

In the original German-language version of the book that would later become *Human Action*, written during his time at the Graduate Institute for International Studies in Geneva, Mises granted even more ground to race science, writing that "we may take as given that the racial element plays a role among the factors that form the personality and, with it, our values and understanding." What he objected to was not the possible truth content of race theory but its misuse. "In the doctrine of National Socialism and its derivative teachings in Italian fascism," he wrote, "there is an unbridgeable gap between the statements of the founders of racial biology and their application to propaganda and use for practical policies." The fascist politicization of race theory should not discredit it permanently. "Because the keywords of race theory are used to justify measures with which it has nothing to do," he wrote, "does not free scientific thought from the responsibility to think through to the end the problem of human races (*Menschenrassen*) in its praxeological significance."[39]

These asides must not be read as some sort of conclusive evidence of Mises's racism. His objections to Nazi racial science were clear, and his passing references placed less significance on the political meaning of race than many contemporary thinkers on the right and left, including John Maynard Keynes, to name one example, an active member of the British Eugenics Society.[40] Important for our purposes is how the followers of Mises took his rather parenthetical opening to the possibilities of race theory and drove the metaphorical truck through it. In their appeal to race science, they found a genetic basis for unequal capacity, unequal achievement, and in Hoppe's work, an explanation for the supposedly natural aversion of races to cohabitation. This last is in direct contradistinction to Mises's own assertion that "millions of mulattoes and other half-breeds are living counter-evidence to the assertion that there exists a natural repulsion between the various races." [41] Yet, faced with the neoliberal problem of how to explain unequal capacity in a universal marketplace, Rothbard and Hoppe diverged from Hayekian arguments about social learning and cultural imitation to seize on the putative objectivity of race science.

As Rothbard and Hoppe embraced the premise of what could be called not polylogic but "polyfacultive" racial difference, they welcomed new collaborations. Most important was with the group that former MPS member Paul Gottfried dubbed the "paleoconservatives."[42] In November 1989 Rockwell and Rothbard made a fateful trip to meet their counterpart paleoconservatives in their headquarters—a city in the middle of farmland a hundred miles west of Chicago called Rockford.[43] The town housed the Rockford Institute, which published *Chronicles* magazine, edited by Thomas Fleming, founder of the *Southern Partisan* and later founder of the Southern League. Rothbard and Rockwell's pitch: the two groups were not as different as they seemed. The end of the Cold War offered a chance to revisit the legacy of the old Right and build a common front against the neoconservatives who wanted to transform anticommunism into an endless war for global democracy.

The outcome of the "paleo alliance" was the John Randolph Club (JRC), founded in 1989 and named after an early nineteenth-century plantation owner and advocate of African colonization. At the first meeting of the JRC, Fleming dubbed the paleo ideology "the new fusionism."[44] Adopting the term, Rockwell said the core of the new fusionism was the belief that there were "iron links between culture, economics, and politics."[45] He might have added science. As noted in the introduction, the new fusionism drew from evolutionary psychology, cultural anthropology, cognitive psychology, and genetics to support arguments about human difference and the need for segregation. As Gottfried recalled later in the speech where he introduced the term "the Alternative Right," paleo thinkers were "preoccupied with sociobiology."[46]

In a "paleolibertarian manifesto" published months before the first meeting, Rockwell declared his distance from the hippies and libertines of the broader libertarian movement, pronouncing "objective standards of morality, especially as found in the Judeo-Christian tradition, as essential to the free and civilized social order." He described "the egalitarian ethic as morally reprehensible" and "the welfare state as organized theft." Populations had to be re-sorted out from below, a process he was sure would lead to greater homogeneity. "State-enforced segregation," he wrote, "was wrong, but so is State-enforced integration." "State enforced segregation was not wrong because separateness is wrong, however," he continued, "Wishing to associate with members of one's own race, nationality, religion, class, sex, or even political party is a natural and normal human impulse." "There is nothing wrong with blacks preferring the 'black thing,'" Rockwell concluded. "But paleolibertarians would say the same about whites preferring the 'white thing' or Asians the 'Asian thing.'"[47]

If the arrangement of bodies in space was the problem, it could be the solution too. In a decade of the 1990s marked by moves toward supranational integration in the form of the European Union, the WTO, NAFTA, and UN intervention, the members of the JRC looked in the other direction. Their goal, as I have described elsewhere, was to bring the dynamic of dissolution afoot in Eastern Europe home to their own United States.[48] Disintegrate and segregate: that was their program. Reinstate homogeneous culture as the basis of political organization. Cut short the disastrous march toward the false god of egalitarianism launched by the social movements of the 1960s. With the Cold War over, the United States must no longer go "abroad in search of monsters to destroy," as Buchanan quoted John Quincy Adams, but should focus on what they saw as the monsters at home. Rothbard identified an "unholy triad" of "left Puritanism," environmentalism, and "victimology." Rhyming with Rothbard's talk of "egalitarianism as a revolt against nature," Fleming called the movement for civil rights "a revolution against our Constitution, a revolution against nature, and a revolution against the God who created nature."[49]

The formula for paleo reconciliation was decentralization. Snidely coopting a favored metaphor of then New York City mayor David Dinkins, Rothbard said that the common goal of the paleos was turning the nation into a "gorgeous mosaic." At a JRC meeting in Dallas he shared his radical libertarian vision of "contractual neighborhoods" where everything was privatized as "world states wither away on a free market."[50] If every last scrap of land and street were privately owned, then the new shapes of communities would be determined by "neighborhood-contracts" between property owners.[51] Instead of birthright citizenship, which he saw as bait for free-riders, "access rights" would be purchased.[52] Rockwell added to the vision of stateless market society or anarcho-capitalism by saying that the rolls of citizenship should be closed. The next step was denying access of immigrants to public services, including public schools.[53] A few years later, the success of Proposition 187 in California would move a step in just this direction, barring undocumented migrants from state services.

In Rockwell and Rothbard's desired future, migration would either be temporary or based on the ability to buy entry to a new jurisdiction. Mobility would downgrade the importance of democracy. "As we begin to work toward the pure model," Rothbard wrote, "as more and more areas and parts of life become either privatized or micro-decentralized, the less important voting will become." Citizenship would be replaced by ownership. "The voting process should be considered trivial and unimportant at best, and never a 'right,'" he wrote, "apart from a possible mechanism stemming from a consensual contract."[54] Rothbard's ideal space for collective deliberation—his equivalent of the town hall meeting beloved by many devotees of the American democratic tradition—was the shareholders meeting. "Voting makes sense most," he wrote, "as the voting of parcels of ownership over resources, e.g. the owner of five percent stock in a corporation properly has the right to five percent of voting power over its assets."[55]

What of those without the resources to move or purchase access—those humans "outcompeted" in the process of evolutionary selection and left with neither stake nor vote? Paleos were performatively disinterested in the question, deriding the poor as "freeloaders" and welfare dependents. "He who does not work, neither shall he eat," Rockwell said at the John Randolph Club meeting.[56] Yet even if one accepted the principle of privatization, decomposition, and the subjection of the poor and their families to potential death by starvation or exposure, the question remained: what should be the basis of the smaller unit? In the 1990s, paleos re-posed one of the basic questions of a century earlier: What is a nation? In response, they did not turn to linguistics, philology, folklore, art history, archaeology, or anthropology, to name some of the disciplines that made nationality real in the nineteenth century. Instead, many turned to another nineteenth-century novelty: the science of evolution and the successor fields of ethology, or animal behavior, and race science. The uncertainty produced by the open-ended problem of political organization was solved through a flight to nature. The paleo embrace of the purported science of race created the foundation for their collaboration with their Far Right colleagues in the JRC and made space for what became alt-right libertarianism.

THE DEFENSE OF WHITE CIVILIZATION

The chief organ of publication for the new fusionist paleo position was the monthly *Rothbard-Rockwell Report* (later *Triple R*), which began publication in April 1990. From the beginning, the *Rothbard-Rockwell Report* displayed an openness to "racialist" arguments, sharing contributors with the *American Renaissance* newsletter, a "journal of race, immigration, and the decline of civility" which began publication the same year to protest the ongoing "dispossession" of whites by nonwhites.[57] Michael Levin was a contributing editor at *Triple R* in the late 1990s at same time that he was contributing articles to *American Renaissance*. A preview of his book *Why Race Matters* was published by the Mises Institute in 1996.[58] Alongside articles and a regular gossip column (often devoted to Bill and Hillary Clinton), each issue of *Rothbard-Rockwell Report* included, usually without comment, capsule summaries of violence committed by people of color.

Rothbard had cited the Harvard psychologist Richard J. Herrnstein on the genetic basis of IQ difference in Gstaad. Herrnstein became much better known decades later when, just before his death, he coauthored with (later MPS member) Charles Murray *The Bell Curve: Intelligence and Class Structure in American Life* (1994). The book, discussed at length in chapter 4, became a talisman in JRC circles, a sign that the science of racial hierarchy was once again viable for popular discussion. "The new turn on race was the talk of the JRC corridors," Rothbard wrote. He praised the authors for breaching the topic of race science, writing that "until literally mid-October 1994 [when *The Bell Curve* was published], it was shameful and taboo for anyone to talk publicly or write about, home truths which everyone, and I mean *everyone,* knew in their hearts and in private: that is, almost self-evident truths about race, intelligence, and heritability."[59] Now it was being addressed in all major publications, including a dedicated issue of *The New Republic* with "Race and IQ" splashed across its cover.[60]

"After *The Bell Curve* controversy, discussion of race and government policies about race will be considerably more open and honest than before," wrote the conservative columnist Sam Francis, another leading member of the paleo alliance, in 1994.[61] He displayed his own version of such "openness" the same year when, in a piece titled "why race matters," he called on Caucasians to reassert "identity" and "solidarity" in "explicitly racial terms through the articulation of a racial consciousness as whites." Arguing that race was a "biological reality," he expressed his faith that "biological science in the near future will show even more clearly how necessary racial, biological, and genetic explanations are to understanding social and historical events more fully."[62]

A senior policy analyst at the Heritage Foundation in the late 1970s and early 1980s, Sam Francis held a worldview that had been shaped, like that of many on the Far Right, by the era of decolonization in general and the slow erosion of white minority rule in southern Africa in particular. At Heritage, he wrote backgrounders for lawmakers defending white-minority government in Rhodesia against international sanctions.[63] The categories of geopolitics and race, often blurred together during the Cold War, were one and the same for Francis by the 1990s. He first delivered his article on "why race matters" as a talk at the first conference organized by *American Renaissance*.[64] The racial chauvinism of the paleos was defiant. "The civilization that we as whites created in Europe and America," Francis was quoted as saying at another American Renaissance conference, "could not have developed apart from the genetic endowments of the creating people, nor is there any reason to believe that the civilization can be successfully transmitted to a different people."[65] Whiteness was both a biological and cultural patrimony.

The early 1990s saw a flourishing of publications devoted to racial science and the supposed dangers facing the white race. Paleo or proto-alt-right neoliberals published regularly in the Rockford Institute's glossy monthly magazine *Chronicles*, which had been in print since 1976. Among the first authors in *Chronicles* were MPS members Paul Gottfried and Ernest van den Haag. Gottfried, a historian who has written on the conservative movement itself, was a bridging figure, beginning with articles in *National Review* and *Modern Age* and later publishing in *Rockwell-Rothbard Report, Chronicles, American Renaissance*, and, as a contributing editor, *Telos*. Paul Craig Roberts, a journalist and former staffer in Ronald Reagan's Treasury Department, had a similar role. He began as an MPS member publishing in *Modern Age*, later *Chronicles*, and ending by renouncing his membership in MPS in 2008 on Rockwell's website because it was "captured by neocons" while spreading theories that 9/11 was an inside job, the Sandy Hook massacre never took place, and the Orlando club attack was a false flag operation.[66]

Chronicles began to focus heavily on questions of immigration and race in the 1990s with covers featuring, for example, the Statue of

Liberty stormed by slant-eyed devils with the title "Bosnia, USA" in 1993, and a glowing article about "secessions" in 1991. Hoppe published excerpts from what would become *Democracy: The God That Failed* (2001) in 1993 and 1995 in *Chronicles*.[67] In the excerpts, he used the language of opponents of the civil rights movement to condemn the "forced integration" that resulted from immigration and the shared use of state-owned and operated roads and schools.[68]

The combination of the race question with libertarianism is what most identified the paleo position. Even more than the work of Herrnstein and Murray, Rothbard, Hoppe and other paleo authors relied on the more unapologetically racist work of Richard Lynn (1930–) and J. Philippe Rushton (1943–2012), who published their psychometric studies linking cranial size, race, climate, and intelligence at the fringes and often beyond the fringes of their own professions.[69] Rothbard used the work of such "racialists" along with the example of Yugoslavia to support his position, published the same year as *The Bell Curve*, that "beyond a small quantity, national heterogeneity simply does not work, the 'nation' disintegrates into more than one nation, and the need for separation becomes acute." He argued that the solution for South Africa was not in less apartheid but more—a "Grand Apartheid . . . not just cantonization, but separate sovereign nations in the territory of the existing Union of South Africa."[70]

OUTREACH TO THE REDNECKS

The John Randolph Club's most direct attempt to bring their hoped-for future into reality came with the 1992 presidential bid of one of their members: the columnist, debate show host and former Nixon staffer Patrick J. Buchanan.[71] Although many libertarians questioned Buchanan's soft spot for protectionism and support for the War on Drugs, Rothbard and Rockwell endorsed Buchanan, deeming him "as close as any real-world candidate could possibly come to paleolibertarianism."[72] Rockwell took a leave of absence from his position at the Mises Institute to join Buchanan's entourage, and Ron Paul, for whom Rockwell had served as chief of staff, stepped aside to clear the path for Buchanan in the primaries.[73]

The Buchanan moment was the culmination of decades of Rothbard's search for a new approach to libertarian politics. He expanded on his strategy in a document he wrote for Charles Koch in 1977 after cofounding the Cato Institute. There, Rothbard lamented that libertarians always defaulted to what he called "'educationism': namely that actions rest upon ideas and therefore that libertarians must try to convert people to their ideas by issuing books, pamphlets, articles, lectures, etc." Rather, while recruiting "cadres" (his term), it was also necessary to conceive of what he called "transition demands." Their goal—"the disappearance of the State and its aggressive coercion"—would "not be achieved overnight." They needed what he called "ideological entrepreneurship" to help seek out "way-stations along the path to victory."[74]

Rothbard returned to these themes at the January 1992 meeting of the JRC when he laid out a strategy intended for Pat Buchanan for what he called "right-wing populism" and elsewhere "paleopopulism."[75] The goal of right-wing populism, he wrote, was to oppose Hayek's approach of "trickle-down educationism" that targeted elites with a style that was "exciting, dynamic, tough, and confrontational, rousing and inspiring not only the exploited masses, but the often shell-shocked right-wing intellectual cadre as well."[76] Showing his willingness to endorse white separatism in a particularly stark way, he used the example of the former Grand Wizard of the Ku Klux Klan, David Duke, who had won over half of the white vote in the gubernatorial race in Louisiana in 1991.[77]

Rothbard's strategy turned Hayekian neoliberalism on its head. Since the 1930s, the assumption was that the masses naturally tended toward redistribution and socialism and careful state design was necessary to constrain them. The audience for this philosophy was elites because it was elites who would design, adjudicate, and enforce the binding rules that prevented democratic legislation from derailing the laws that protected private property and free competition. Rothbard wanted to turn the dynamic around: to use the masses to disempower the elites. His reversal was based on a simple insight: the masses no longer leaned socialist. Much had changed in the postwar era. Although Rothbard did not put it this way himself, we could point out that, alongside aggressive anticommunism, union density had halved from the 1950s to the 1990s, the introduction of 401(k) pensions in the late 1970s that rose and fell with the stock market, and the use of the language of makers and takers condemning so-called dependency on state benefits had helped produce a hospitable environment for his message. What Melinda Cooper calls "supply-side populism" reversed New Deal thinking to continue the transfer of public wealth through "subtractive" means of tax cuts, depreciation allowances, deregulation, and credits, irrigating an illusion of individualist self-making even as the wealth of asset owners was propped up by the reengineering of fiscal policy.[78]

To the paleos, the only true-believer socialists remaining were at the top: the politicians, civil servants, lobbyists, and bureaucrats, who were sustained by an ever-larger state—"the Establishment," as Rothbard dubbed it in the 1960s. "The basic right-wing populist insight," he wrote, "is that we live in a statist country and a statist world dominated by a ruling elite"; the elite comprised "a coalition of politicians and bureaucrats allied with, and even dominated by, powerful corporate and Old Money financial elites (e.g., the Rockefellers, the Trilateralists); and the New Class of technocrats and intellectuals, including Ivy League academics and media elites."[79] If the elites were the last line of defense for socialism—and the new line of offense in a revived social democracy after the Cold War—then the core message for a paleolibertarian to send was clear: fuck the elites.

Against "the Hayek model" of "converting the intellectual elites to liberty, beginning with top philosophers and then slowly trickling on down through the decades to converting journalists and other media opinion-molders," Rothbard called for a "one-two punch." Build up a loyal cadre while rousing "the masses of people against the elites that are looting them, and confusing them, and oppressing them." He invoked the example of Senator Joe McCarthy and his capacity "to short-circuit the power elite...and reach out and whip up the masses directly." The goal was one that had evaded the libertarian movement thus far: "a strategy of Outreach to the Rednecks."[80]

Rothbard debated what they should call themselves beyond the categories of "paleo" and "new fusionist." "Perhaps we could call ourselves radical reactionaries, or 'radical rightists,'" he said in front of the JRC, "the label that was given to us by our enemies in the 1950s. Or, if there is too much objection to the dread term 'radical,' we can follow the suggestion of some of our group to call ourselves 'the Hard Right.'"[81] Buchanan was the tiger the paleolibertarians hoped to ride to a stateless society. The racial coding of many of these issues was clear, including the gesture to David Duke and the invocation of "rednecks" about which the author John Ganz has written about revealingly.[82] Rothbard's advice ahead of Buchanan's next run for president in 1996 was even more explicit. "This is a revolution of white Euro-males," he wrote, "and Pat needs to focus on their grievances and concerns: their focus should be his focus as well." The concerns were taxes, regulation, environmentalism, welfare, gun control, foreign aid, the attack on Christianity and "immigration by hordes of foreigners not assimilated into American culture."[83] This was the new front after the Cold War: upward against the elites and their attempts to usher in social democracy by the back door and outward against the immigrants threatening at the gates.

RACE SCIENTISTS AND LIBERTARIANS ON THE TURKISH RIVIERA

After two failed presidential runs by Patrick Buchanan and Murray Rothbard's death in 1995, the paleopopulist alliance between right-libertarianism and the self-described "race realists" has been carried by the Mises Institute and, since 2005 by Hans-Hermann Hoppe's Property & Freedom Society (PFS). The PFS meets annually in the ballroom of the Kadria Princess Hotel in Bodrum on the Turkish Riviera. Hoppe founded the PFS as a rejuvenated version of the JRC aspiring to be the "international spearhead" of an "anti-statist counterculture." He hoped it would replace what he described as an MPS undermined by think tankers, government "agents and propagandists" and other "right-wing social democrats." Attending and speaking at MPS meetings in the 1990s, Hoppe had found to his dismay that there was "no discussion in the hallowed halls of the Mont Pèlerin Society of U.S. imperialism... or of the financial crimes committed by the Federal Reserve Bank—and," in what would be an important inclusion, "no discussion of any sensitive race issue."[84] Hoppe's PFS was to be a staunchly new fusionist alternative to the MPS, more open to naturalized hierarchies of human capacity. "Under a regime of 'separate but equal,'" he wrote in the contribution to a volume edited by David Gordon of the Mises Institute, "people must face up to the reality not only of cultural diversity but in particular also of visibly distinct ranks of cultural advancement."[85]

Hoppe sought to claim the legacy of the Austrian neoliberals. He cited Mises in the mission statement and, at the society's inaugural meeting, repeated Hayek's often-quoted words that "we must make the building of a free society once more an intellectual adventure, a deed of courage. What we lack is a liberal Utopia."[86] Since 2006 the PFS has hosted key figures in the alt-right and so-called academic racist movement, including *American Renaissance* founder Jared Taylor, "human biodiversity" theorist and journalist Steve Sailer, VDARE.com publisher and anti-immigration extremist Peter Brimelow, racial scientist Richard Lynn, and Richard Spencer, who gave the lead-off speech at the 2010 meeting on the topic of the movement he helped coin two years earlier: "the alternative Right in America."[87]

The conferences at the Turkish hotel have matched discussions of central bank independence, limited liability, and entrepreneurship with a discourse on race that grew ever more grotesque. At a meeting in 2010, an aged Richard Lynn repeated his theory that climate was the most important determining variable of intelligence in human evolution, while Jared Taylor confirmed with his fellow panelists that Australian Aborigines have the world's smallest brains, and Hoppe added that equatorial populations faced no challenges and ate "insects" while northern populations killed "big game."[88] Hoppe expanded on these junk science yarns in a book, *A Short History of Man: Progress and Decline*.[89]

As remedies for the supposed maladies of egalitarianism and the pursuit of social justice feared by neoliberals everywhere, the distinction between the vulgar race theory of the PFS and Hayekian subjectivism and cultural evolutionary thinking seems absolute. Yet the contributions of Spencer at the PFS meeting in 2010 suggested otherwise. During the question period, a woman in the audience challenged the speakers' emphasis on race for its supposedly un-libertarian redirection of attention back to groups and nation-states. "We're like the astronauts," she said. "We don't even see these borders." Spencer responded that "as an Austro-libertarian, value is subjective. It's something you can make. Groups are extremely important. You can't get away from the idea that identity and these kinds of associations form a basis of authority for people, that they might very well want to choose. It might be economically inefficient for someone to have a community that they decide is going to be Jewish.... I don't want to stop them from doing that. That is their subjective understanding of value." Elsewhere in the discussion, Spencer argued that pointing out genetically determined differences in IQ was "an important defensive component, but no one ever bases a political movement or a movement of identity or a new European consciousness or a new right wing on IQ."[90]

One could see in Spencer's response that the alt-right version of libertarianism does not choose sides but combines the insights of the cultural and racialist Austrians. Subjective value gleaned from the lifeworld is built on a substrate of shoddy science about race. This synthesis runs through more recent discourse of the Ludwig von Mises Institute, whose president, Jeff Deist, has insisted on the need for libertarians to remain mindful that "blood and soil and God and nation still matter to people."[91] Harking back to Rothbard's 1992 writings, Deist has called for a "libertarian populism" and suggested that "even in a hyper-connected digital age elites struggle to maintain support for globalism against a tide of nationalist, populist, and breakaway movements. Libertarians should embrace this reality and reject universalism for the morally and tactically superior vision of radical self-determination."[92] Deist saw Trump's victory in 2016 as offering libertarians "the gift of populism . . . our job is to unwrap it: to turn the nation's contempt for politicians into contempt for politics itself."[93]

One of the fallacies of understanding neoliberalism and libertarianism, especially in its extreme forms, is to say that it is simply an assertion of individualism. In fact, because these ideologies prioritize individualism, they become immediately concerned with investigating and proposing the conditions under which individualism can exist and be protected. This includes attention to laws and rules, quite obviously, but also to other parameters such as culture and heredity. Rothbard was especially attentive to this. In 1990, he wrote, "we must not fall into a nihilist trap. While only individuals exist, individuals do not exist as isolated and hermetically sealed atoms. While the State is a pernicious and coercive collectivist concept, the 'nation' may be and generally is voluntary. The nation properly refers, not to the State, but to the entire web of culture, values, traditions, religion, and language in which the individuals of a society are raised."[94]

The conventional way to read Hayek's savanna story is a normative one: a tale of the need to evolve from the tribe to the Great Society, from face-to-face interactions governed by the principle of solidarity to anonymous exchanges mediated by competition and the price mechanism. Yet, as we have seen, Hayek left open another reading when he proposed that the "moral heritage" is itself something contained within a given community or group. Racial Austrians did not reject

Hayek's savanna story about small group solidarity. Some differed by seeing the savanna as the space for the creation not of a universal human nature but a particular racialized one. In their telling, populations that persisted in warmer climates failed to develop higher forms of cognition and physical ability because of the relative absence of challenges in acquiring food and surviving. So-called climate theories of racial origins underpinned the racism of alt-right libertarians by the end of the twentieth century. In this version of the human origin story, there was a savanna story, but more important a "boreal" European woodland story and even a tundra story that left enduring human group differences.[95] That none of these versions of human evolution stand up to the actual science of physical anthropology bears little on the story we are telling here. What is important for us is that—in ways underappreciated by critics so far—basic truth claims about political economy and society became grounded in hard sciences.

In 2017, one month after the deadly Charlottesville protests, Hoppe gave a talk at the PFS that formalized the schism in the neoliberal movement over matters of culture and race and completed the arc traced in this chapter. He described the alt-right as the "successor of the paleoconservative movement that came to prominence in the early 1990s," and praised its insistence that "libertarians must above all be realistic and recognize from the outset, as the alt-right does, the inequality not just of individuals but also of different cultures as an ineradicable datum of the human existence." Hoppe argued that the waves of affirmative action and feminism that emerged from the 1960s had turned "white married Christian couples with children" into "the most severely victimized people," while "single black Muslim mothers on welfare" were "the most protected." Echoing Rothbard's strategy for right-wing populism from a quarter century earlier, he said to "get rid of all welfare parasites and bums," "crush the street criminals and gangs," and "stop mass immigration."[96]

Echoing Rothbard's "revolution of white Euro males," Hoppe said that "native whites" must be "the main addressees of a populist libertarianism."[97] As opponents, he added the new figure of the "anti-fascist mob," or antifa. "Public anger must be aroused," he wrote, "and there must be clamoring far and wide for the police to be unleashed and this mob beaten into submission." In 2018 Hoppe wrote the foreword for a book by a man who blogged under the title *Radical Capitalist*. The book was called *White, Right, and Libertarian*. In a nod to Chilean dictator Augusto Pinochet's "death flights," on which political opponents were executed, the cover featured a helicopter with four bodies dangling from nooses, their heads showing the logos of communism, Islam, antifa, and feminism.[98]

As should be clear by now, behind the abstract talk of liberties and freedoms in much of twenty-first century neoliberal and libertarian discourse lies a much grubbier story of hunting and gathering, primordial beginnings, and adamantine differences. Only by realizing this can we understand the mystique of evolutionary psychology in the work of right-wing gurus like Jordan Peterson or the statistical obsessions of the so-called race realists on the radical right. Arguments about politics always rest on claims about human nature.

The message of the savanna stories that neoliberals told was that the tribe will never go away. Because this is the case, homogeneity is preferable to reduce conflict. Similar threads ran through their debates about immigration. The next chapter shows that stories of the ethnostate and the economy did not run on parallel tracks: they were woven together. We cannot understand the Far Right without seeing their vision of capitalism.

CHAPTER THREE

Ethno-Economy

> The fact is that a belief in free markets does not commit you to free immigration.
>
> —Peter Brimelow

In Neal Stephenson's *Snow Crash* (1992), a novel that channeled perfectly the libertarian imagination of the post–Cold War moment, the territory once known as the United States has been shattered into privatized spaces: franchise nations, apartheid burbclaves, and franchulets, a world of what I have called "crack-up capitalism." The threat in the plot is the Raft, a maritime assemblage several miles across: a decommissioned aircraft carrier lashed to an oil tanker and countless container ships, freight carriers, "pleasure craft, sampans, junks, dhows, dinghies, life rafts, houseboats, makeshift structures built on air-filled oil drums and slabs of styrofoam." The Raft "orbits the Pacific clockwise" bearing a cargo of "Refus" or refugees, welcomed aboard by an entrepreneurial tech evangelist who has just cornered the global fiber optic grid and has schemes to subjugate the population through a computer virus administered as a bitmap narcotic. The Raft's passengers are dehumanized and anonymized: a mass of insects "dipping its myriad oars into the Pacific, like ant legs" at whose arrival the coastal residents of California live in terror, subscribing to a "twenty-four-hour Raft Report" to know when the "latest contingent of twenty-five thousand starving Eurasians has cut itself loose" to swim ashore.[1]

Stephenson's descriptions are stomach-turning, indulging in a grotesque racist imagery of nonwhite danger. The Raft was the fodder for, as he wrote, "a hundred Hong Kong B-movies and blood-soaked Nipponese comic books." As the race scientist and former *National Review* journalist Steve Sailer noted, the Raft also had an obvious antecedent: the "Last Chance Armada" of Jean Raspail's 1973 novel, first published in French, *The Camp of the Saints*.[2] In that book, a disabled messianic leader from the Calcutta slums boards millions of indigent Indians on a lashed-together fleet of old ships to travel West "in a welter of dung and debauch." The novel revels in what one scholar calls "pornographic prose" in its depiction of coprophagy, incest, and pedophilia aboard the armada.[3] The plot ends in an orgy of violence after what the author sees as the suicidal embrace of the armada by the foreigner-friendly French population.

The first English translation of *The Camp of the Saints* was published by Scribner's in 1975 to many positive reviews. The cover image showed a single Caucasian hand holding up a globe from grasping brown hands with a catch line reading: "a chilling novel about the end of the white world." The book returned to public discussion during the first successful presidential campaign of Donald Trump as an alleged inspiration to his advisers Steve Bannon and Stephen Miller, but it was already a common touchstone decades earlier. It was reissued in 1986 by the white supremacist Noontide Press and in 1987 by the American Immigration Control Foundation (AICF), which, along with the Federation for American Immigration Reform (FAIR) helped mainstream anti-immigrant arguments in part by piggy-backing on the mailing lists of right-wing magazines to help seed a national movement.

In 1991 John Randolph Club founding member Sam Francis described the book as "a kind of science fiction novel" that had become American reality. "The future is now," he wrote.[4] The vision of the maritime refugee indexed with the evening news in the early 1990s. There were more than thirty thousand interceptions of Haitians at sea in 1992 and nearly forty thousand Cubans in 1994; the same year, the

Golden Venture ran aground in Rockaway Beach, carrying three hundred Chinese would-be migrants.[5] Raspail's novel "forecasts the recent landing of the *Golden Venture*," as one letter to the *Washington Times* put it in 1993.[6] The Social Contract Press reissue featured a photo of Chinese men wrapped in blankets after disembarking from the vessel in the background.[7] Introducing the novel, the nativist ideological entrepreneur and FAIR director John Tanton wrote that "the future has arrived," citing the *Golden Venture* and other instances of maritime flight that had taken Raspail's plot "out of a theorist's realm and transposed it into real life."[8] Fiction can be more powerful than fact," wrote JRC member and American Renaissance founder Jared Taylor in a review of *The Camp of the Saints*. "The novel," he wrote, "is a call to all whites to rekindle their sense of race, love of culture, and pride in history—for he knows that without them we will disappear."[9]

The Camp of the Saints had a special place in the paleo imagination. Ahead of the first JRC meeting, the Ludwig von Mises Institute's Lew Rockwell claimed partial credit for the book's circulation in the United States in 1975.[10] In his talk "Decomposing the Nation-State" at the Mont Pelerin Society in 1993, Rothbard wrote that he had previously dismissed the novel's vision, but "as cultural and welfare-state problems have intensified, it became impossible to dismiss Raspail's concerns any longer." He referred to his proposal of privatizing all land and infrastructure discussed in the last chapter as a solution to the "Camp of the Saints problem."[11]

When the JRC met in Chicago in December 1992, the conference was titled "Bosnia, USA" and Hans-Hermann Hoppe spoke in the lead-off session named after *The Camp of the Saints*.[12]

The year between the first and second meeting of the JRC had been momentous. The Los Angeles riots in April, Buchanan's run for president, and Rothbard's proposal of a strategy of right-wing populism made 1992 look like, in the words of author John Ganz, "the year the clock broke."[13] Another notable event was the publication of an article in *National Review* by the scheduled keynote speaker at the club:

the journalist Peter Brimelow, a naturalized U.S. citizen born in England in 1947.[14] When the article was published as a book by Random House in 1995 with thanks given to Rockwell and Jeffrey Tucker at the Ludwig von Mises Institute (as well as his agent Andrew Wylie), *Alien Nation* was described as a "non-fiction horror story of a nation that is willfully but blindly pursuing a course of suicide."[15] Historian Aristide Zolberg writes that the book "marked the ascent to respectability of an explicitly white supremacist position... that had hitherto been confined in the United States to shadowy groups."[16] *Alien Nation* came in the immediate wake of the passage of Proposition 187 in California, blocking access to education and health services for undocumented immigrants, one of the earliest instances of local governments "trying to retake immigration control into their own hands."[17] "No writer has argued more effectively for this change of policy than Peter Brimelow," wrote Brimelow's former colleague at *Forbes*, David Frum. "No reformer can avoid grappling with [his] formidable work."[18]

In 1999, Brimelow took his project online—"fortunately the Internet came along," as he put it later--founding the website VDARE.com, named after the first child born to white settlers in North America, Virginia Dare. Serving as what the *Washington Post* called a "platform for white nationalism," the website has hosted prominent advocates of scientific racism like Jared Taylor, J. Philippe Rushton, and Steve Sailer as well as alt-right activists Richard Spencer and Jason Kessler.[19] An amplifier for themes and tropes of the Far Right, a search of the website yields more than twenty-thousand posts with the term "white genocide," more than thirteen thousand with "race realism," and six thousand with "Great Replacement."[20] Brimelow is also proximate to more mainstream figures in the United States. He was hosted at the home of then-president Donald Trump's economic adviser Larry Kudlow in 2018 and held a role at the same time at Fox reporting directly to Rupert Murdoch.[21]

Brimelow has become Jean Raspail's spokesperson for the 1990s and 2000s. But how has he made his case? An intellectual portrait of Brimelow lets us ask the question that animates this book: Where does the resurgence of the Far Right come from? Scholars attempting to explain how apparently fringe political ideologies have moved to center stage since the election of Trump in 2016 have split into two camps. The first locates the origins of the Far Right in culture: racism, chauvinism, xenophobia, the "tribalism" of "white identity politics," or a longing for "eternity."[22] As a group, these commentators seem to ignore the admonition from Frankfurt school sociologist Max Horkheimer repeated so often that it threatens to become a cliché that "whoever is not willing to talk about capitalism should also keep quiet about fascism."[23]

Capitalism can be hard to find in this literature. A recent book on "the far right today" does not mention the term once.[24] Four other books on the alt-right and white power movement barely mention it, and a fourth only to say that the alt-right is "skeptical of global capitalism."[25] References to "identity" outnumber "capitalism" at a ratio of several dozen to one. The assumption seems to be that Far Right ideology is either post- or pre-material: it inhabits a space of culture detached from issues of production and distribution. This is startling given the fact that the radical Right's central issue is nonwhite immigration, an eminently economic issue with a vast specialized literature.

By contrast, the second school of interpretation finds the origins of the Far Right in the spirit of capitalism itself. Rather than a rejection of neoliberalism, they see the Far Right as a mutant form of it, shedding certain features—like a commitment to multilateral trade governance or the virtues of outsourcing—while doubling down on Social Darwinist principles of struggle in the market translated through hierarchical categories of race, nationality, and gender. This chapter contributes to this body of literature by showing how Brimelow's strain of "rogue neoliberalism" defended ethnically-selective immigration restrictionism through a doctrine fusing economistic logic with cultural essentialism. His work helps us see how the nation is understood as both a racial and economic asset to the Far Right.

Brimelow is described variously as a "white nationalist," "restrictionist," or "Alt Right figurehead."[26] Yet he is almost never described the way he described himself: as a libertarian conservative or even a "libertarian ideologue."[27] It is rarely, if ever, noted that he was a fixture in the standard networks of neoliberal intellectuals seeking to rebuild the foundations of postwar capitalism.[28] He spoke at a Mont Pelerin Society (MPS) regional meeting in Vancouver in 1983 alongside Margaret Thatcher's speechwriter and later *National Review* editor John O'Sullivan.[29] Brimelow's interviews and lengthier features in *Forbes* in the late 1980s and 1990s drew almost exclusively from the MPS roster. This included profiles and interviews with Thomas Sowell (twice), Peter Bauer, Milton Friedman (twice for *Forbes* and twice for *Fortune*), and Murray Rothbard.[30] His longer features were built around the research of Gordon Tullock, Hayek, Friedman, and MPS member Lawrence White.[31] He wrote a glowing review of Milton and Rose Friedman's memoirs, recounting Milton's first trip overseas to the inaugural MPS meeting and praised the couple's contributions to "the free-market revolution in economics that has overthrown the statist-Keynesian-socialist consensus."[32]

To describe Brimelow as nativist and white nationalist may be correct, but it threatens to banish his concerns from the domain of the rational and the economic. In fact, he was a typical member of a transnational milieu linking Thatcherite intellectuals taking their own version of a cultural turn around the Institute of Economic Affairs' Social Affairs Unit with social scientists like Charles Murray and Richard J. Herrnstein concocting theories linking race, intelligence, and economic capacity as well as neoconservatives from the United States to Singapore to Japan rediscovering the relevance of "Asian values" for capitalist success.[33] For the new fusionists of the free-market Right, the economic was not a pristine space quarantined from matters of biology, culture, tradition, and race. Rather, these thought worlds overlapped and melded with one another.

We see below how Brimelow's nativism cross-fertilized with the discourse of competitiveness in the 1980s and 1990s. He turned to theories of genetic racial hierarchy even as he promoted the publication of the Economic Freedom of the World index in 1997, suggesting that high-ranking countries might be "good places to put some money," and that "freedom pays."[34] For Brimelow, the nation was an economic boon because it decreased transaction costs within its borders, especially in an information economy where there was a consensus about the centrality of human capital and an emergent discourse about the challenges of building "social capital" in diverse polities.[35] One can also see how the ordinal ranking of nations according to credit-worthiness and risk in global markets deepens a doubled sense of nation as both economic and cultural entity.[36]

This chapter places Brimelow in the context out of which he came: the financial press of the 1980s, the decade of smash-and-grab capitalism, mergers and acquisitions and hostile takeovers after which "one third of the largest corporations in the US had disappeared as independent entities."[37] His first book was not about politics or race. It was called *The Wall Street Gurus: How You Can Profit from Investment Newsletters*, marketed alongside books like *The Warning: The Coming Great Crash in the Stock Market* and *Wall Street Insiders: How You Can Watch Them and Profit*.[38] Like the authors of those newsletters, investment was simultaneously a strategy of money-making and leveraging symbolism and accruing influence. We can understand his turn to whiteness as the outcome of a portfolio analysis. The nation was a safe asset. The pro-white play looked like a payday. Brimelow's xenophobic libertarianism was less blood and soil than human capital and economic freedom.

Seeing Brimelow more clearly helps us see the Far Right more clearly too. The milieu of 1980s deregulated capitalism out of which he emerged was also the context for the coalescence of the mutant form of neoliberalism found on VDARE.com and other platforms of the alt-right today. His emphasis on a "metamarket" contained in specific populations between borders helps illuminate the Far Right's "reactionary internationalism."[39] While the call to seal national borders seems to bear no resemblance to the putatively neoliberal call for "open borders," this article shows how Brimelow's position on immigration came out of a quarrel *within* the neoliberal Right, or what he called the "small, embattled minority" that shared a "fascination with free markets"—a minority in which he placed himself.[40] Some noticed this at the time. In 1995, the *New York Times* observed that "in the libertarian wing of the conservative mansion can be found the only people anywhere in our political debate who favor completely open borders.... But the most intense opposition to immigration is also located in the conservative movement."[41] What was clear at the time has become obscured since: that an influential strand of the U.S. Far Right came out of a neoliberal civil war. The turn to restriction was itself underwritten by an economic rationality. In 1993, the notorious white nationalist Wilmot Robertson wrote a book calling for *The Ethnostate.*[42] Delving into the case of Brimelow, we find a related but different demand that foregrounds the importance of capitalism in the Far Right imaginary: the idea of an ethno-economy.

AN EARNEST PROVOCATEUR

Peter Brimelow was an immigrant twice over. After reading economics and history at the University of Sussex in the UK, completing an MBA at Stanford, and working as a financial analyst at Richardson Securities in Winnipeg, he joined the masthead of Toronto's *Financial Post* in the investments section in 1973.[43] He wrote regular pieces on business and oil stocks alongside reviews on varied topics from the collected letters of a family in Georgia in the Civil War to *The Gospel According to Harvard Business School.*[44] One column would ask if you could "beat the market" ("some say yes, some say no") while others asked "why the blacks have declared war on Jews."[45] Brimelow's writing appeared in the "fusionist" publications of the time, including *Human Events,* where he published a positive piece about white minority-led Rhodesia and another advocating a flat-rate income tax.[46]

Brimelow presented as a clubbable British import from the United Kingdom, growing a confection of hair that could only be described as a mane from under which he would peek, smiling wryly. He first cited *The Camp of the Saints* publicly in the late 1970s in a column written from New York, where he was, somewhat off-brand, subletting an illegally converted Soho loft from artists. He summarized the book's plot as "an effete West unable to prevent itself being overwhelmed by an unarmed invasion of third world immigrants." Previewing the points he would develop over the next several decades, he wrote that "in a low key, this scenario is underway in the US now. Quite apart from the 1965 Immigration Act, which discriminates against northern Europe, one million Mexicans alone arrive illegally in the US each year. Lately hundreds of Haitians have been showing up in open boats and demanding political asylum."[47]

Brimelow was on the masthead of the *Financial Post* until the end of 1980, when he moved to *Barron's*, but he returned at the beginning of 1988 to contribute a weekly column after his book on the chances of territorial crackup in Canada, *The Patriot Game*, was published by Hoover Institution Press (where he remained a media fellow into the late 1990s).[48] Brimelow transposed the problems of multilingualism and division he had written about in Canada to the United States. Demographic balance had shifted after the 1965 Immigration Act, he wrote in 1988, which had "effectively choked off European immigration and favored the Third World." Politically, "the majority, the overwhelmingly European and Christian descendants of pre-20th century immigration" was pitted "against the minorities, blacks and more recent arrivals." He quoted the opinion of a character in Tom Wolfe's best-selling novel *The Bonfire of the Vanities* (1987) that "the melting pot has never created any alloys as far as I can tell, or very few." Brimelow agreed: "the US today is in many ways a heterogeneous empire, not a nation-state."[49]

Brimelow was credited with a kind of contrarian wit by some of his supporters, who either naively missed or cynically misread the earnestness of his ideological project. In a remarkable piece from 1989, his *Financial Post* editor glossed a recent column in which "Brimelow offered a deliciously provocative idea: perhaps it's time to close the gates of North American immigration to people who are not WASP." We would be dupes to take him at his word, the editor enlightened the reader: "Brimelow wrote the column as if he was serious but he is a polemicist." He was actually "doing a magnificent job satirizing those despicable people who judge everybody by their race." Brimelow had been doing this earlier, we are told, when he "sort of embraced the view...that blacks are intellectually inferior to whites, who are inferior to Orientals." In pretzel-like logic, the editor declared that "when Brimelow says WASPs built North America he is using antithesis (or if you like extended oxymoron) to force us to recall the numbing hopelessness of the black slaves on which the Southern cotton economy was built; to remember the hard labor of low-paid and now-forgotten Chinese coolies who laid the Western railroads; and perhaps recognize the tenacity of the Scottish communities of Cape Breton."[50]

This was, of course, an idiotic misunderstanding. Brimelow was not engaged in Swiftian satire. He meant exactly what he wrote. "Let's have fun, playing Brimelow's game," the editor wrote. It was a game, but the editor was the one being played. Like hosts of editors before and after him, the newspaper's platform was coopted to broadcast radical views under the cover of provocation. Brimelow used his perch at the *Financial Post, Forbes,* and *Fortune* to mainstream the view that the immigration and reproduction of Brown and Black people was the new all-encompassing threat North America faced after the end of the Cold War. In column after column, Brimelow built up a theory of nativism built on market logic, a mutation of conservative and libertarian thought we have come to call the alt-right: the dream of a zone in white skin.

HARD BORDERS, HUMAN CAPITAL

At the turn of the 1990s, Brimelow's pieces hit the same notes as his fellow neoliberals. On the one hand, the death of the Soviet Union was obviously, as he put it, a clear vindication of Ludwig von Mises in the interwar debates about the possibility of socialism.[51] On the other hand, it was not clear that capitalism had actually won. "At first glance, the spectacle of joyful Germans waltzing through the Berlin Wall seems conclusive proof that Soviet-style socialism has failed," Brimelow wrote in December 1989. But "If socialism is dead, then why isn't it lying down?" "Fukuyama is wrong," Brimelow wrote, "History is not over in the sense he meant it. One of the antagonists has simply mutated." He predicted "a green face instead of a red face" for socialism as "popular scares such as acid rain and global warming" served to justify ever more "government control."[52] "Alienism," in the term he borrowed from fellow JRC member Joe Sobran to describe those who were open to nonwhite immigration, became for Brimelow the prime example of mutant socialism in action.

Although the theme of immigration is not one of the favorites of neoliberal discourse, there was material there to work from. Take Ludwig von Mises, whose normative political geography was shaped first by the Habsburg Empire, famously the largest free-trade zone in Europe, and a space for the free movement of labor. Taking his bearings from the period before First World War when the passport in Europe was rare, he called for open borders to allow the movement of workers to where their energy and skills could be used best. The distribution of nations was fated to change under the influence of economic forces: "There are nations whose areas would be more densely and others more thinly settled. This relative overpopulation must be dissolved now through movements of migration."[53] Mises took an antiterritorial perspective on the question of nationality. Defining nations as linguistic communities, he felt that they could be dispersed without losing their sense of connection. His defense of an absolute right to mobility was functional. Sticky attachments to place would impede optimal global productivity. The effects of perfect mobility would be total. Given the new technological capabilities, he wrote, "unrestricted free trade must lead to a change in the conditions of settlement on the entire surface of the earth."[54]

It was only in Mises's writings by the 1940s that he began to depart from his earlier polemical calls for the total free movement of goods, capital, and labor. In his wartime writings, he began to concede that total freedom of migration was not only unlikely—it might even be unwise. His first concession was to military exigency. One could not allow nationals from belligerent powers to enter the Western nations: "under present conditions America and Australia would simply commit suicide by admitting Nazis, Fascists, and Japanese."[55] The second reason was related to nonwhite populations. While he distanced himself from people who opposed nonwhite immigration in defense of "Western civilization," he conceded that

> we must not close our eyes to the fact that such views meet with the consent of the vast majority. It would be useless to deny that there exists a repugnance to abandoning the geographical segregation of various races. Even men who are fair in their appraisal of the qualities and cultural achievements of the colored races and severely object to any discrimination against those members of these races who are already living in the midst of white populations, are opposed to a mass immigration of colored people. There are few white men who would not shudder at the picture of many millions of black or yellow people living in their own countries.[56]

By the 1940s, out of pragmatism more than first principles, Mises partially legitimized closed borders for nonwhite migrants as a near-permanent feature of the world order.

Hayek made similar concessions to human weakness. In a series of three letters to the *Times* in 1978, he supported then candidate Margaret Thatcher's call for an "end to immigration." To make his case, Hayek harked back to his native Vienna, where he was born in 1899, recalling the difficulties created when "large numbers of Galician and Polish Jews" arrived from the East before the First World War and failed to integrate easily, thus provoking outbursts of racialized resentment. It was sad but true, Hayek wrote, that "however far modern man accepts in principle the ideal that the same rule should apply to all men, in fact he does concede it only to those whom he regards as similar to himself, and only slowly learns to extend the range of those he does accept as his likes."[57]

The topic of immigration arose intermittently at Mont Pelerin Society meetings. The leading opponent of nonwhite immigration, British Conservative MP Enoch Powell was a member and spoke at several of its meetings.[58] In Hong Kong in 1978, the same year Hayek wrote to the editor, Margaret Thatcher's speechwriter (and later editor of the *National Review*) John O'Sullivan gave a talk called "Migration to Utopia," reflecting on the recent episodes of settlement in Britain. Leaning on the work of Peter Bauer, he suggested that the United Kingdom offered something like a natural experiment with an earlier wave of migration by people of African descent from the Caribbean followed later by people of largely South Asian descent, especially from Central Africa. Asking how one could account for the relative economic success of the latter compared to the former, he said that one would have to appeal to Bauer's "aptitudes, social customs, motivations" more than any social circumstance. Because of the disparity in this internal reservoir of capacity, there could be no equality of outcome, regardless of the degree of state intervention. Attempts to make things equal would inevitably fail, thus only enabling further expansions of state intervention. The best solution was to let the market organize populations: if they chose to self-segregate then so be it. If they chose to spend hypothetical educational vouchers on "Hindu, Sikh, Muslim or even Rastafarian schools," then let them.[59]

In 1984, another British neoliberal Tory, Andrew Shenfield, described immigration as "a special difficulty peculiar to our times." "Freedom of movement of men and goods was a fundamental principle of classical liberalism" and earlier waves of immigrants, he said, were easily assimilated in North America. But "in our day the sources and scales of immigration have been transformed, partly by mass air transport and partly by the population explosion among poor non-European peoples." The guest worker model was not an option because "in practice it is not easy to use the reserved right of sending them home." States themselves could be blamed because he said it was "the welfare state which they have foolishly and illiberally established that is the magnet for the feared hordes." The problem was that "immigration by people of such different races and cultures in enormous numbers might transform the character of a host nation." "National character may be a slippery concept," he wrote, "but there is something in it. National culture is certainly a reality. The very liberties of America, Britain and France are rooted in their cultures, the product of centuries. Do they not have a right to preserve them?" The borders might have to close. After all, "It is good liberal doctrine that freedom of movement of goods, to which there should be no hindrance, reduces the need for movement of men."[60]

While these occasional interventions by mostly British neoliberals came and went, the topic of immigration did not appear clearly on the agenda until the late 1980s and 1990s. Brimelow described his own intellectual conversion through formative encounters with three leading neoliberal intellectuals at that time. He drew the same lesson in all cases: of the importance of the human factor and the endowments of culture in economic success.

The first encounter was with Peter Bauer, the British-Hungarian Oxford economist known as the most long-standing critic of development aid, who Brimelow interviewed for *Forbes* in 1988.[61] Bauer opposed the categories of the high age of modernization, arguing, for example, that the term "the Third World" had no coherence beyond denoting the common status of the world's poorer nations as recipients of foreign aid. Bauer believed that crude economic measurement of aggregates such as GDP made unities out of a heterogeneous medley of the world's populations. He also disputed the very category of "country." "The habitual reference to countries," he wrote in 1969, "is apt to obscure the fact that our concern is appropriately with groups of people not with geographical entities."[62]

Economic inequality was a consequence of cultural and group differences, and the stubborn persistence of these differences proved the folly of egalitarianism, Bauer argued. Much of the world was simply born poor—in both money and culture—and poor they would remain. Speaking at the Institute of Humane Studies-sponsored Second Symposium on Human Differentiation in Gstaad, where Rothbard cited Herrnstein and declared egalitarianism a "revolt against nature," Bauer noted that "differences in economic abilities and attitudes are especially wide between people who belongs to different cultures," seeing this as the biggest obstacle to economic development.[63] "What holds back many poor countries," he put it bluntly, "is the people who live there."[64] The cover graphic of Bauer's most famous book, *Dissent on Development*, expressed his pessimism, depicting a rainbow in shards.[65]

"Most problems besetting the poorer countries are of their own making," Brimelow summed up Bauer's thesis for *Forbes*.[66] There was no need to feel any sense of moral obligation nor did poorer countries hold out any prospect of economic salvation. Recalling his conversation with Bauer, Brimelow said that the economist's focus on people made him realize that "you can't reason from population growth to economic growth necessarily" and "you don't actually need immigration to smooth out any demographic imbalances: the greying of the baby boomers, the social security problem, as long as you have technical innovation." The consequences were large: "what this means is that massive immigration is not necessary for economic reasons."[67]

Brimelow and Bauer's assessments ran contrary to the mainstream conservative position of the late Cold War. Most pertinent was the editorial page of the *Wall Street Journal*. While the political demand of "open borders" is often invoked with imprecision, this is literally what the *Journal* called for in the copy of their paper published for the Fourth of July in 1984. Against "the 'nativist' Americans who still dominate Mountain States politics and the 'Club of Rome' elitists of the Boston-Washington corridor," the editors wrote, "we propose a five-word constitutional amendment: There shall be open borders."[68] Two years later, in the shadow of debates over the Simpson-Mazzoli Act, which tightened penalties on employing undocumented workers, the *Journal* ran the demand again with added barbs for the militarization of the southern border with their "Darth Vaders . . . in helmets equipped with infrared telescopes to better track today's tired and poor."[69]

As befit a financial publication, the *Wall Street Journal* had no scruples about defending its position in economic rather than humanitarian terms. The end of the Cold War had ushered in "a world in which human capital is increasingly the coin of international 'competitiveness,'" it wrote in 1990.[70] The *Journal* ridiculed the cultural arguments made by nativists and the blinkered economic reasoning of the "Limits-to-growth types."[71] Their position was a refutation of the "trembling no-growthers" concerned with overpopulation and limited resources.[72]

The economist who came closest to the *Journal*'s position was Brimelow's most important antagonist: University of Maryland economist Julian Simon. In 1989, Simon published *The Economic Consequences of Immigration*. Like Bauer, he turned to the human factor but drew different consequences. "Natural resources are increasingly less important with each passing decade," he wrote, "The crucial capital nowadays is 'human capital'—people's skills plus the stock of knowledge."[73] A review in the *Journal* hailed the book for exploding "virtually every popular dogma of the seal-the-borders brigade."[74] Simon's position on immigration followed from his position on population and environmentalism. Humans were "the ultimate resource," as the title of his most famous book read.[75] He believed that the solution to ecological problems was more, not less, population growth, since it would be humans who would find a technological fix for environmental challenges.

"It was as a fellow libertarian ideologue that I first met Simon," Brimelow wrote, "at a 1990 Manhattan Institute seminar for his new book." Published in 1995, *Alien Nation* was in effect a 350-page argument with Simon, the person mentioned most frequently. Brimelow's target of persuasion were people like himself: right-of-center habitués of the space between business, journalism, and public policy, attendees of think-tank lunchtime events and evening galas like the Manhattan Institute lecture in November 1988 named after the head of Citibank, Walter Wriston, where resident fellow Charles Murray introduced a talk by Tom Wolfe, who titillated his audience with an account of "the penetration of the money fever to every level of society" down to the beepers, Mercedes Benz medallions, and imitation gold chains of the "wolf packs of young men from Brooklyn."[76] Brimelow wrote that "one of the joys of New York life" was attending events where people like CUNY professor (and JRC member) Michael Levin "say the unsayable, loudly," like suggesting "to a black intellectual that his race's problems might be caused by an hereditary IQ deficiency."[77]

Amid the reigning mood of tittering taboo-prodding on the right, Brimelow took it as his task to question the shibboleths of free trade and the free movement of people. Confronting Simon's idea that "you have to accept the free movement of people if you believe in free trade/free markets," he asked, "You do? It's a more radical proposition than appears at first sight." "The fact is that a belief in free markets does not commit you to free immigration," Brimelow wrote. "In fact, on a practical level, free trade tends to operate not as a complement for immigration but as a substitute. If you have free trade, you don't need immigration." Brimelow looked globally and historically for support: "the Japanese have factories in the Philippines rather than Filipinos in Japan. Victorian Britain, with its foreign policy of 'splendid isolation' from the quarrels of Europe, combined total free trade with almost no immigration, a policy that satisfied Liberal 'Little Englander' isolationists and Tory Imperialist global interventionists alike."[78] The vision of free trade as substitute for free migration had an intellectual pedigree. Neoliberals had made this argument since the 1930s when the position was first outlined by the Austrian trade economist and later Harvard economics professor Gottfried Haberler.[79]

Brimelow saw correctly that the 1990s were a time of combining more freedom of movement for goods with less freedom of movement for people. He observed that one of the arguments for NAFTA was "that it would help reduce the current immigrant flood by providing alternative employment south of the border." This allowed for an ideologically consistent restrictionist libertarianism: "this is a crucial theoretical concession. It means that there is a point at which intervention to stop immigration is justifiable on economic grounds—not just because there's a backlash from the dreaded nativists."[80] One could allow for nativism and still be in line with free market principles.

Brimelow's trick was to accept Simon's premise and turn it around. If Simon allowed for the centrality of human capital then he must allow for the centrality of the differing quality of human capital from immigrant to immigrant. He argued that the 1965 Immigration Act had "accidentally instituted a perverse selection process. It effectively favored lower-skilled immigrants." He said that Simon "simply ignored this."[81] Working from Simon's premises, Brimelow pointed out he could come to a very different conclusion. It is notable that Simon conceded the point himself. A close reading of his 1989 book shows that he too believed that low-skill immigrants represented "lower-quality human capital for American workers to cooperate with" and would actually reduce productivity. "If one asks only whether additional immigrants today will help us economically tomorrow or next month," Simon admitted, "the answer probably is 'no,'" but said this was "just as a baby is a burden at first."[82]

Immigrants were investments. Simon himself did not endorse the *Wall Street Journal*'s maximal call for open borders. At a 1988 meeting of the Mont Pelerin Society meeting, which he joined in the early 1990s, he proposed an alternative: sell immigrant visas.[83] In the Japanese academic and Mont Pelerin Society member Sayo Kaji's response to the paper, he observed that "free immigration, meaning the movement of people over international borders in response to market signals, is an ideal against which no Mont Pelerinians would go in principle. Difference of views develops from how one perceives the real world."[84] The concession to "the real world" was the space of the debate between Brimelow and Simon. The alleged open borders advocate and the restrictionist firebrand both measured people by the yardstick of economics.

MILTON FRIEDMAN AND THE METAMARKET

Peter Brimelow's *Alien Nation* laid out a free market defense of immigration restrictionism. It was closed borders libertarianism that also relied on an appeal to what Brimelow called "the metamarket." "A commitment to free trade and free markets does not mean that you would sell your mother if the price were right," he wrote, "The free market necessarily exists within a societal framework. And it can function only if the institutions in that framework are appropriate. For example, a defined system of private property rights is now widely agreed to be one essential precondition. Economists have a word for these preconditions: the 'metamarket.' *Some degree of ethnic and cultural coherence may be among these preconditions.* Thus immigration may be a metamarket issue."[85] "We are all free marketeers now," he wrote in *Forbes*. "But the free market is not all things. It must function in a framework of institutions and values. That framework needs attention, too."[86] Brimelow first invoked the idea of the "metamarket," which was not in fact a common term in economics beyond Mont Pelerin circles,[87] in response to his third encounter with a prominent neoliberal, this time none other than Milton Friedman.

In 1988, Brimelow conducted his first of three interviews with Friedman.[88] In a *Financial Post* column summarizing the interview in 1989, Brimelow reflected that the "metamarket" comprised property rights but that "there may be cultural prerequisites as well as institutional prerequisites for free markets." "It may be just a matter of homogeneity, which reduces frictions," he wrote. "Or it may be more specifically that some cultures can handle the marketplace's atomism and impersonality better." He mentions bringing this up with Friedman. To his surprise, the economist "agreed instantly."[89] Friedman remarked to Brimelow that "It's a curious fact that capitalism has developed and really only come to fruition in the English-speaking world.... I don't know why this is so, but the fact has to be admitted.... Beyond a certain point [capitalism] may not be [exportable.]"

The one positive example Friedman raised was Hong Kong, but "there the limited-government framework was provided by the British.... Whether the Chinese themselves can generate that framework is very much an open question."[90] Brimelow used Friedman's response to buttress his own case, arguing in economic terms that "immigration may not be a simple matter of augmenting the factors of production. It may make the climate for the use of those factors less favorable."[91] Completing the clean sweep of neoliberal heavyweights, Brimelow also appealed to Hayek in *Alien Nation*. "Hayek used to advance a sort of sociobiological argument for the apparently immortal appeal of socialism," Brimelow wrote. "Cities and civilization have come very late in human history, he pointed out. Almost all mankind's experience has been in small hunter-gatherer bands. Face-to-face relationships are still much more comprehensible to us than impersonal ones."[92]

Appealing to the lessons of the savanna story, Brimelow suggested that ethnic diversity triggered the caveperson within. "To extend Hayek's argument," he wrote, "it is obviously easier to demonize a landlord if his features—language, religion—appear alien."[93] Homogeneity smoothed economic transactions by tipping its hat to primordial instinct. We would compete better if we felt somewhere deeply that we were all on the same team. Within the terms of Brimelow's argument, the nation was not valuable for its own sake. Its utility was its instrumentalization toward economic ends. In the final reckoning, the nation was only the most enduringly successful version of the corporation. As he wrote, "the emergence of the nation-state on the world scene is quite analogous to the simultaneous emergence of the corporation in the development of capitalist economies. Both can be traced to lower transaction costs, efficiencies in the transmission of information and the superior economies of specialization." Ethnic homogeneity had a material payoff: "the nation-state, where everyone understands one another, is an efficient way of organizing human beings. In economists' jargon, they have lower transaction costs."[94] This is the main theme of Brimelow's race-centric libertarianism: xenophobia was not just required for social cohesion. More important, as the financial journalist assured his audience, ethnic exclusion made good business sense.

Alien Nation received positive reviews in the libertarian press. Gregory Pavlik, assistant editor of *The Freeman*, director of the op-ed program of the Foundation for Economic Education and fellow John Randolph Club member, gave Brimelow a rave. He agreed that immigration regulations were "domestic social engineering efforts that aim at a radical transformation of American society from its European mores, folkways, and culture." "Along with the elevation of Third World lifestyles under the leftist rubric of 'multiculturalism,'" he wrote, "current supporters of U.S. immigration laws and so-called open borders, are buttressing anti-Western trends by importing masses of largely unassimilable minorities." Pavlik felt that Brimelow validated the charge of "contemporary libertarian critics of open borders [who] contend that immigration serves to bolster the cost and size of the welfare state." It was not the fact of the immigration but the kind of it: "the current shape of immigration is politically determined," he wrote, "it actively limits the immigration of skilled Europeans who are more likely to assimilate—as well as add to the economy." It was, in literal terms, a conspiracy to undermine the country and add support to the socialist elites.

Pavlik noted correctly that Brimelow was not making a case for protectionism. In fact, he was arguing "that free trade can replace immigration in public policy, allowing us to enjoy the benefits of the international division of labor without the social dislocations and destructiveness of mass immigration." He compared this to Victorian Britain, where there was "unlimited free trade and virtually no immigration." This gave evidence that "the international division of labor and the mobility of capital tends to eliminate the need for large-scale immigration."[95] Pavlik saw clearly Brimelow's vision for the alternative globalization of the libertarian Right: free movement for goods and capital but not for people.

ENEMIES OF THE ETHNO-ECONOMY

Peter Brimelow's core argument was that restricting non-European immigration was economically rational. If this were so, why would anyone advocate a more unconditionally inclusionary policy? Why assail the metamarket? In response, Brimelow contended that the motivations of the "alienists" were both deranged and pecuniary, both suicidal and self-interested. In their drive to accumulate private profit, they were setting about destroying the framework that supported overall prosperity.

In a polemical and cryptic charge in the first line of *Alien Nation*, Brimelow dubbed the 1965 Immigration Act "Adolf Hitler's posthumous revenge on America." In an attempt to combat racism, he wrote, the United States "triggered a renewed mass immigration" that would "transform—and ultimately, perhaps, even... destroy" the victor of the Second World War itself. Citing and transforming the famous aphorism of Bertolt Brecht as he had since the late 1970s, Brimelow wrote that "U.S. government policy is literally dissolving the people and electing a new one."[96] Immigration policy was turning the United States into what he called "a freak among the world's nations because of the unprecedented demographic mutation it is inflicting on itself."[97]

On the one hand, Brimelow saw the demand for liberal immigration policy as an irrational expression of neurosis: "a reflexive, masochistic submission, at a deep psychological level, to the demands of others." He contended that some "alienists" believed that "American whites must be swamped by immigration to make it impossible for them to act on their racist impulses."[98] Here was the *Camp of the Saints* logic he had written about already in 1978: "white guilt" triggering a self-paralysis, a kind of willing surrender to the depredation at the hands of those they had oppressed themselves. But on the other hand, would whites promote a system biased against whites only out of collective masochism?

Here Brimelow said no and brought class back in by the back door. He ultimately relied on the idea of a "new class" ascendant after the Second World War, associated in different forms with James Burnham and Milovan Delis. He cited neoconservative thinker Irving Kristol on the rise of a new class of managers: "the government bureaucracy; media educational establishment; the elite." It was this class supposedly that was leading "the contemporary campaign against the nation-state." He suggested this was true because of the innate sense of superiority and desire of the elites to distance themselves from the "peasants" who felt patriotic feeling but also because, as rent-seekers, they valued their own positions at the controls. In Brimelow's argument, "the New Class disliked the nation-state for exactly the same reason it disliked the free market: both were machines that run of themselves with no need for New-Class-directed government intervention."[99]

Thus, immigration was a deliberate project of what Brimelow called "deconstructionism," dissolving the homogeneous population to eliminate the elites' last rival and ensure the continuity of their own power while garnishing the tactical checkmate with moral superiority. Meanwhile, there was an added bonus: it made them rich. Wealthy employers wanted cheap workers. In this reading, the white elite support for immigration was not based on humane principles but cynical ones: "the American elite's support for immigration may not be idealistic at all, but self-interested—as a way to prey on their fellow Americans."[100]

Brimelow argued that the exchange of collective prosperity for the enrichment of a narrow stratum of the wealthy was accomplished by a sleight of hand that deflected attention from material redistribution toward what the political philosopher Charles Taylor called, in a famous essay published just three years earlier, "the politics of recognition."[101] Socialism had shifted from a focus on economic equality to racial diversity, Brimelow contended. By shifting from the demand for a more productive social system to one that promised to deliver "ethnic equity," socialism was now "justified in the name of extirpating 'discrimination.'" "It's a sort of bureaucratically regulated racial spoils system," Brimelow wrote, premised on evenness of representation via quotas and affirmative action, which amounted to "government-mandated discrimination against white Americans."[102] This was a postmaterialist or nonmaterialist ideology he described as a mutant socialism. It traded in chromatic signs and skin tones: a socialism of pigmentation instead of redistributed wealth.

Brimelow's portrait was far-fetched in many ways. Most glaring was that it was not any supposed turn to racial harmonization but the tax cuts for top earners praised by Brimelow for decades that had produced gross economic inequality and the emergence of a hyperwealthy class. In 1995, the median wealth of an African American household was 17 percent of a white household. If this was mutant socialism in full swing, it was laughably ineffective. That Brimelow's depiction was fantasy is obvious but, as ideology, it was internally consistent. Manifest is that Brimelow's nativist appeals spoke the language of economics as much as timeless autochthonous essences.

LIVERPUDLIAN THUGS AND ZULU COMPUTER SCIENTISTS

In the 1970s, Jean Raspail's *The Camp of the Saints* crystallized the Right's terrified consciousness of what political catastrophes might follow the end of empire. In the 1990s, it stood for something else: the West disoriented at the moment of apparent victory. Raspail's *Last Chance Armada* and Stephenson's *Raft* were specters of a question: What kind of nation? But behind that was another one: What kind of capitalism? In 1974, Garrett Hardin published a famous article on what he called "lifeboat ethics," subtitled "the case against helping the poor."[103] In *Alien Nation*, Brimelow adopted Hardin to cast the North American continent not as *terra firma* but as a maritime vessel. "The United States is not a pile of wealth but a fragile system—a lifeboat," he wrote. The United States was a particular lifeboat, "towing the economy of the entire world." "And lifeboats can get overcrowded and sink."[104]

This vision of decline allowed for dependence and interaction—but at arm's length. "Lifeboats can tow large numbers of survivors along in their wake," he wrote, "The lifeline everyone can hang on to, in this case, is trade." But trade did not mean it was "at all necessary for Chinese peasants to come in person to America in order for the American system to 'minister' to them effectively. In fact, it may be easier if they don't."[105] The comedown after the Cold War's end was intense: the West itself had become a raft. For new fusionists like Brimelow, there was a feeling of paradise betrayed: a moment of radical change uncannily revealed to hide a new host of threats. One can see this among other denizens of the neoliberal think tanks. At a meeting of the Cato Institute in Moscow in 1990, ice sculptures of hammers and sickles dissolved into puddles as Paul Craig Roberts, the author of a book on the end of communism called *Meltdown*, beamed for the camera.[106] Just a few years later, Roberts warned of an "alien future" in which "whites are turning over their country to Third World immigrants" and will soon have to worry about being targets of "ethnic genocide."[107]

Brimelow channeled the shift of mood from triumph to danger and demanded an ethno-economy. His lifeboat recalled James Buchanan's satellites and the contractual communities envisioned by the John Randolph Club. What I call the "inkworks" of negotiated, contractual governance was joined by "bloodworks," or connections based on kinship, heredity, and organic filiation. Human capital in his model was tied to cultural endowment, which was the core input for material productivity and prosperity. Immigration policy needed to bend to the law of the market. In a review of *Alien Nation*, Sam Francis summarized the argument when he said that Brimelow proved "we... do not 'need' immigrants, at least for economic purposes. And if immigration isn't necessary for the economy, we have to wonder what it's good for at all."[108] Cultural claims were not required if one could make the point on the foundation of economic reason. Counterposing a culturalist nativist demand for closed borders, as is often done, against a cosmopolitan market-justified demand for a (partially) open door misses the fact that both were rooted in specific understandings of the economic. Future studies of the Far Right must be sure, as Horkheimer suggested almost a century ago, not to remain quiet about capitalism.

What redefinition of human nature emerged from this reduction of people and culture to economic inputs? The JRC's premier politician Pat Buchanan offered one answer when he ignited a firestorm in 1991 in an interview with David Brinkley when he remarked offhandedly that "if we had to take a million immigrants in, say, Zulus, next year, or Englishmen, and put them in Virginia, what group would be easier to assimilate and would cause less problems for the people of Virginia?"[109] Reflecting its self-consciously ecumenical embrace of labor inputs regardless of skin color, the *Wall Street Journal*'s Paul Gigot responded that "the Zulus, who are the ones who want to immigrate, would probably work harder than the English."[110] Buckley dedicated a whole column to the exchange and overlaid the economic question with the racialized specter of violence. "If a million Zulus were to come on over and demand to be taught in Zulu," he wrote, "we would face a real demand-supply problem. We take it for granted that a million Zulus would not, in their disappointment, do to us what they did in 1879 at Isandhlwana, which was to express their resentment of the English by initiating what is called the Zulu War, killing 806 Europeans and 471 Africans in a single engagement."[111] Brimelow also defended Buchanan in *Alien Nation* with gruesome embellishments. "It should not be necessary to explain that the legacy of Chaka, founder of the Zulu Empire," he wrote, "who among other exploits killed all his concubines' children, sometimes with his own hands, massacred some seven thousand of his own subjects to mark his mother's death, sliced open a hundred pregnant women to satisfy a fleeting interest in embryology and ordered executions at whim daily until his assassination in 1828—about the time de Tocqueville was getting ready to visit the US to research *Democracy in America*—is not that of Alfred the Great, let alone that of Elizabeth II or any civilized society."[112] The exchange would seem forgettable, another episode of taboo-pushing by the professional provocateurs of the Right, were it not for two further responses that help illuminate the contours of the contemporary debate.

The first came from a reviewer of *Alien Nation* who asked, "what if those million Englishmen were Liverpudlian thugs and the million Zulus were Ph.D. candidates in computer science?"[113] In the page of *Commentary*, bastion of the paleo's rivals, the neocons, Francis Fukuyama said that it "may or may not be right that a million Zulus would work harder than a million English, but a million Taiwanese certainly would, and would bring with them much stronger family structures and entrepreneurship to boot."[114] The alternative to Brimelow's ethno-economy was not a broader conception of the human but what American Enterprise Institute fellow Ben Wattenberg dubbed first in 1990 "designer immigration," the selection of immigrants according to their economic utility, regardless of cultural background.[115] "Designer immigration" was the term Fukuyama used. And it was the one that Julian Simon, advocate of visas for sale, used too.

The open question that remained was what criterion one should adopt in a "world in which human capital is increasingly the coin of international 'competitiveness,'" as the *Wall Street Journal* put it. Cultural background was one. But the response to Brimelow showed that even if one intended culture and race as proxies for economic capacity, it was all too easy to label this (correctly) as a form of nativism and racism. There was another candidate, more attuned to the twinned rise of the biological sciences and computer technology. As the next chapter shows, race returned to public conversation at the end of the twentieth century as a way to talk about the best forms of selective adaptation to the needs of the knowledge economy.

Intelligence—as measured in IQ—became a central category for the new fusionists. Thinking through what I call neurocastes would be a way to be both primordial—in attention to evolutionarily determined human groups—and modern in attending to the pressures put on individuals and nations. The modern racism of the new fusionists would trade in the categories of informational capitalism: it would be an IQ racism.

CHAPTER FOUR

Neurocastes

> Something worth worrying about is happening to the cognitive capital of the country.
>
> —Richard J. Herrnstein and Charles Murray

In 1958, the British sociologist and Labour politician Michael Young published a dystopian novel—and a novel dystopia—with an enduring coinage in its title: *The Rise of the Meritocracy, 1870–2033*. Writing from the first decades of the twenty-first century, an "imaginary Michael Young of 2034" describes an earlier era when "intelligence was distributed more or less at random. Each social class was, in ability, the miniature of society itself; the part the same as the whole."[1] This began to change around 1963, when "schools and industries were progressively thrown open to merit, so that the clever children of each generation had opportunity for ascent" into the class of "brain workers." What we could call neurocastes began to emerge at this point: a new social hierarchy based on intelligence.

Introducing the "unpleasant term" that made him famous, Young wrote that by the 2030s it was time to "frankly recognize that democracy can be no more than aspiration, and have rule not so much by the people as by the cleverest people; not an aristocracy of birth, not a plutocracy of wealth, but a true meritocracy." Meritocracy was not subordinate to popular sovereignty but to science. Prefiguring a half century of discussions about artificial intelligence and automation,

Young described how "cyberneticists" modeled machines on the minds of men, achieving a breakthrough in 1989 when a computer called Pamela with an IQ of 100 became the national yardstick, a gold standard of brainpower.

Yet the meritocracy was plagued by a problem. By definition, only those deemed elites had the capacity to grasp fully the necessity of their own elevated status. Resisters to the new paradigm included the religious and the socialists who made common cause with those "just intelligent enough to be able to focus their resentment on some limited grievance." There were also "intellectual egalitarians... so much afraid of being envied that they identify themselves with the underdog, and speak for him."[2] In a twist ending, the narrator, so confident that the lower classes have internalized their position, is killed in a general strike and armed insurrection of "Populists" led by women on May Day 2034.

Young's book was republished in 1994. Reviewing it for the *National Review*, the *Fortune* columnist and amateur intelligence researcher Daniel Seligman wrote that Young's "vision of the future has been resoundingly confirmed by the recent data... what would earlier have read as a wickedly provocative speculation about the future now looks a lot like mere reality."[3] Elsewhere, he cited the research of the psychologist and opponent of affirmative action, Linda Gottfredson, to argue that the occupational pyramid in the United States had become an "intelligence hierarchy."[4] Neurocastes seemed to be emerging in America.

Talk of "the Information Age" and the "information economy" took off in the 1990s. In 1991, Robert Reich described an economy dominated by a new class of "symbolic analysts . . . analyzing and manipulating symbols—words, numbers or visual images."[5] The vision of the economy as a collection of nodes transmitting packets of information overseen by left-brained engineers had been the basis of cyberpunk fiction since William Gibson coined the term "cyberspace" in *Neuromancer* (1984).[6] In 1988, Bruce Sterling depicted the leader of

Singapore announcing to the crowd, "This is an Information Era, and our lack of territory—mere topsoil—no longer restrains us."[7] The next year, Tim Berners-Lee, brought this closer to reality when he combined hypertext and a local network from his office at CERN in Geneva to create the World Wide Web. "We think of 'creative' work as a series of abstract mental operations performed in an office, preferably with the aid of computers," Christopher Lasch wrote the year Young's book was reissued. This creative work was becoming the métier of a new elite who "live in a world of abstractions and images, a simulated world that consists of computerized models of reality."[8]

The New Economy seemed like it would inaugurate a new reign of the intelligent. Running in parallel, neuroscience took on a new prestige as the 1990s were declared the Decade of the Brain and the launch of the Human Genome Project accelerated what *Nature* called in 1995 "the rise of neurogenetic determinism."[9] "There is no doubt," Seligman wrote, "that the literate public has been assimilating a few large truths: that genes play a greater role in human behavior than previously posited; that human beings are somewhat less malleable than had been assumed; that human nature is making something of a comeback." "Hereditarianism is on the march," he proclaimed, "Nature is clobbering nurture."[10]

New fusionists plugged into the twin discourses of the New Economy and neuroscience in the 1990s, showing specific favor for IQ. The neurocastes produced by the information economy seemed to prove both the existence of an exclusive hardwired stratum of the elite and the futility of efforts of leveling up outcomes through welfare, public education, or the affirmative action programs that they saw as the burdensome inheritance of the 1960s Great Society. As Sam Francis wrote, recommending Seligman's work in 1995, "Unless the dogma that human beings and their behavior are almost completely the products of their social environment is accepted without question, then the central faith of the managerial state—the feasibility of the ameliorative planning, reconstruction, engineering, and management of social and economic institutions by centralized government—is in vain."[11] Peter Brimelow wrote that group differences in brainpower put any attempt at equalizing outcomes "on a collision course with reality." The IQ gap between races was ineradicable, he wrote, and "race bureaucrats" were misguided to think this could be remedied by "quotas and censorship."[12] The appeal to science was their trump card against state-led social uplift.

No book was more important to the rise of IQ talk for the new fusionists than the one that Seligman reviewed alongside the reissue of *The Rise of Meritocracy*: Richard J. Herrnstein and Charles Murray's *The Bell Curve*, which hit bookstores in September 1994. *The Bell Curve* was the most controversial book of the decade. "No book since the Kinsey Report has received so much attention," William F. Buckley remarked at the time.[13] Accusations ranged from labeling it "anachronistic Social Darwinism" by the Harvard biologist Stephen Jay Gould to the *New York Times* columnist Bob Herbert's claiming that it was "a genteel way of calling somebody a ni**er."[14] The same newspaper dubbed Murray "the most dangerous conservative in America," a charge the Conservative Book Club adopted later as an advertisement for the book.[15] Special issues of magazines were given over to the book's arguments, and it spawned multiple monographs in response as well as an official rejoinder from the American Psychological Association.[16]

Like Young's book, *The Bell Curve* offered a version of the meritocratic caste paradox whereby "the more open the society becomes, the more it becomes a closed caste system."[17] The castes were defined by cognitive ability and the book diagnosed a "cognitive stratification" occurring in the United States. More intelligent members of society were being siphoned from their communities of origin into enclaves of elite education and high-income employment, leaving the low-intelligence populations to multiply, encouraged by the perverse incentives of a welfare system that rewarded large families. "Going on welfare really is a dumb idea," they wrote, "and that is why women who are low in cognitive ability end up there; but also such women have little to take to the job market, and welfare is one of their few appropriate recourses when they have a baby to care for and no husband to help."[18]

The Bell Curve made an argument about geography. Neurocastes were accelerating territorial fragmentation as populations of comparable brainpower clustered together. Existing policies were making it worse. "Demographic trends are exerting downward pressure on the distribution of cognitive ability in the United States," they wrote. Alongside the subsidization of reproduction for groups of low average intelligence, immigration policy was "the other major source of dysgenic pressure" as people entered the United States according to the "nepotistic and humanitarian criteria" of family reunification and refugee policy rather than "competency rules."[19] Duller populations flooded in and sprawled across the country as dwindling proportions of the intelligent concentrated in tight pockets. (The argument chimed with those described in the last chapter. "Peter Brimelow will be a very strong ally," Herrnstein wrote to his agent, Amanda "Binky" Urban, as they were planning the book.)[20]

The Bell Curve was not primarily about Black-white differences, but it strove to spark epiphanies on that topic, saying that "racial and ethnic differences in this country are seen in a new light when cognitive ability is added to the picture." Factoring in cognitive differences caused apparently racialized patterns of structural inequality or discrimination in employment and education to vanish. For example, they wrote that "the average black who worked year round was making less than 77 percent of the wage of the average employed white. After controlling for IQ, the average black made 98 percent of the white wage."[21] Because they were less intelligent on average, the authors implied, Black Americans were being paid what they deserved.

For many, *The Bell Curve*'s blunt statements about the quasi-permanence of relative average group differences in intelligence and its call "for America once again to try living with inequality" crystallized the punitive mood of a decade that matched the "end of welfare as we know it" with mass incarceration—pointedly replacing the carrot with the stick as the tool of social order.[22] The prison population nearly doubled in the 1990s after more than doubling in the 1980s.[23] By casting IQ as the single most important factor for one's life chances and identifying Blacks as having the lowest average intelligence in an era when "the remaining differences in intelligence are increasingly determined by differences in genes," Herrnstein and Murray's brand of "realism" seemed to grimly affirm an open-ended future of deepening racialized divides in achievement and wealth.[24]

The book was understood by many as IQ racism: the mobilization of science, and in part, racial science, against the goals of the welfare state. As evidenced by its reception by the paleos of the John Randolph Club, it affirmed the new fusionist belief in the scientific validity of race and the futility of state action in reducing inequality. JRC member Pat Buchanan captured the essence of the argument when he observed, "I think a lot of data are indisputable.... It does shoot a hole straight through the heart of egalitarian socialism which tried to create equality of result by coercive government programs."[25]

Reviewers criticized *The Bell Curve* for mistaking heritability for immutability, for underplaying the consequences of historically rising IQs, for confusing correlation with causation, for torturing and misrepresenting the data, and for overstating the fact of equal opportunity in the United States.[26] Among the most high-profile of the book's reviews—to which Murray found it necessary to respond in an afterword to later editions—were those that pointed out what the *New York Review of Books* called its "tainted sources."[27] Critical coverage focused on the book's scattered references to the journal *Mankind Quarterly*, founded and run since 1961 by open white supremacists, and to its pervasive reference to research by recipients of support from the Pioneer Fund founded in 1937 for the improvement of the white race.[28]

Mankind Quarterly was the flagship journal of a group of anthropologists and psychologists, most of whom specialized in psychometric techniques of intelligence measurement. Labeled by some the "academic racists" and by others the "pro-differences camp," these scholars argued for innate, immutable, nontrivial disparities in ability between genetically defined races long after such arguments had receded from mainstream social science.[29]

Although race science was discredited in mainstream anthropology, it lived a shadowy existence among older practitioners and in outré publications like *Mankind Quarterly*. Over time, the race scientists would claim to find new support in the hard sciences, specifically genetics and neuroscience. The Human Genome Project, which appeared at first to pitch another shovelful of dirt on the grave of race science, has played some role in exhuming it.[30] Home DNA kits, Airbnb partnerships with genetic screening kits, the embrace of the genomic categories of race by progressive scientists: few would have expected the creeping takeover of race discourse by science in the twenty-first century.[31]

The eroding consensus on the social construction of race has strengthened the hand of the new fusionists. If races, even if redefined as populations, do exist scientifically, and there are group differences between them, then shouldn't this have consequences for how humans organize themselves? The basic principle of democracy is one person, one vote, a fundamental assertion of equivalence and equality. But what if people vary enough in their capacity to think and make rational decisions to make this proposition dangerous?

Neoliberals had long comforted themselves about the consequences of universal suffrage in a population with unequal endowments in two ways. The first was by pointing out that actual existing democracy was not governed by simple majoritarianism. As Milton Friedman observed at a workshop in 1986, if 51 percent of the people cannot vote to kill the other 49 percent, then a system of government is not actually "majority rule."[32] Liberal institutions, laws, and norms overlaid the brute decision-making moment of pulling the lever or scratching an "*x*" in a box.[33] Their second consolation was that voting did not matter much anyway. The real allocation of resources in a capitalist democracy happened in the market. Every dollar was a ballot, as the metaphor had it, and power was distributed unevenly with rewards reflective of entrepreneurial ability with a dash of luck.[34] The great meddler with the principle of consumer democracy was the welfare state. It apportioned rewards irrespective of ability. In fact, it seemed to work perversely: it rewarded those least able. Libertarians revolted against this contravention of the performance principle as well as what they saw as the license it gave for an ever larger and more intrusive state. As we will see, taking racial difference seriously allowed new fusionists to first add ammunition to their battle against the redistributive and caring state and, failing that, in some cases, to propose the need to create new polities freed from less-abled populations.

The Bell Curve is usually engaged on the terrain of science. I engage it on the terrain of capitalism. I show that the book tapped into a constellation of funders who shared a vision of inegalitarianism and an opposition to the redistributive social state. I trace its lineage to the alliance of rump race scientists and libertarians who kept the flame of IQ racism alive after the world's traumatic reckoning with race science after the horrors of National Socialism. The IQ racism of the new fusionists subjected human capital to quantification and lumped populations into neurocastes, collectivizing them to produce a discourse of Volk capital.

SILICON VALLEY RACE SCIENCE

Silicon Valley was a hot spot for race science in the 1960s and 1970s. As Malcolm Harris shows in his sprawling political history of Palo Alto, the founder of Stanford University was both a breeder of horses and an enthusiastic believer in the possibility of breeding humanity. The "Palo Alto System" developed by Leland Stanford is described by Harris as an apt way to think about the longer project of selecting high-performing winners and abandoning less capable losers in the febrile investor environment of what became Silicon Valley.[35] The Institute for Humane Studies (IHS) located in Menlo Park, and the Hoover Institution on the Stanford campus, were active participants in this project. Among the lesser-known but key players, mentioned in the first chapter in passing, were the Vienna-educated political scientist Stefan Possony and Nathaniel Weyl.[36] Possony, a scholar of military and nuclear strategy best remembered for claiming to inspire Ronald Reagan's Star Wars program in collaboration with the hard science-fiction author Jerry Pournelle, was a senior fellow and director of international political studies at the Hoover Institution from 1961 until his retirement in 1985.[37] He attended the Walter Lippmann Colloquium in 1938 and testified in defense of South Africa's policy of racial segregation at the International Court of Justice in 1965. "Mankind with all its diversities has never accepted a single writ," he said while citing Hegel and defending apartheid, "To impose a single formula would be ideological imperialism."[38] Weyl, a communist in his youth, testified against Alger Hiss and turned firmly to the Right in the 1950s, becoming an author of anticommunist polemics.

In the 1960s, Weyl turned to the study of group differences with a focus on intelligence. He soon became an important link between the world of race science and organized libertarianism. One of his correspondents was F.A. "Baldy" Harper, a founding member of the Mont Pelerin Society in 1947 and first president of the IHS. Harper concocted the institute with grand ambitions in 1961. With funding from the philanthropic pocketbook of the Volcker Fund which had paid for his trip to Mont Pelerin in 1947, Harper hoped to create what one leading libertarian account called a version of Princeton's Institute for Advanced Studies for "in-depth study and research on the principles of liberty that the movement needed to grow." The focus would be on much more than economics. Consulting with leading neoliberals, Harper heard from Hayek that psychology should be centered along with philosophy and from Rothbard that answers about "natural law ethics" should be sought in "human biology."[39]

This scientific approach chimed with Harper's own idiosyncratic epistemology which combined nods to the divine with a devotion to the natural principle of variation. In the appendices to Harper's most complete piece of writing *Liberty: A Path to Its Recovery* from 1949, he wrote reverentially of the father of modern statistics Adolphe Quetelet (along with the father of both statistics and eugenics Francis Galton) for the discovery that the variation of natural traits could be graphed on a "smoothly bell-like curve."[40] His interest in variation did not translate directly into a belief in racial group differences; historian John H. Jackson notes that Harper suggested something of the opposite, emphasizing variation even within so-called races.[41] Yet the two symposia on "human differentiation" in the early 1970s discussed in earlier chapters signaled Harper's openness to more biologized understandings of human nature.

More evidence can be found in 1972, a year before Harper's death by heart attack at the age of sixty-eight, when his ambitions for the IHS had been pared down to a headquarters in his garage in Menlo Park financed by the institute's chairman, the tycoon Charles H. Koch. (Koch would later move the institute to George Mason University in Fairfax, Virginia, where it currently has a $17 million annual operating budget.)[42] In a letter to Weyl, Harper reported that a member of the IHS council, John R. Baker, had "written a book on human racial differences which is the product of many years of work."[43] A devotee of Hayek, with whom he collaborated in the Society for Freedom of Science in the 1940s, Baker was a biologist who became a staunch defender of white minority rule in Southern Africa after the war and joined the editorial board of *Mankind Quarterly*.[44] An outspoken defender of the hierarchy of intellectual ability and scientifically verifiable racial traits, Baker was a central figure in what one historian calls "the renaissance of racist eugenics" in the 1960s and 1970s.[45]

The book Harper referred to was titled *Race*, and it set out to rehabilitate racial typologies reliant on outdated criteria like the size and shape of crania.[46] One scholar described Baker's ideology as "an odd amalgam of libertarianism and genetic elitism, not unlike the formula of *The Bell Curve*."[47] Of course, Baker was not alone in this odd amalgam of scientized neoliberalism—it is the essence of the new fusionism that is the subject of this book. When Harper asked Weyl about his feelings about the Gstaad conference on human differentiation, Weyl lamented the oversight of disenfranchisement based on the level of human evolution. "Do we conceive of man as species in evolution—one ranging from surviving fossil peoples with brains possibly too small to permit rational thought up to a Leonardo, a Shakespeare, a Goethe or an Einstein?," he asked. "If so, are their rights modified by their ability to exercise them rationally?" Weyl believed they should have discussed "whether belief in the inequality of men"—which they all shared—"is compatible with belief in the equal right of all men to freedom and property."[48]

Weyl's invitation to the Gstaad conference had come from George Resch, Harper's assistant at the IHS, who had brainstormed the idea of the institute with Rothbard and Leonard Liggo with whom he also coedited the short-lived journal *Left and Right* in the 1960s.[49] If Harper was reticent on topics of racial difference, Resch was the opposite. He swapped thoughts with Weyl on the proposals of Silicon Valley's most prominent advocate of scientific racism, William Shockley, whom Weyl described as a friend.[50] After winning the Nobel Prize in 1956 for helping invent the transistor, Shockley used his position at Stanford to propagate theories of group difference in intelligence and ideas such as paying low-IQ men to be sterilized. Resch was not convinced, suggesting that Shockley's "bribe of $1000 per IQ point below 100 to get people to submit to a voluntary sterilization seems a bit wild." "Judging from the Negro proletariat with which I've had any contact," Weyl wrote, "I guess they could be 'bought off' for a good deal less than $10–$15,000."[51] He and Weyl agreed that Shockley was also too optimistic about the "benefits" of gene mixing. Weyl wrote in 1971 that "his theory that on average you can increase the IQ of a practically pure bred [*sic*] Negro population by 1 point for every injection of 1 percent of White genes seems to me wild."[52] Weyl and Resch outflanked Shockley from the Right. They felt he was not racist enough.

Weyl connected to other nodes of the world of race-curious libertarianism. He exchanged letters with William H. Regnery II of the Intercollegiate Studies Institute (ISI), who commissioned him to write for their magazine on "the relative importance on the individual of heredity and environment" but warned that they could not include any "discussion of Negroes" because they were "constantly monitored by Group Research, the Anti-Defamation League et al."[53] Regnery would go on to be a major funder of white nationalism and scientific racism.[54] Robert A. Schadler, national director of the ISI wrote to Weyl to congratulate him on an article he had written, "Racial Differences in the Range of Brain Capacity," for *Mankind Quarterly*.[55] Schadler invited him to present but, echoing Regnery, urged him to use tact. "I regret that it will be necessary to downplay your insights into genetics and ethnic differences," he said. "ISI is not yet in a strong enough position to withstand the attacks such a presentation could bring." Accepting the invitation, Weyl shared his thoughts about race science and intelligence alongside one of the stalwarts of the Austrian school of economics, Hans Sennholz, at the ISI summer school in 1971.[56]

Weyl's most notable interaction on the topic of race and libertarianism was with the future founder of the Mises Institute and John Randolph Club, Lew Rockwell. Working as an editor at the conservative press Arlington House, Rockwell published a book that Weyl wrote about minority rule in southern Africa called *Traitors End*.[57] Proposing the book, Weyl said that it would "collate and present the available data on the comparative IQ scores, educational progress EEG patterns, kinesthetic neonatal maturation rates and brain histologies of the various races inhabiting the area."[58] Rockwell made the book a selection of the Conservative Book Club in 1970.[59] Reviewing it for *Mankind Quarterly*, the magazine's founder, Robert Gayre, or "Sir Gayre of Gayre and Nigg," as he styled himself, condemned the role of communists in discrediting the study of race as "racist, nazi and fascist" and said the book "should be read by all who wish to understand the hidden forces which today are exploiting the race problem to their own interests."[60]

Rockwell corresponded with Weyl about publishing another book called *Culture, Race, History* but ultimately begged off, saying that "it would be discounted and attacked even more vehemently by the liberals as 'racist' if we were to publish it (though I must say I agree personally with practically everything in it)."[61] Instead, Rockwell suggested that he follow up with a different volume called *Integration: The Dream That Failed*. Noting that "in the large cities, integration and other forces have turned the public schools into jungles," Rockwell suggested that "the book would examine integration in the schools, churches, armed forces, neighborhoods, etc. and the havoc it has wrecked and the hatreds that it has generated." Previewing the position he would package as "paleolibertarian" with the JRC in the 1990s, Rockwell clarified what he wanted: "I envision the book taking the position that both forced integration and forced segregation are wrong in America, and that both have failed. The only rational alternative being voluntarism with charity which would probably result in de facto segregation for the majority of both races and integration for the minority who want it."[62]

In his unpublished draft, which survives in typescript in the archives of the Hoover Institution, Weyl agreed. Given freedom from state interference, populations would self-segregate by intelligence and race, leading to an optimum outcome as better-endowed couples produced the future intellectual elite. He described affirmative action as "the injection of hordes of Negroes of low intelligence into the colleges and universities," which would dilute the gene pool and produce "a negatively-selective mate-selection matrix." "Creativity, innovation and world leadership are concentrated in the highly industrialized, urbanized societies in the colder portions of the globe," he wrote, using a euphemism for the traditionally Caucasian geographic regions. They were the "creative leaven of mankind" and must be allowed to self-select without egalitarian meddling.[63]

The IQ racism that linked Weyl and the libertarian world was premised on the acclamation of a natural elite and an inflexible hierarchy of hardwired intellectual castes that mapped on to race. Weyl's book that most clearly anticipated *The Bell Curve* was *The Geography of Intellect*, coauthored with Possony in 1963. (The similarity may be more than coincidence. Herrnstein wrote to Weyl in 1991: "I have followed your work for years and count myself as a fan.")[64] Published by conservative Regnery Press in the same year it published Wilhelm Röpke, William F. Buckley, and Russell T. Kirk, the book began by declaring that "the resource which seems most critically in short supply on a global scale is human intelligence" and noted that intelligence was unevenly distributed both across space and across races.[65] The authors argued that the dominant political form of the postwar world—welfare democracy—was making matters worse. "Genetic deterioration of the human race is frequently paralleled by growing lip service to democracy," they wrote, and lamented that the end of empire meant the departure of white elites from sub-Saharan Africa with little chance of them being replaced as "mental capacity tends to be adequate among peoples and races adjusted to cold and temperate climates, but inadequate among those adjusted to hot climates."[66]

"The Caucasoid are becoming a diminishing proportion of the world's peoples," Weyl wrote to *MQ*'s editor Robert Gayre in 1964. "In Latin America, negroes, Indians, mestizos and mulattoes are reproducing more rapidly than the white creative minority."[67] He wrote that he and Possony were offering solutions to the problems of the developing world, including: "1) artificial eugenic insemination to upgrade African Negro mental capacity; 2) restoration of the white presence in one form or another; 3) structuring the development along simple lines not mentally exacting or any combination of the above."[68]

Consistent with the IQ racism that would blossom in the 1990s, Weyl and Possony proposed different hierarchies than one might expect. In 1962, Weyl wrote an angry letter to William F. Buckley complaining about the leading conservative intellectual's blanket use of "racist" and "white supremacism" as analogous slurs. White supremacism was a red herring, Weyl contended. "I would not personally agree that the case for Caucasian superiority over such races as the Mongolian is at all strong or convincing," he wrote. Indeed, Weyl and Possony began their book by writing that "the greatest contribution to the total intellectual life of the modern world seem to have been made by the Jews."[69] Second, Weyl suggested that racism "may mean any one of several things." "The significant form of 'racism' to intelligent people is the proposition that significant mental, and perhaps emotional differences exist among races and are to a large extent genetically caused." As opposed to Nazi doctrine, he wrote, "race is not considered as a mystical entity, but as a natural product of evolution, mutation, adaptation to environment, etc."[70]

Beyond the placement of Ashkenazi Jews and East Asians at the top of the hierarchy, a key trait of IQ racism is that it dealt in averages—the iconic bell curve—rather than isolated cases. Theoretically that should mean that, like Harper, one should recognize variation within groups as undercutting attempts to make judgments about groups at large. Yet when it came to policy, a crude shorthand was necessary. "There are large areas in which we must judge aggregates not individuals," Weyl wrote. He used the example of immigration: "If the US needs more intelligent people, should it not increase the quotas for Mongolians at the expense of less favored groups?"[71]

IQ racism was a practical science, always intended as a tool of policy, urging attention to intelligence in the interest of maximizing productivity in what its adherents saw as an economy moving toward a focus on intellectual tasks. "If cybernetics and automation mean a revolutionary and drastic rise in the minimum threshold of mental ability in the economic system," Weyl and Possony wrote, "they will magnify the social problem of the submarginal man." Like Young before them, Murray and Herrnstein after them, and innumerable Silicon Valley technolibertarians since, they projected forward to a future when labor would be conducted ever more by "cybernetic and automation control systems." As machines rendered more workers obsolete, they would make the workers who design and operate the machines ever more important.[72] IQ racism reflected the needs of an emergent knowledge economy.

RICHARD LYNN: BETWEEN PSYCHOLOGY AND FREE MARKET THINK TANKS

The worlds of IQ race science and paleolibertarianism were woven together in the United States in the 1960s and 1970s. The strands also crossed the Atlantic. A case in point was Richard Lynn, with whom Weyl corresponded, sending him a draft paper on "Ethnic and Racial Differences in Intelligence" in 1975.[73] Parallel to Weyl and Possony, Lynn sketched out the contours of a market-oriented IQ racism, a project later followed by Murray and Herrnstein. After *The Bell Curve* was published, critical reviewers singled out Lynn for special attention. The little-known psychologist was thanked for his advice in the acknowledgments and cited twenty-four times in the text.[74] Born in the UK in 1930 and educated at the University of Cambridge, Lynn taught at the universities of Exeter and Dublin before taking a professorship at the University of Ulster in Coleraine, Northern Ireland, in 1972, where he also received Pioneer Fund grants to his home address listed as "the Ulster Institute for Social Research."[75] He was an associate editor of *Mankind Quarterly* and the propagator of theories of immutable racial differences in intelligence, self-control, and the capacity to build civilizations.[76]

While Lynn's prominent role in the "pro-differences" camp of rump race scientists is common knowledge, less well known is his long connection to the world of free-market think tanks. This story stretches back to the 1960s and constitutes a forgotten chapter of the neoliberal "war of ideas."[77] Lynn's first translation of his academic work into public advocacy came in 1967, when he contributed a chapter for a volume published by the Institute of Economic Affairs (IEA) and edited by its director, Ralph Harris, and the economist John Jewkes, both members and presidents of the Mont Pelerin Society. The IEA was the prototypical neoliberal think tank. It was established by the poultry entrepreneur Antony Fisher in 1955 and explicitly designed to enact Hayek's suggestion of addressing the "second hand dealers in ideas" of academics, teachers, and journalists as a way to shift the climate of opinion from a social democratic variety of capitalism moderated by solidarity and pooled risk to one guided by the principles of competition and individual risk.[78]

Lynn's article for the IEA presented a case against the postwar welfare state based on what would become known as evolutionary psychology—a version of Hayek's idiosyncratic take on sociobiology but with a different outcome. "Primitive man," he told his reader, "lived in small mutually hostile groups. During the course of evolution, the competition and aggressive instincts became progressively strengthened on the survival-of-the-fittest principle. The groups which had most of them tended to win, expand and establish themselves in the best territories."[79]

The selection over time for what Lynn called "the instinctive competitive drive" or "achievement drive" had shaped human nature and sat uneasily with the demands for collective cooperation in a system—such as postwar Britain—with high levels of public ownership and economic planning. People were liable to respond with one of three responses: retreat, escape, or counterattack. He saw signs of the first in investors disinclined to start new businesses because of high taxation and overregulation and the second in the outmigration of skilled workers and the wealthy.[80]

The third response—counterattack—was a good description of the strategy adopted by IEA and its supporters in the Conservative Party. Lynn's next contribution to the campaign was related to education policy. In 1970, he wrote an essay for one of the so-called Black Papers published from 1969 to 1977, originating in Tory circles, that protested the move toward comprehensive schools and the elimination of merit-based "streaming" in public education. Later praised by Margaret Thatcher, the Black Papers were an early salvo of the emergent New Right notable for being "a direct response to the student revolution of 1968" and a warning against the wrong-headed "ideology of equality" they associated with their opponents on the left.[81]

Lynn insisted that the "natural inequality between the intelligent and the dull still persists" against the wishes of "the egalitarians." He defended the inevitability of social hierarchy and the fact that streamed schools were "part of the method of training children for competitive western society." Lynn drew larger conclusions, arguing that "much of the country's economic malaise seems to arise because the British are not competitive enough."[82] Intellectual hierarchy and interpersonal and economic competition must be the lodestars of public policy. Lynn built his themes of the evolutionary and functional need for competition on assumptions about genetic determinism. In a 1969 article in the magazine *New Scientist* about the emigration of skilled workers, he drew "attention to the serious danger which a prolonged brain drain could entail for the genetic quality of the population remaining in Britain" and contended that "intelligence is principally determined by inheritance."[83]

Even as he gravitated toward intelligence, Lynn experimented with other variables as predictive indicators of economic growth and success. In 1968 and 1971 he published on the power of relative levels of anxiety and arousal to explain national hierarchies of economic output. By compiling data on alcoholism, mental illness, suicide, calorie intake, coronary heart disease, car crashes, and weather patterns, he claimed to have determined that moderate levels of anxiety were beneficial for economic performance.[84] His conclusions were published in the prestigious journal *Nature* and were covered by the *Times* of London.[85]

It was only after the early 1970s that Lynn narrowed his focus to what would become the monocausal variable of intelligence. In 1972, he wrote to Herrnstein to credit his article in *Atlantic Monthly* on IQ for influencing him.[86] Lynn wrote that he had "never realized the brilliance of Binet's innovation [in inventing IQ tests] until you pointed it out in the early pages of your article." He invited Herrnstein for a stay at the University of Ulster and paid him the compliment of redirecting his line of study permanently toward intelligence measurement research.[87]

Lynn's willingness to apply psychological insights to the counterattack against the egalitarianism of the welfare state and make audacious claims that shifted scale from the classroom to the national economy persuaded the IEA's Harris to pursue deeper collaboration with him. In May 1970, Harris proposed to Lynn that they try to establish "something along the lines of a Foundation for Research into Human Behavior."[88] Lynn responded positively to what he called first a "Foundation for Social Research" and later proposed renaming either the Galton Institute after the "ideologically fairly neutral psychologist" (who was also the founder of the field of eugenics) or Charles Spearman, a pioneer of intelligence research and discoverer of "g" or general intelligence.[89] Lynn and Harris secured the assent of prominent members of the pro-differences camp, Hans Eysenck and Cyril Burt, to sit on an advisory council and Lynn suggested employing a young journalist named John O'Sullivan who, as mentioned earlier, would become a speechwriter for Margaret Thatcher, editor-in-chief of *National Review*, and a member of the board of directors of Brimelow's anti-immigration website VDARE.com.[90]

Lynn proposed that one route to realizing their institute would be coopting an existing organization. "Have you had a look at the Eugenics Society?," he wrote to Harris, "I think it is a magnificent idea to make an attempt to take over this society."[91] While the attempt to "take over" the British Eugenics Society failed, Harris and Lynn did find a supporter in plastics mogul Nigel Vinson, who gave them a one-year £100,000 interest-free loan through the Institute of Economic Affairs for their new endeavor.[92] Vinson would cofound the Centre for Policy Studies in 1974 along with Thatcher and Keith Joseph and reenter the news decades later (now as Lord Vinson) for backing the climate denial think tank, the Global Warming Policy Foundation, launched in 2009.[93]

In courting donations from corporate managers at Esso, General Electric, and elsewhere, the duo included Lynn's research on "the decline of the national intelligence" and explained that they planned to address problems of motivation and the disincentive function of high rates of taxation. Although the latter would not become widely discussed until its effective branding in the diagram of the Laffer Curve by the economist Arthur Laffer in the late 1970s, it was the topic of research of the German behavioral economist, Günter Schmölders, who was also made the president of the Mont Pelerin Society in 1968.[94] The topic of the first MPS general meeting Schmölders organized, in Munich in 1970, was "the image of the entrepreneur" and Lynn's research fit well into this effort.[95] In his 1974 profile of eight prominent businessmen, Lynn compared the entrepreneur to "the creative scientist and the artist."[96] Returning the favor to Vinson for his donation, Lynn included him in the gallery.

Lynn continued to work with neoliberal think tanks after the plans for the Galton Institute ended in 1972. Most notable was Lynn's receipt from 1988 to 1990 of $190,000 ($350,000 in present-day dollars) for his research from the Pioneer Fund funneled through the Atlas Economic Research Foundation (later Atlas Network), an umbrella think tank founded by IEA impresario Antony Fisher in 1980.[97] In a 1987 letter to Harry F. Weyher, president of the fund from 1958 to 2002, Lynn explained that he originally approached John Blundell, the president of the IHS, who "was quite happy to receive the grant."[98] Blundell eventually demurred, however, when "after consulting with his colleagues he became nervous of the title and scope of the project and felt that some supporters of his Institute might react adversely to it." Lynn explained that Blundell's "institute is concerned principally with free market economics and some of these people are uneasy about the possibility of adverse publicity arising from association with work on racial differences in intelligence." "I expect you will have encountered the widespread sensitivity on the intelligence issue," Lynn wrote to Weyher, "and the desirability of keeping a low profile on the subject."[99]

The documentation for one of Lynn's grants—of $30,000 approved in January 1990—was "for the continuation of a study to be supervised by Professor Lynn of an evolutionary theory of the characteristics of the intelligence of Mongoloids and its extension to various populations."[100] While Lynn had studied educational systems in Japan in the 1980s, what he published after the duration of the grant was a two-article survey in *Mankind Quarterly* on "race differences in intelligence."[101] Paid with money funneled through Atlas, he was pursuing his research into race science. To borrow a metaphor from his own field of evolutionary science, Lynn was the missing link between the worlds of racial intelligence research and free market think tank advocacy. He cleared the path that Herrnstein and Murray would walk later.

CHARLES MURRAY: FROM *HOMO ECONOMICUS* TO HUMAN DIFFERENCES

The Bell Curve was made possible by the financial support of neoliberal think tanks and the institutional support of Harvard University. Charles Murray received a generous annual stipend of $90,000 ($200,000 in present-day dollars) from the Lynde and Harry Bradley Foundation while working from home as an affiliate of the Manhattan Institute and Herrnstein received his salary from Harvard. They received additional grants administered as subgrants through Harvard from the Carthage Foundation and the Smith Richardson Foundation, among others.[102] Herrnstein courted the Alexis de Tocqueville Institution for additional funding and approached a third rail when he suggested they could "in a pinch, ask the Pioneer Fund for help."[103]

But Murray's route to intelligence theory was not a straight one. The path to *The Bell Curve* charted a disciplinary transition from an approach grounded in behaviorism to one grounded in the cognitive psychology of IQ racism. Murray rose to prominence first for his 1984 book *Losing Ground*. Published first as a pamphlet by the Heritage Foundation, the book was written under the aegis of the Manhattan

Institute, another think tank founded by Fisher and directed by Hammett, the former general director of the Center for Libertarian Studies.[104] The book asked why the War on Poverty launched in the 1960s seemed to have been lost. Murray pursued the answer through his background in public policy auditing and his methodological tools of cost-benefit analysis, rational choice theory, and behaviorism.[105] Murray's keywords were "rules of the game," "environments," "inducements," "short term rationality," and above all "incentive structures" and "status rewards." He argued explicitly that the poor were not making decisions based on innate, inherited, or culturally derived qualities. Rather, they were universal actors pursuing pleasurable activities until the pain of sanctions deterred them from doing so.

Murray went out of his way to argue against race as a causal variable. Beyond specific areas where "white guilt... shaped status rewards," he contended that problems of Black people were simply problems of poverty. He gave no credence to arguments about heritability of intelligence or the genetically based intractability of group difference. As he pointed out later, he even cited Stephen Jay Gould's *The Mismeasure of Man*, a book he later scorned. The rhetorical strategy of *Losing Ground* was to depict an environment where state intervention misled the poor into pursuing life strategies that may bring short-term satisfaction or relief but were ultimately self-destructive. "Everything interacts," as he put it, and the only variable that could be isolated—and needed to be reduced—was state expenditure on programs that scrambled incentive structures.[106] The member of the underclass was not understood as a part of a separate species but as *homo economicus*, maximizing rationally but unproductively.

Murray's focus in *Losing Ground* was on the conscious—and often subconscious—decisions made by individuals within the framework of rewards and punishments. While the underclass was certainly pathologized, Murray's model still adhered at some level to the classical liberal model of bootstrapping and individual effort and self-control. The underclass was mired in patterns of self-indulgent behavior enabled by a misguided welfare state. But it was not permanently trapped. His suggestion of shock therapy in the form of ending all welfare payments to single mothers—inducing a turn to either family, fathers, or adoption—was taken straight from the pages of behaviorism. The organism would adapt once the environment had changed. As he recalled in 2018, "When I wrote *Losing Ground,* I was still optimistic about the malleability of human beings."[107]

Murray's approach in *Losing Ground* resembled the early work of his later collaborator, Herrnstein. Slurred as "pigeonman" by his critics, Herrnstein spent his early career in the Harvard psychology department's Pigeon Lab beneath Memorial Hall as the successor of the doyen of behaviorism, B. F. Skinner.[108] Like the early Murray, Herrnstein believed that "human society has yet to find a working alternative to the carrot and the stick."[109] Yet by the early 1970s, Herrnstein had begun to express open doubts about the limits of the behavioral approach. In *IQ in the Meritocracy,* he shared his conclusion that behaviorism had not only failed to deliver on its early promise to guide environmental modifications to improve social outcomes, but it had also led to a destructive hubris about the possibility of such modifications, which marginalized and even denied the meaningfulness of human differences.[110]

Herrnstein's transformation came through a return to IQ. "My confidence in the environmentalist doctrine broke down," he wrote in 1974, "when my study of the subject of intelligence testing (or more broadly mental testing) persuaded me that the facts about people, far more than those about animals, point to the role of genes in human society."[111] Years later Murray would also reject behaviorism—and, by extension, his own earlier methodology—when he denounced Skinner's ideas of conditioning "as only the most extreme form of the view that human behavior can be shaped at will by properly constructed environmental influences."[112] The opening pages of *The Bell Curve* played the same refrain.[113]

When did the change take place? By Murray's own account, he was converted to Herrnstein's perspective when he was invited to comment on a panel at the American Psychological Association in 1986 on the relationship between IQ, unemployment, and crime.[114] The panel was organized by a married duo of sociologists from Johns Hopkins University, Robert Gordon and Linda Gottfredson. Another commenter was Raymond Cattell, a major figure in intelligence research who, by the 1970s, had begun promoting a philosophy of "Beyondism," which prescribed intrusive programs of both negative and positive eugenics and praised the evolutionary value of colonialism.[115]

Also commenting was Murray's future collaborator, Herrnstein. The panel was the first of Gordon and Gottfredson's planned Project for the Study of Intelligence and Society, which has been aimed at establishing a "sociology of intelligence." The travel of the participants was paid for by the Pioneer Fund.[116] Gottfredson, Gordon, Cattell, and Herrnstein were part of a small community of intelligence researchers who clung to the overwhelming importance of a single version of general intelligence, or Spearman's "g," as the predictor of life outcomes at a time when mainstream psychology had moved away from this position. In their work, intelligence became a master key to understanding the success and failure of populations.

While Murray would later claim with some justification that *The Bell Curve* was "not about race," the APA panel unquestionably was. Gottfredson presented on what has remained her leitmotif: the large and stable gap in Black/white IQ differences means efforts at parity in more advanced professions through affirmative action and preferential treatment are bound to fail in their intended goal and will lead to both lowered overall productivity and increased (justified) resentment from nonwhites.[117] Gordon applied a similar rationale to crime, arguing that the most accurate determinant for Black/white differences in crime rates is not income or education but intelligence, and would likely remain so.[118]

Murray bought the argument. As he wrote of himself (in the third person) in a coauthored letter in 1991, "he became increasingly aware of how many of his assumptions in *Losing Ground* had to be rethought."[119] The switch from behavior to intelligence was profound. Individuals constrained previously by an external deficiency of resources were now constrained by an a priori internal deficiency. Equipped with the scientistic single-variable explanation of IQ, it was no longer necessary to acknowledge complexity. "Everything is connected" became "a few hard truths."[120] The word "simple" appears more than fifty times in the text of *The Bell Curve*. Leaving behind the abstract assumption of universal *homo economicus* for a partially genetic understanding of human differences, Murray argued that equality was elusive because it was impossible. Groups were unequal in their endowments and would remain so indefinitely.

Abandoning what Gottfredson called "the egalitarian fiction" and Murray called the "egalitarian premise," which they both saw as a toxic legacy of the 1960s, would require "facing up to inequality," as the conclusion to *The Bell Curve* was originally titled.[121] Murray's correspondence with Herrnstein during the writing of *The Bell Curve* suggests the zeal of the recent convert to a new methodology. He joked at one point of being "corrupted by people like you" to Herrnstein, whose overwhelming focus on IQ seemed to offer a simple answer to what had been complicated questions about the persistence of the underclass.[122]

Although Black/white differences were not the central subject of *The Bell Curve*, it was the demands of the African American population that brought the demand for equality and the "reality" of group differences to the sharpest point. Nowhere was this more the case than in the issue of affirmative action, which Murray and Herrnstein described as "leaking a poison into the American soul."[123] The centrality of the issue to the duo is backed up by evidence. Already in 1982, Herrnstein wrote in a private journal that "sooner or later someone will pull together the arguments against affirmative action and publish them in an establishmentarian paper or magazine."[124] In Murray's only two published articles in intelligence research, from

2006 and 2007, the self-trained cognitive psychologist attempted to prove that the Black-white gap in intelligence had stopped narrowing decades ago, meaning that the Supreme Court defense of affirmative action, premised on the eventual convergence of zblack and white achievement, would have to be overturned.[125]

Murray's turn to IQ capitalized cannily on the increasing public visibility of neuroscience. It chained itself to a sense of novelty—namely, biological determinism—which was notably just as much part of the Victorian zeitgeist as the stigma toward the "undeserving poor" he had preached previously. The irony of the revival of racial science to oppose the welfare state is that the welfare state was designed, in part, to address fears of the degeneration of the race. The traditional modern response to fears of degeneration or the deteriorating genetic quality of a population was to increase state intervention, including through public programs of nutrition, maternal training, public health, child benefits, family planning, and access to birth control. In extreme forms, this entailed forms of negative eugenics, including sterilizations of criminals and the mentally ill and, eventually, the extermination policies of Nazi Germany. How did Murray and other new fusionists seek to reverse the dysgenic trend without such measures? In the early twenty-first century, dystopian visions of the "downward pressure on the distribution of cognitive ability," as Herrnstein and Murray define it, have not stayed on the monograph page but become an active part of political arguments.[126]

HAVING A GO AT REHABILITATING EUGENICS

The Bell Curve was never merely an academic undertaking. It was a counterattack on what the authors saw as the corrosive doctrine of equality as sameness, a doctrine Murray later wrote had its political roots in "the legal triumphs of the civil rights and the rise of feminism."[127] As early as 1967, Herrnstein wrote to the editor of the *Atlantic Monthly* that it was "almost wildly implausible that the two races [Black and white] could be equally intelligent." "If negroes are inferior, then what is going to happen if they remain at the bottom of the social heap after every legal, political, educational and social advantage is granted them," he asked, saying, "I worry about this sometimes, mainly because the people who should be thinking about the range of eventualities have gotten themselves locked into a quasi-ethical trap when they should be free to function pragmatically."[128] The goal of *The Bell Curve* was to bring home, as Murray put it in a pamphlet for the AEI in 1998, "the reality of human inequality, a reality that neither equalization of opportunity nor a freer market will circumvent."[129]

"It is time," the book concluded, "for America once again to try living with inequality."[130] The authors believed that science was the best pedagogical tool for the task. "Do not underestimate the degree to which the Left's agenda has been founded on the equality premise," Charles Murray said in his keynote address at the Atlas Network's Freedom Dinner in 2006. "Do not underestimate the degree to which losing that premise will throw the Left into disarray." The key to securing inegalitarianism was grounding it in science. "The explosive growth of genetic knowledge," he said, "means that within a few years science will definitively demonstrate precisely how it is that women are different from men, blacks from whites, poor from rich."[131]

Murray's project linked him across the Atlantic to British neoliberals. He was hosted by the IEA three times and was granted space for two four-thousand-plus-word essays in *The Sunday Times*, published as pamphlets by the IEA's Health and Welfare Unit and in a free-standing volume with commentaries.[132] Murray's work on "the underclass" chimed especially well with the focus on "law and order" in an offshoot organization from the IEA called the Social Affairs Unit (SAU). Directed by Mont Pelerin Society member Digby Anderson, the SAU made academic-style inquiries into sociology and psychology with special attention to morality and values.[133] The titles had a punitive neo-Victorian tone, including *This Will Hurt* (1995) and *The Loss of Virtue* (1992).[134] A year after Lynn's two-part series on racial differences was published in *Mankind Quarterly*, Lynn contributed a chapter to an volume edited by Anderson in which he suggested that "the genetic constitution" of a child was "a significant determinant" of their capacity for socialization.[135]

In the early 1990s, as *The Bell Curve* was being completed, Herrnstein and Lynn took part in a series of informal conferences with other members of the "pro-differences" camp in an effort to return discussion of racial group differences to the mainstream. After one such meeting in 1991, held in a Best Western hotel on Long Island, Lynn wrote to Herrnstein about his plan to "have a go at the rehabilitation of eugenics," saying that "it seems extraordinary that basically sound principles that we need to find ways to correct genetic deterioration should have become so widely accepted in the first four decades of the century and subsequently have become lost." Reflecting on a trip to recently postcommunist Poland, Lynn wrote that "it was depressing to contrast this hopeful future with that of the U.S. where I think probably the transition to a non-white majority is unstoppable and therefore we have to think of the U.S. as finished in the medium term future."[136]

Responding to Lynn's cri de coeur about the decline of the white race, Herrnstein wrote: "I agree with what you say about eugenics. The old work is full of ideas and claims which, if they were written today, could get a person into real trouble. Most intellectuals think that eugenics has somehow or other been discredited or disproved. It continually amazes me that even biologists deny having eugenic sentiments, as if they were shameful." After another meeting two years later, Lynn wrote again to Herrnstein: "As far as the theme of the meeting is concerned, I side with the pessimists. I think it is inevitable that whites will become a minority in the US sometime in the middle decades of the next century and this will entail a considerable deterioration in the quality of social, cultural and economic life." Apparently untroubled by Lynn's visions of racial degeneration, Herrnstein sent him the introduction and four additional chapters of *The Bell Curve* three months later, thanking him for his "useful comments" on the chapters that Murray sent him directly.[137]

Lynn also had proposals about feeding the ideas of the pro-differences camp to the policy entrepreneurs of the neoliberal think tanks. In October 1990, Lynn wrote to Herrnstein, "one of our most important tasks is to convince the people in the US political economy Think Tanks of the significance of the heritability of intelligence and criminality, and of race differences for the social problems confronting the US. These Think Tanks have considerable influence on informed public opinion and on politicians, far more than we in psychology do, and if some of them could be converted public understanding of these problems would be greatly advanced." As potential partners and targets, he cited the Cato, Manhattan, and Pacific Research Institutes, the Hoover Institution, and the Institute for Humane Studies.[138]

In fact, the book that Herrnstein and Murray were writing would achieve precisely this goal. Although the director William Hammett reportedly asked Murray to leave the Manhattan Institute in objection to the subject of race and intelligence research, the more high-profile and long-standing American Enterprise Institute (AEI) adopted him along with his funding.[139] Murray drew more money to the AEI after his arrival. In 2003, he became the inaugural W. H. Brady Scholar in Freedom and Culture after a $15 million gift by the Brady Foundation.[140] On retirement in 2018 he cemented his position as the symbolic head of new fusionism when he became the F. A. Hayek Emeritus Chair in Cultural Studies. His most recent book extends the project of *The Bell Curve,* exploring "the biology of gender, race, and class."[141]

Lynn himself has become an iconic figure in the formation known as the alt-right. In the spring of the year *The Bell Curve* was published, Lynn wrote an article for the white nationalist organization American Renaissance, founded by JRC member Jared Taylor. He has been cited over four hundred times on their website and blurbed Taylor's book *White Identity,* saying that it sounded "a much needed wake-up call for whites to regain their sense of racial consciousness."[142] Lynn's books have been published since 2006 by the Nazi sympathizer Richard Spencer's Washington Summit Publishers, and he remains among the psychologists cited most often by open racists and white supremacists online to validate their claims of genetic hierarchy.[143] His work has been cited hundreds of times on VDARE.com and *American Renaissance.*

In 2010, Lynn presented a new book that paid direct homage to Herrnstein and Murray in its title: *The Global Bell Curve.*[144] Summarizing Herrnstein and Murray's earlier findings crudely but not inaccurately, Lynn said that "they presented a racial hierarchy in the United States of IQs of racial-ethnic groups." He held that his book asked if "this same hierarchy appear elsewhere in the world" and concluded that it did. He claimed that IQ differentials offered the conclusive answer to the question of global inequality. Describing poorer parts of the world, he said, "The problem lies in them. They have some deficit. Something inside them stops them from earning as much money as we do."[145] Although Murray would never express himself so baldly, Lynn captured the same truth that he and other new fusionists relied on science to propound. This was a naturalization of a racial, ethnic, and gendered hierarchy of ability consciously designed to roll back the egalitarianism of the 1960s. Responding to—and distorting—the surge of interest in human capital theory in mainstream economics, Lynn wrote in his later publications of the "genetic human capital" of populations.[146]

The neurocaste is an epistemology in search of a philosophy of governance. Despite his partnerships with free-market think tanks, Lynn preaches a highly interventionist role for the state in enhancing genetic superiority. Murray, by contrast, makes his politics clear. The first book he wrote after *The Bell Curve* was titled *What It Means to Be a Libertarian: A Personal Interpretation.*[147] In their coauthored book, Herrnstein and Murray suggested a kind of radical application of the subsidiarity principle with the decentralization of social services and their relegation down to the community level there to be performed spontaneously (as he claims to hope) or not (which may also be the case).

The clearest application of a libertarian IQ racism to policy was in immigration law. Murray proposed an end to both "chain migration" and automatic citizenship for those born in the United States. In 2006, he wrote that "massive immigration of legal low-skill workers is problematic for many reasons, and some of them have to do with human capital. Yes, mean IQ does vary by ethnic group, and IQ tends to be below average in low-job-skill populations. One can grant all the ways in which smart people coming from Latin American or African countries are low-job-skill because they have been deprived of opportunity, and still be forced to accept the statistical tendencies."[148] The inference was that an IQ-conscious immigration policy would acknowledge the "statistical tendencies" and screen for incoming people from "low-job-skill populations" in Latin America and Africa.

The new fusionism is in action beyond the United States. The equivalent of *The Bell Curve* in Germany was authored by the former Bundesbank board member, SPD politician, and amateur intelligence aficionado Thilo Sarrazin and published in 2010. Its dystopia was contained in its title: *Germany Abolishes Itself*.[149] The book has sold more than 1.5 million copies and has been seen as laying the intellectual groundwork for the success of xenophobic parties like Alternative for Germany (AfD). In the book, Sarrazin used the same body of intelligence research as Herrnstein and Murray, including Lynn, to argue against immigration from Muslim-majority countries on the basis of IQ. Sarrazin also appeals to much more mainstream indicators such as the PISA scores of educational achievement measured by the OECD since the early 2000s, which have become a kind of national obsession in many countries, and in Germany in particular.[150] Among his influences, Sarrazin cited Heiner Rindermann, a cognitive psychologist who has coauthored pieces with Mont Pelerin Society member Gregory Christainsen arguing that "cognitive capital" as directly measured by intelligence tests is the most important determinant of national prosperity and, using the same language as Murray and Herrnstein, that the relative intelligence of a nation's "cognitive elite" is a sound predictor for GDP.[151]

Sarrazin is a familiar face in organized neoliberal circles. He has been hosted more than once by the Hayek Institute in Vienna and the Hayek Society in Germany. In 2017, he shared the stage with the German sociologist Erich Weede at the Hayek Society's Freedom Forum in Berlin. Weede, who cofounded the Hayek Society and was granted its Hayek Medal in 2012, follows Lynn in seeing intelligence as the primary determinant of economic growth.[152] At the Freedom Forum, both he and Sarrazin argued for free trade and free investment flows combined with tight borders to preserve strong property rights, bemoaning the burden placed on state budgets by immigrants who "bring little or no human capital with them."[153]

Closed borders, the duo argued, were necessary to save globalization. "Knowledge, goods and ideas" should be free to migrate, Sarrazin said. People, however, did not have to move "in large numbers." That had already "brought nothing but deterioration."[154] "Cultural heterogeneity is a burden," Weede wrote elsewhere, and "mass immigration risks endangering traditions."[155] While the extension of production chains and cross-border trade had led to the economic uplift of distant foreign populations as a group, immigration only helped the small number who made the risky voyage. "Even under pure humanitarian (Rawlsian) criteria," Weede wrote, "it would be bad if mass migration threatened global free trade."[156] People must remain fixed so that capital and goods could be free.

As good spokespeople of the new fusionism, the speakers argued that the hardwired inequality of human endowments made economic inequality ineradicable. "Those who want to correct the unequal consequences of genetic fate," Weede wrote, "must flout individual rights and thus contribute to justifying totalitarianism." Inequality was "destiny and necessity."[157] For the sake of stability and prosperity, the world's poor must remain segregated from the world's intelligent rich. In a publication for the Ludwig Erhard Foundation, Weede suggested two alternatives for a reformed immigration policy drawn from fellow Mont Pelerin Society members. One was Gary Becker's proposal of selling visas for a fee. The second was from Richard Posner: screen would-be immigrants with IQ tests.[158]

The new fusionism of Lynn and Weede goes beyond the work of Murray and Herrnstein. Ranking national populations by IQ renders them static and removes the world's peoples from the reality of cross-border mobility by sorting them into neat containers. Frozen inside borders and arrayed in a hierarchy, the human capital of groups becomes something new—a flawed discourse of Volk capital.

DYSGENESIS IN THE INFORMATION AGE

Dysgenesis is a category that echoes through the writings of new fusionists: the decline in quality of populations over time. The concern is a quintessentially modern one. It arose in the second half of the nineteenth century when states first began to acquire an overview of their populations through projects of national statistics gathering.[159] One of the classic tales of dysgenesis and degeneration was published one century before *The Bell Curve*. In H. G. Wells's *The Time Machine*, brute Morlocks, descendants of earlier proletarians, live underground and breed the pasty-faced and rubber-limbed Eloi, descendants of the lazy upper class, for food. This was a dystopia that befit the era of high-industrial capitalism in the West. The engines of the economy were the factories, and its fuel came from the mines and the forests. When discussion of "degeneration" was widespread in the late nineteenth century, the world was rising the cresting wave of industrialization. Recruited into armies, workers revealed themselves as shorter than their fathers and grandfathers. Lungs were perforated and weak from exposure to coal smoke. Meanwhile, white-collar employees were growing effete and ineffectual, suffering from a nervous illness dubbed neurasthenia.[160] The scientific racism of this time was based on the measurement of limbs and skulls, skin tone, and musculature. Intelligence was part of the story but in a minor key. The term "intelligence quotient" or IQ was not even coined until 1912.

By the 1960s, matters were very different. Sociologists had already begun to speak of the "postindustrial society."[161] Computers promised to transform work processes, and the service industries of education, medicine, finance, marketing, and basic research were all on the rise. The year before Weyl and Possony published *The Geography of Intellect*, Fritz Machlup, a colleague of Hayek in Vienna and longtime Mont Pelerin Society member, published a book on the "production and distribution of knowledge in the United States," introducing a new coinage: "the knowledge economy."[162] By the last third of the twentieth century, brainpower seemed to be a more relevant factor for the economy than physical strength.

The IQ-centrism of the new fusionists is a fitting form of racial science for the postindustrial age. It was built on mainstream concerns about the knowledge and innovation economy, national competitiveness, and analogies of human beings to information processors. Thriving on the craze for standardized outcomes, rankings, benchmarks, and indicators, IQ-centrism offers a simple and powerful story about the world that naturalizes and hardens existing hierarchies, reinforces folk understandings of difference, and disempowers efforts of collective reform. Perhaps most effectively, it does so with the elegance of a single number—IQ as a biologized credit score.

The postfascist race science embraced by the new fusionists is concerned, above all, with the question of hereditary group differences in intelligence. There is a particular focus on the connection between intelligence and time preference, or the willingness to delay gratification and plan for the future.[163] This is important because, in the end, postfascist race science is about economic performance and competition. It is about quantifying the potential and capacity of members of groups to both perform historically and in the future. The IQ fixation fits perfectly in an era of indicators and measurements. It renders human worth objective and calculable. For the new fusionists, it became a way to determine human utility for reasons often but not only of immigration. Race in this case is an idiom that works because it conjugates with the economic assumptions of zero-sum competition over a shredded safety net of rankings, benchmarking, indices, productivity monitoring, and precarity that has produced a new sense of all against all, from the bottom of the socioeconomic pyramid to the top.

IQ talk worked in two directions in the 1990s. It contended that the nonwhite groups coming "here" in the United States and Western Europe were inferior and specific nonwhite groups "there" were superior. It served as a ready explanation for both the domestic slowdown in industrialized countries since the 1970s and the parallel rise of economic powers in East Asia, from Japan to the "tiger economies" of Hong Kong, Taiwan, South Korea, and Singapore.[164] It is a fitting coincidence that the end of the twentieth century in Michael Young's dystopia confronted an economic challenge from China.[165] IQ racism created a seductively simple global map, explaining the uneven histories of the capitalist world through an indicator etched in our genes.

What Murray called at the MPS meeting in the Galápagos in 2013 "the rediscovery of human nature and human diversity" was intended to promote a doctrine of governance that worked against redistribution and the social state.[166] At another MPS meeting in 2010, Denis Dutton wrote, "Political utopians have treated human nature as indefinitely plastic, a kind of fiberboard building material for political theorists. Evolutionary psychology advises that political architects consider the intrinsic equalities of the wood before they build."[167] Yet the science does not point in the direction they claim. In *The Bell Curve*, Murray and Herrnstein made absolute statements about "genes" when, in their own analysis, racial status was not based on genetic analysis but self-identification. Indexing intellectual capacity onto supposedly commonsense categories of race validated folk understandings of the race concept and encased them in the carapace of incontestable fact. The conclusion of actual geneticists (reaffirmed now by genomics) that there is more variation within so-called racial populations than between them is glossed over for the sake of the polemical point. For the sake of a new scientific language to express his unchanged message of the need to repress expectations and apply stigma to contain the "underclass," Murray mainstreamed arguments of intelligence research that now proliferate across the edges and, increasingly, the center of political discourse. As with the nightmares of the Raft and the Last Chance Armada, projections of dysgenesis intentionally create an atmosphere of end-times, of accelerating and even imminent collapse. The next chapter explores the worlds of those who embraced capitalist eschatology most openly, who saw the apocalypse coming while selling you the only way to survive it.

CHAPTER FIVE

Goldbugs

People make bad money, and that money makes bad people.
—Peter Boehringer

Thus far the book has dealt with two of the three "hards" of the new fusionists: hard borders and hardwired human difference. Each opened the door for collaboration between neoliberals and those further to their Right. This chapter turns to the third: hard money. Monetary issues have long divided neoliberals. Can you trust a central bank to manage currency? Can the growth of the money supply be made automatic? Should fixed or floating rates reign in global currency markets? Must money be backed by precious metals?[1] While the debates fill many turgid journal pages, they are also rendered in the period style of *The Omega Man* (1971) in a paperback that appeared in 1979 with its title in glossy embossed red letters: *Alongside Night.*

The novel opens in a near future where the Fed is struggling to prop up the value of "New Dollars," banknotes that "resembled Monopoly money" worth so little against the "gold-backed eurofrancs" that European shoppers are flooding Manhattan. The gold price rises by a third every day as people scramble for stable assets. The protagonist is a young man named Elliot Vreeland. His father is the Nobel Prize–winning economist Martin Vreeland, a hybrid of Milton Friedman and Friedrich Hayek, who summers in New Hampshire but hails from Vienna. An outspoken critic of the government's monetary policy,

Vreeland père becomes a target of the Secret Service as the crisis deepens. Anticipating his arrest, he sends his son to fetch his cache of gold coins sewn into a leather belt held by a bald, bearded man named Al at an adult video store in Times Square. Al becomes Elliott's entry point into a radical libertarian underground called the Cadre whose greeting Elliott hears chanted in the streets: "Laissez-Faire!... Laissez-Faire!... Laissez-Faire!"

The Cadre is part of the Agorist Underground, a hard money offshoot of the neoliberal movement that rejects the rule-based monetary management of Milton Friedman. Their initials are the chemical symbol for gold, the precious metal they see as the only vessel of value and means of orderly exchange. Taking seriously the anarchist injunction to "build the new society inside the shell of the old," these so-called goldbugs have constructed a vast underground base called Aurora, which one enters after signing a "Submission to Arbitrate" with a third-party legal service. Fixtures include a vendor of nuclear warheads; a cafe named after Friedman's famous statement that There Ain't No Such Thing as a Free Lunch (TANSTAAFL); NoState Insurance; and the First Anarchist Bank and Trust Company or AnarchoBank, which issued its own coins and advertises "The Wonderful World of 100% Gold Reserve Banking." In Aurora's version of freedom, residents surrender the right to choose when to leave and agree to extensive surveillance, including, of course, IQ tests.

The internecine neoliberal fights over money surface in the book's finale. Lured into the orbit of government by the prospect of wielding technocratic authority, the Hayek-Friedman figure accepts the role of comptroller or "economic czar" to oversee the introduction of a new gold-backed currency after a loan from the European Common Market Treaty Organization (EUCOMTO). To the goldbugs of the Cadre, he is a traitor seduced to compromise with state power. When the rescue of the New Dollar fails, the Cadre's own AnarchoBank steps in and their currency is soon the only one accepted. Taxis list their rates in the new money and unpaid members of the military queue to be employed by the Cadre and paid in gold. All services are privatized. The NYPD keep their blue uniforms but add red armbands reading "Security." The book ends with the Cadre offered recognition as the legitimate government of the United States, a status they refuse on principle. Across the nation, the black flag of anarchism rises alongside the Gadsden flag with the rattlesnake and the logos "don't tread on me" and "laissez faire" on a golden field.[2]

Alongside Night presents a world where the direst predictions of what Melinda Cooper calls "debt millenarianism" have been realized.[3] The trigger was the U.S. departure from the gold standard in 1971, a decision that many predicted would open the floodgates of money production and, in a morally loaded term, "debauch" the currency. The group that I call catastrophe libertarians pitched a form of survivalism, a way to prepare for the inevitable crisis. What made their survivalism different from those of other "preppers" was the conviction that the apocalypse might be a source of profit. One libertarian described the goldbug ideology as "the embracing of disaster." He recalls people "who believed that when the crisis happened they could take a $20 gold piece and buy a block in midtown Manhattan." "To listen to some of them is to hear people who not only worry about disaster but would welcome it," he wrote, "Because they would be ready, which means that they would be right."[4] Being right would be lucrative. "In 1973, Ludwig von Mises died," recalled one radical libertarian, and Austrians "outbid each other with predictions of the righteous monetary thunderbolt of the market at last bringing justice to the statists (and profits galore for those who went 'long' on gold and silver)."[5] Twin pleasures—the vindication of winning an argument and the payday of economic enrichment—are at the heart of the Far Right's capitalism, nowhere more evident than among the goldbugs.

HOW TO PROFIT FROM THE APOCALYPSE

Histories of neoliberalism begin at different points, to serve different purposes. Some begin with the coup in Chile in 1973 and the rise to power of Augusto Pinochet, showing how neoliberalism always hit the Global South first. Others begin with the breaking of the UK miners' strike, or the slashing of top marginal tax rates in Reagan's America, to capture the class contours of the project in the North. Others go back further to the dissolution of the Habsburg Empire and the efforts to assemble a space where property and sovereignty were distinct, or the transformation of the IMF and the World Bank into the disciplinary arm of the U.S. State and Treasury Departments after Mexico's default and the onset of the Third World debt crisis in 1982.

One could also begin from a less well-known event: when a book called *How to Profit from the Coming Devaluation* hit the national bestseller list in 1970. The book was by Harry Browne, an investment advisor and a pioneer of the nearly forgotten genre of the investment newsletter.[6] Browne acknowledged Murray Rothbard as one his most important influences and dedicated a later book to Rothbard and other MPS worthies Henry Hazlitt, Ludwig von Mises, and Milton Friedman.[7] The author of *Alongside Night*, J. Neil Schulman, credited Browne as the inspiration for his novel. He wrote it to show libertarianism not as an intellectual project but an activist one. His characters were not libertarians because they "spout all the theories" but because they had "something concrete to offer: safe areas, free trade zones, communication and transportation immune from the State, ways to beat the system."[8] Schulman had a point. Histories of neoliberalism are often too focused on the heady debates of monographs and seminar rooms and not enough on the practitioners, tipsters, and hustlers who often drive radicalization, recruit new believers, and, in not a few cases, shift popular common sense. Understanding the marriage of libertarianism and the Far Right requires entering the profane space of the newsletter, the advice manual, and eventually, the website, the feed, and the chatroom.

How to Profit from the Coming Devaluation was published by Arlington House, a small press out of New Rochelle, New York. One of the editors was Lew Rockwell, encountered in earlier chapters as Rothbard's collaborator in the founding of the Mises Institute in 1982, the creation of the paleo alliance in the early 1990s and the publisher of Nathaniel Weyl on the precarious state of white minority republics in Southern Africa and commissioner of *Integration: The Dream That Failed*, which attacked the desegregation of schools based in part on Weyl's extensive research on the supposedly hardwired genetic gaps in intelligence between racial groups. Running the Conservative Book Club for Arlington House in the late 1960s and early 1970s, Rockwell tapped into the new demand for right-wing publications in the years of backlash against the civil rights and student movement and the nascent counterrevolution to the cultural revolution. *How to Profit* was a runaway success for Arlington House. Rockwell tried to follow up the success with a series of copycat titles, including *Panics and Crashes, and How You Can Make Money Out of Them; How to Buy Gold Coins;* and *How to Buy Gold Stocks and Avoid the Pitfalls.*

What the books had in common was the prediction of an impending social and economic collapse and the need to secure hard assets, preferably in precious metals, and make plans for the safety of oneself and family. Survivalism was both an investment strategy and a business opportunity. As one person involved wrote, "the mid-1970s witnessed a tremendous increase in 'hard money' books, newsletters, seminars, coin companies, survival retreats, food storage, and related businesses."[9] The mixture of topics is captured in an issue of *Libertarian Review* from 1976. It included selections from German neoliberal economist Wilhelm Röpke alongside advertisements for a cassette program on "basic relaxation and ego-strengthening" by Ayn Rand's designated heir Nathaniel Branden and fine print offerings of "survival information" from *Inflation Survival Letter.* Pamphlets for sale ranged from the innocuous "how to minimize your taxes" to the more alarming "layman's guide to survival firearms" and "how to hide your valuables." It included a piece by Rothbard advertised as "the dean of libertarian economists" as well as pieces by Gary North on "How to Buy Rural Property—Part I and Part II" and future MPS member and standard-bearing goldbug Mark Skousen on investment advice.[10]

The idols of the catastrophe libertarians were the investors who knew how to profit from apocalypse and the books were guides to how to join their ranks. Browne's book, like the others, portrayed the modern period as a fall from metallic-monetary grace. At the end of the nineteenth century, all major national (and imperial) economies had subscribed to a gold standard that limited the amount of currency in circulation and was believed to place built-in constraints on state expenditure. The gold standard collapsed with the First World War only to be resurrected with difficulty in the peace. The Wall Street crash of 1929 and the Great Depression created a liquidity crunch with accompanying spikes in unemployment and plummet in prices. The decline was only reversed when Great Britain abandoned gold convertibility in 1931 and the United States followed two years later, removing the limit on money creation and the expansion of credit and liberating governments to spend freely. After the Second World War, a novel compromise arrangement was devised whereby the U.S. dollar was returned to convertibility to gold while the rest of the world's major currencies had fixed but adjustable rates in relation to the dollar.[11]

The so-called Bretton Woods system ended on August 15, 1971, when Richard Nixon decreed that the United States stop converting dollars into gold. This is Day X for goldbugs, marking the descent into what German libertarian and MPS member Roland Baader called "monetary socialism" (*Geldsozialismus*) under which, they felt, the printing presses funded programs for the present at the cost of building up federal debt, which would lead in time to global monetary collapse.[12] The end of the gold standard was mourned by many neoliberals, and Browne as well. They felt it freed states from salutary constraints. "Governments don't like gold because it tells them when they do wrong things," Browne wrote in 1970. "Without the gold, they might be able to stretch their misdeeds a little further. But it will not stop the consequences. They're inevitable."[13] Leaving the bonds of gold meant runaway inflation and, by implication, devaluation of currency and savings. Degenerating morality was both consequence and cause of the collapsing monetary order. The erosion of the traditional family, the multiplication of children born out of wedlock, the rise of no-fault divorce: all were seen as bloating state spending, entitlements, and transfers and accelerating the coming crisis.[14]

Browne's book was followed by a series of books with similar titles, including Doug Casey's *Crisis Investing: Opportunities and Profits in the Coming Great Depression,* Harry Schultz's *Panics & Crashes and How You Can Make Money Out of Them,* and Howard Ruff's *How to Prosper During the Coming Bad Years,* the last described as "the bestselling financial book in history."[15] Browne even copied himself, hitting the top of the *New York Times* bestseller list in 1974 with *You Can Profit from a Monetary Crisis.*[16] *Crisis Investing* hit number one in 1980. These authors were part of a scene of authors of investment newsletters. Before the internet expanded in the 1990s, direct mail and the mailing lists associated with them were a prime means of approaching the common person, getting around the gatekeepers of the mainstream media.[17] None other than nativist neoliberal Peter Brimelow wrote a book called *The Wall Street Gurus* in 1986 with the subtitle *How You Can Profit from Investment Newsletters.* He described brokerages being blindsided by the power of the recipients of newsletters. Stock prices would move based on the flood of phone calls they would receive on the advice of a newsletter.[18]

In the print world of goldbugs, investment advice was not just about a stock portfolio or savings account but one's entire lifestyle, understanding of politics, and encounter with the past and the future. It was a starting assumption of the writings that monetary collapse was inevitable. The question was not if the death of money would take place but when. Because of this, one must prepare not just financially but tactically. Browne's book ended with admonitions to create some kind of "retreat," from a "well-stocked camper" to an "elaborate hideaway." An essential part of the goldbug formula was instilling a basic mistrust in the utterances of public authorities. Politicians of all parties only shifted blame to keep the greater confidence game going. "You will hear—right up to the crisis," Browne wrote, "all the typical platitudes, asserting that the dollar is absolutely sound, that 'we have nothing to fear but fear itself,' that 'depressions are caused by fear mongers' etc. but we have seen the fundamental economic principles that transcend confidence and mass psychology." "Your patriotism will be appealed to," he wrote, "but react by saving yourself, not the government. You are not responsible for what has happened; it is the government that has destroyed the currency." "You have only one mission," the book concluded, "*to survive and prosper.*"[19]

Goldbug investment advisers and other counsels of market apocalypse channeled a kind of folk version of Public Choice theory. They argued that money creation was a tool that political elites used to reproduce their own power. The rhetoric of achieving social justice through social spending was hollow: a sleight-of-hand to conceal the politician's real goal of buying votes with taxpayer dollars. The most extreme version of this argument came from the outright conspiracy theories of authors like Gary Allen and Larry Abraham, cited and propagated by goldbugs over the years. In their 1976 book *None Dare Call It Conspiracy*, Allen and Abraham argued that finance capitalism was the "anvil" and communism the "hammer to conquer the world." They argued that debt was used to create power over people on the path to a global oligarchy, joining the party elites of the Soviet-led world with the financial elites of the West.[20]

Until 1974, the practicalities of hoarding gold for the end-times were complicated by the fact that it had been illegal to possess it privately in the United States since 1933, when individual gold holdings were requisitioned by President Franklin D. Roosevelt. Yet in his 1970 book, Browne noted an important loophole: you could hold gold coins if they were old enough to be considered antiques. Thus was born a critical nexus. Though the two are rarely recounted at the same time, the history of libertarianism in the United States cannot be separated from the business of selling collectible coins. The most high-profile libertarian in the country, Ron Paul, sold coins for decades, and his partner, Burton Blumert was proprietor of Camino Coins in Burlingame, California, as well as the founder of the Center for Libertarian Studies, cofounder of the John Randolph Club (JRC), chair of the Mises Institute, and publisher of the *Rothbard-Rockwell Report*. Paul partnered with Blumert from the time he stepped down from Congress in 1984 until he returned to Congress in 1996.[21]

Later JRC member Gary North also started out in the coin and newsletter scene. He moved from a position at the Foundation for Economic Education in the early 1970s to sell silver coins with Browne, conducting "seminars" in cities to move their product. He attended the famous founding conference of Austrian Economics in 1974 in South Royalton, Vermont, sponsored by the Institute for Humane Studies, before joining Ron Paul's staff in 1976 to write his newsletter followed by a position writing Howard Ruff's newsletter in 1977. His own newsletter was making him so much money that he changed states to avoid income tax.[22] As a "Christian Reconstructionist" as well as an adherent of the Austrian school, North believed that money and morality were inseparably connected and rooted in biblical teachings. The adoption of welfare functions by the government—financed by fiat currency—drove humanity further from God and closer to the abyss.[23] In 1979, he wrote his own copycat Browne book titled *How You Can Profit from the Coming Price Controls*.[24]

The apocalypticism and counterfactual claims so familiar from the online Far Right of the early twenty-first century had a precedent in the goldbug investment newsletter, which also offered packaged insights that appeared to go against the grain, to offer you the edge that nonsubscribers lacked, the one the mainstream media did not want you to have because otherwise everybody would beat the market. They cultivated an aura of esoteric knowledge and an abiding suspicion of conventional wisdom. They also often used stark, frightening language used to propel the reader into action to save themselves. A common word used was "survival." Rothbard himself wrote multiple articles for

Skousen's *Inflation Survival Letter.*[25] The binary of survival or death mirrored the binary of buying or selling a share but, in this case, one's own existence was the asset in question. Life itself was the stake.

THE METAL VIEW OF HISTORY

As suggested by the outsized significance of Nixon's decision to leave the gold standard, goldbugs wrote their own history of the twentieth century. One way of tracking their parallel timeline is through Ron Paul's newsletters, the editorship of which was another line on Lew Rockwell's resume. The surfacing of the Ron Paul newsletters created a minor scandal in 2008 during Paul's surprisingly robust run for the Republican presidential nomination. Excerpts from what was originally called the *Ron Paul Investment Newsletter* suggested correctly that they were shot through with racist and xenophobic sentiment but scholars dug no further than the few startling anecdotes.[26] In fact, the articles, most of which lack a named author but whose style strongly resembles Rockwell's own, offer a thick description of the end of the Cold War and the beginning of the 1990s from the paleolibertarian perspective, prefiguring in many ways the Far Right politics of decades later.

Notable first is that the newsletters recount something other than the titanic clash of communism and capitalism. Rather, they track a persistent struggle by hard money purists against the architects and manipulators of fiat money. Into the 1990s, goldbugs saw their primary enemy in the "monetary socialists" of both parties who manipulated and bought off refugees, immigrants, and populations of color as their patsies and useful idiots. Even before the collapse of the Soviet bloc, the chief threat was not communists but what the authors called "Trilateralists," "globalists," or the "Paper Aristocracy," who they contended orchestrated inflation to expropriate the common saver, fund welfare dependents, and finance foreign wars.[27]

Consistent with the conspiracy theories of Gary Allen, who the newsletter praised in 1988,[28] they warned of what Rothbard's protégé

Hans-Hermann Hoppe called in an interview "the coming world state" led by a transatlantic elite of "the Trilateral Commission, the CFR [Council on Foreign Relations], and the various Business Round Table groups" who were using European integration as a step toward their final goal of "One World State with a world tax system, a world central bank, a world currency, a world welfare state, a world regulatory agency for all stock markets, world economic planning, abolition of private firearms, population control, world public education (for indoctrination), a world court, world secret police, and a world army."[29] Referencing Roman Polanski's 1968 film in which a woman is unwittingly impregnated by Satan, the newsletter authors dubbed the global scheme a "Rosemary's baby."[30]

Having watched a decade of structural adjustment in the Global South, Paul's paleos expressed open concern that the same thing would happen to the United States. One author, who also wrote for the Mises Institute, observed in 1988 that "a world central bank can force every country in the world, including the US to accept whatever political agenda the bankers have." If this were realized, "the US will be in the same position as the Brazilians, Peruvians, and the Bolivians: debt-ridden, inflationary and controlled by foreign political and banking powers."[31] When the newsletter's authors titled an article "can it happen here?" in 1989, they did not mean fascism in the United States as in the classic Sinclair Lewis scenario but structural adjustment boomeranging home from places like Venezuela: "It's only a matter of time before the US will be getting marching orders from the IMF as well."[32] A gold standard would be ideal but unlikely given the situation, so the best thing to do was impose a "personal gold standard with the maximum amount of fully owned, personally held, low-premium gold bullion coins. Only they can protect you from the dollar run wild."[33]

A month after the Berlin Wall fell in November 1989, the *Ron Paul Investment Letter* made its predictions for the new decade: "In the 80s, communism disintegrated; in the 90s Keynesian welfarism will implode." This would be accompanied by chaos: "Racial violence will fill our cities... as a bankrupt welfare state fails to provide the cash, mostly black welfare recipients will feel justified in stealing from mostly white 'haves.' Race hatred will grow... the New Money will be issued... the American republic will be replaced with Democratic Fascism." The goal of the newsletter was to equip the reader to "rebuild from the rubble."[34] Race war was a running theme. Paul's paleos turned even more pointedly to the need to prepare for race war from the end of 1992, marked by the election of Bill Clinton and the continuing fallout from the spring's Los Angeles riots. They signaled the sharpening of tone in December 1992 by changing the name of the *Ron Paul Investment Newsletter* to the *Ron Paul Survival Report* "for the Age of Clinton."[35] The authors elaborated the logic. "In the latter half of the 1990s," they wrote, "survival will have to be our first priority, rather than conventional investing."[36]

The *Survival Report* left no ambiguity about the source of threat: Black foreigners lured by liberal policy and welfarism. A single issue of the newsletter in 1993 captured the constellations of concerns. One article raised a *Camp of the Saints*-like specter, warning of "thousands of Haitians" (called elsewhere "AIDSians") "now building boats to sail to the United States of Welfaria after the inauguration. Many are HIV positive and come for free medical care as well. During the campaign, Clinton promised to welcome the Voo-dooistas and here they come."[37] Another spoke of Somalia. The author claimed that "every black nation in world history has the same problems as Somalis, including tribal warfare, primitivism, socialism, totalitarianism and starvation." "This is not simply because the inhabitants are black," he assured the reader, but because of the supposedly perverse effects of white paternalism. "Blacks in general, both in the US and Africa," he wrote, "have become dependent on others. In America, blacks have allowed themselves to become enslaved in a welfare system. Black countries of Africa do the same thing by demanding and getting foreign aid from Western countries."[38]

The immediate measures suggested to Paul's readers were outlined in one of the few articles published with attribution—by James

B. Powell, a consultant for Globacor, a firm whose president had published a book called *The Coming Investment War—How to Win It.*[39] Powell's invocation of the near future was vivid. "We are convinced that the 1992 riots in Los Angeles and other US cities are just the preshocks of the holocaust which is coming to America's urban areas," he wrote, "As with the Rodney King trial in 1992, we can expect our nation's urban areas to become tinderboxes.... The lesson from Los Angeles and other areas is clear: in a major crisis, you are both your first and your last line of defense. You must also be your own store, your own bank, your own doctor, and your own everything else."[40]

Powell suggested vigilante defense of communities. "On the second day of the 1992 riots," he wrote, "groups of armed men from the inner city began to move outwards toward the affluent suburbs." The formations were "typical of their kind throughout the world. They were ruthless and ready to kill but they were looking for quick, easy scores. Where they found them, they engaged in an orgy of pillage and destruction, leaving death and ashes in their wakes. But where they met with determined resistance they left in search of easier pickings." Powell recommended retrofitting a three-quarter-ton Chevy Suburban in case of the need to escape and stockpiling surplus MREs (meals ready to eat), which would be available for purchase from the military at a discount after the unexpected briefness of Operation Desert Storm, which ended in January 1991. "Make your home a fortress," he advised. "Be ready both physically and psychologically for a total breakdown with possibly very little warning."[41]

Like Powell, the *Ron Paul Survival Report* specialized in end-times entrepreneurialism marketing the means of "surviving the barbarians at our urban gates."[42] They opened a gold hotline and advised on "How to store your gold at home" and recommended books on "How to Bury Your Goods" and "How to Hide Almost Anything."[43] They reported that Peru was selling passports. "People concerned about survival are naturally interested in a second citizenship and passport," they wrote, and Ron Paul told readers to "drop me a note and include your telephone number and I'll get you some interesting information."[44]

The most important aspect of preparation was buying coins. "If a full-blown emergency is declared," they wrote "there is no effective defense short of holing up in an extremely remote area or leaving the US entirely, assuming travel beyond US borders has not already been banned." As in *Alongside Night*, money was the only other means of protection. "Keep a supply of small denomination gold and silver coins at home," the newsletter urged. "A national emergency could be declared in the event of hyperinflation or depression and gold and silver may replace currency as the most widely accepted trading medium in the underground economy."[45] Because "a gold recall is a strong possibility," it continued, "it was necessary to buy the actual metal." And who better to buy it from than the man they described as "the numismatic giant with more than 30 years of experience who manages Ron Paul and Co.," Burton Blumert.[46]

Blumert saw the dissolving Soviet Union as a vision of the future, describing people paying for supplies for gold in the Ukraine. "When our own chaos comes," he was reported as saying, "you won't be able to shop in the Safeway with silver dollars, it will all be one giant flea market.... And when you go to the flea market, and to the money dealer, you want to have those items which are sound, known, and actively traded. That means one-ounce American Eagles, Krugerrands, maple leafs, 100 Coronas, etc."[47]

Beyond its practical utility, Blumert saw gold as the filament of morality. "Most of the moral, economic, and political decay of our society," he wrote, "can be traced to the debauchery of the money system."[48] "The magnificent gold coins produced in this country before 1933 reflect a morality missing in these times," he wrote.[49] "Street violence is indeed related to the moral and ethical climate of a runaway government," he added, seeing "antagonism between the races [as] a consequence of the affirmative action programs, set-asides and quotas of the past several decades."[50] The link between gold and moral-political order was clear for Paul's paleos. They saw the resolution of the revolt of the 1960s in a new consensus around egalitarianism and the equal right of all to things like education, divorce, right to housing, and support from the state in times of hardship matched with a discourse of equal ability. They believed that welfarism and egalitarianism were wrong and that both were made possible by the liberation of money production from the constraint of the gold standard. The relaxation of collective morality through indicators like children born out of wedlock, single parents, and the rising rate of divorce increased the demands for state provisioning. Fulfilling these demands could be done, as they saw it, only by freeing the mint and thus accelerating the degradation of society toward collectivism.

Paleos felt the egalitarian demands for freedom of expression were debilitating in practice and were also based on false premises. Egalitarianism required the suppression of the fact of human difference in capacity. "Central planning always needs a good excuse, and in American politics race has emerged as good as any," they wrote. Like Murray and Herrnstein, who argued that raising wages of Blacks would distort the just rewards due to them by dint of their lesser average intelligence, the *Survival Report* argued that "the government is attempting to prevent blacks from being disproportionately affected by the economic laws of nature."[51] The danger of race war was one of the brightest through lines in the *Survival Report*—a new front of battle after the Cold War. "The race problem could be liberalism's undoing," they wrote, "The welfare state has encouraged the worst tendencies of the most backward people in our society. Our cities have been wrecked, our schools destroyed, suburban malls invaded, and our culture corrupted."[52] They recommended the work of *American Renaissance* founder and JRC member Jared Taylor.[53]

Paleos were always on the lookout for the exits, whether through recourse to Swiss insurance companies or Peruvian passports. For all the references to the founders, remaining on American soil was only ever a provisional commitment. Even the demand for national sovereignty was not unconditional: "The international gold standard does deny to governments the 'sovereignty' to do something—i.e., inflate—that they should not be able to do at all. The gold standard is the monetary equivalent of denying them the ability to set up Gulags."[54] These "nationalists" believed that national sovereignty should be constrained by a priori commitment to hard money. The true paleo heroes of history were those who mined gold from the earth and linked the value of their money to it. To hazard a neologism from the Greek prefix for gold, we could call what paleos promote an auripatriotism—a national feeling whose referent is not this or that territory, ethnos, or language but whichever monetary system backs its currency with the precious metal they perceive to be the natural currency of modern humanity. It's a peripatetic patriotism, alighting where it is safe and fleeing when it is in danger.

Up to its final issue in 1996, the *Survival Report* prognosticated the coming breakdown and assured readers that "we are already living on borrowed time, and past the point where quick fixes will cure the problem." Only monetary meltdown would usher in the reintroduction of the gold standard, which would render impossible "such policy disasters as the welfare state, foreign aid and wars, and the Mexican bailout."[55] "Just as the Soviet system had to come to an end, as predicted so many years ago by Ludwig von Mises, so will the welfare state have to collapse," prophesied the final issue in 1996.[56]

THE PALEOS GO TO GERMANY

As indicated by its roots in the gold-digging West, "hard money" libertarianism had always been a particularly American phenomenon with limited offshoots abroad. This changed in the year the *Survival Report* stopped publication. That year in Brussels, a bureaucrat drew back the cover on a two-foot-high fiberglass sculpture. It showed a previously unknown glyph that would come to define the lives of hundreds of millions of people. It was what the *New York Times* called "a vaguely avant-garde e"—a curved line transected by two bars like the dollar, the pound, the yen, and later the rupee. The new banknotes, unveiled at the same time, depicted no people or identifiable monuments, only bridges, doors, and windows. The euro grew in scale at the stroke of midnight December 31, 2001, when lights turned on to illuminate a three-story sculpture of the symbol in the center of Frankfurt, the site of the European Central Bank, which managed the currency. The sculpture around which the continent's economy turned was the creation of a German conceptual artist, Ottmar Hörl, whose previous work had included portraits of nine hundred and forty-three cows in the Bavarian district of Passau, the installation of four thousand garden gnomes in the Munich city center, and hundreds of sculptures of Martin Luther, Karl Marx, penguins, and sea lions.

What new entity had been birthed with its new symbols? The rendering of the money of approximately three-hundred million people into scrap paper and souvenirs and its replacement with new tokens drawn up at the desk of an Austrian graphic designer was straight out of the pages of hard sci-fi. Bruce Sterling's stories in the late 1980s and 1990s featured characters trading "Euro-yen" and the "evil global currency" of the "ecu," the latter complete with a hologram of René Descartes looking "impressively French and rational."[57] William Gibson's *Virtual Light* (1994) has "Euro-money." *Snow Crash* features trillion-dollar bills named after Reagan's attorney general (and lifetime MPS member) Ed Meese.[58] Lionel Shriver's *The Mandibles* (2016) features the *dólar nuevo* ("The ink isn't right, either. It's brighter. Greener. Garish").[59] Jerry Pournelle's CoDominium series features a merger of the United States and Soviet Union, its flag an "eagle with red shield and black sickle and hammer on its breast; red stars and blue stars around it."[60]

Reflect on the idea of the European Union for a moment and you realize it was no less radical for nations that fought two wars in a generation—France, Belgium, Italy, Holland, and Germany—to unite not only under a shared flag of ringed yellow stars but later under shared money conjured from nowhere. To say the goldbugs were triggered would be understatement. "If Europe is united," the *Survival Report* wrote, "a world government cannot be far behind."[61] Monetary integration under what it called "the EuroMonster" had pride of place in their chamber of horrors. It deemed the European Central Bank "the acorn from which the oak of a world central bank will grow."[62]

Despite the conflation of European integration with neoliberalism by some critics, many actual existing neoliberals were violently opposed to European integration—and especially the euro.[63] The month before the switch to the euro, which took place formally on January 1, 1999, Mont Pelerin Society member Gerard Radnitzky published a "requiem for the deutsche mark." For skeptics like himself, he wrote, the euro was "the artificial currency of a virtual Euroland." "The Politburo seems to have moved from Moscow to Brussels: twenty unelected commissars 'govern' Euroland."[64] Why fear the European superstate? Radnitzky elaborated at the first MPS meeting after the fall of the Berlin Wall, held in Munich. He put it in twinned terms: "creeping socialization" and "creeping democratization." Both led to more decisions made collectively and less individually: "we have every reason to dread the giving of more power to a European parliament which very likely would have a majority which is semi-socialist if not just fully socialist." He cited as warning signs not just the New International Economic Order but also "the attempt to create an International Green Economic Order."[65]

Radnitzky was a philosopher of science. His website included a photograph of himself tête-à-tête with Karl Popper. Some of Europe's other libertarian opponents were of a more worldly persuasion. The website of Radnitzky's colleague, Bruno Bandulet, who was involved with the anti-euro microparty Bund Freier Bürger (League of Free Citizens, BFB) in the 1990s, featured a VHS tape with a picture of himself on the front holding a small bar of gold advertised as the "investment of tomorrow" in glittering letters.[66] Bandulet ran an investor newsletter called *Gold & Money Intelligence* since 1979. In 2016, when Alternative for Germany (AfD) entered the Bundestag as the opposition party, its member from Munich, later appointed parliamentary budget chair, was also a precious metals consultant and investment advisor. At the time they were polling at 16 percent. By 2024 Peter Boehringer was still in Parliament, and they were polling as high as 22 percent, second only to the Christian Democrats.[67] It is by keeping an eye on the more profane figures in the neoliberal firmament like Bandulet and Boehringer that we can see how goldbug politics came to Europe and helped seed the startlingly successful politics of the recent Far Right.

We can date the arrival of the paleos in Germany to 1998 with the publication of the first issue of *Eigentümlich Frei* (loosely translatable as "free by nature"). Its young editor-in-chief, André Lichtschlag, born in 1968, placed the magazine in the anarcho-capitalist tradition of Rothbard and David Friedman, which was little known in Germany.[68] Rothbard's two main texts were translated for the first time only a year later.[69] *EF* made a self-conscious play for younger readers, featuring a cover with a comic book image of three figures: a punk, a casually dressed middle-aged man, and an elderly gentleman with a cane and cigar, gesturing at the different generations of libertarians. Their logo was the Statue of Liberty, a provocation in a political landscape more often defined by criticism of the United States. Among the magazine's frequent contributors and advisory board members were German MPS members Radnitzky, Hardy Bouillon, Detmar Doering, Roland Baader, Gerd Habermann, and Erich Weede, most of whom were also part of the Friedrich Hayek Society, founded in Berlin the same year.[70]

Faithful to its anarcho-capitalism, one of the magazine's motifs was attacking democracy. In one of the first issues, Radnitzky quoted Milton Friedman that "there is evidence that a democratic society, once established, destroys a free economy" and added that democracy had become a "pseudoreligion" with "self-destructive" qualities infected with the "poison of redistribution."[71] Lichtschlag wrote proudly that the libertarian attitude toward democracy ranges from "skeptical to hostile.... Democracy is in their eyes the system of the lynch mob."[72] In a column for *Die Welt*, he proposed that recipients of welfare be stripped of the vote. He cited Hayek in defense, who wrote in 1960, "It is also possible for reasonable people to argue that the ideals of democracy would be better served if, say, all the servants of government or all recipients of public charity were excluded from the vote."[73] "Today," Lichtschlag wrote, inverting a quote of Willy Brandt's from the 1960s, "'risk less democracy!' is the only escape from the path to totalitarianism."[74]

As *Eigentümlich Frei* embarked self-consciously on the path of the "paleo" alliance pioneered by Rothbard and Rockwell, a parallel New Right was also on the rise in Germany. The flagship organization of the "national conservative" movement, the Institut für Staatspolitik (IfS), was launched in 2000 by Karlheinz Weißman and led by Götz Kubitschek alongside their magazine, *Sezession*, and their publishing wing, Antaios.[75] At the first meeting of the IfS, *EF* author Roland Baader spoke alongside Alain de Benoist as the two groups of the Right sought common ground.[76] Making the paleo pitch in *Sezession*, Lichtschlag called for a "libertarian-conservative" alliance against what he called the "state-eco-soc-fem-antifa-doctrine."[77] As a bridge, he proposed the work of a veteran of the U.S. paleo alliance, Hans-Hermann Hoppe, whose book *Democracy: The God that Failed*, was published in German in 2003.[78] The German New Right obliged. *Sezession* printed an excerpt from Hoppe's *Democracy* book, and he contributed to the other organ of the New Right, *Junge Freiheit*.[79]

Hoppe brought the spirit of the paleos back to his native Germany. Speaking at the seventeenth conference of the International Society for Individual Liberty in Berlin in 1998, he preached his doctrine of closed-borders libertarianism, saying that "in an anarcho-capitalist system, there would be no free migration without permission of the property-owners" and described the state itself as a "currency counterfeiter."[80] In an interview in *EF*, Hoppe explained immigration as part of the reason why, as Lichtschlag paraphrased him, "our social democracies will end up breaking apart exactly like the red and brown people's democracies of the past." He described *Democracy* as an attempt to start a "conservative-libertarian counter-movement" against the "the pubescent multi-culti-anti-authoritarian-everyone-can-do-what-they-want-and-I-respect-no-authority-libertarians." It was a "fighting document (*Kampfschrift*)," he said, "for private property and especially the right, based in private property, to expulsion, exclusivity, discrimination and ostracism." Hoppe used the example of racially restrictive covenants in the United States: "When blacks move into a white community, the property prices fall. The property owners in these communities are acting economically rational when they discriminate." He defended discriminating against homosexuals and communists on the same grounds. "Certain forms of behavior, even when they are non-aggressive," he wrote, "lead to expulsion and into the ghetto. So what?"[81]

The "three hards" of hard money, hard borders, and hardwired culture were central to the paleo ideology. It was a philosophy of exclusion. Echoing the main theme of the JRC a decade earlier, Hoppe wrote that "the central intellectual line of connection between old conservatives and libertarians is the theme of regionalization, decentralization, including secession." He recommended Peter Brimelow's site VDARE.com and his book *Alien Nation* along with Jean Raspail's *The Camp of the Saints* and noted that the salutary "demand for ethnocultural homogeneity" was being accommodated by "the development of proprietary communities—'gated' or 'restrictive' communities or covenants—owned by a founder-developer and leased to follower-tenants." He recommended "individual provinces, regions, cities, towns and villages...proclaim their status as 'free territories'" to prevent from being swamped by immigrants.[82]

Until the late 1990s paleos felt they had a real challenge with communication. Newsletters and small journals, even if they were popular, had limited reach and minimal ability to react in real time to major events. Rothbard raised this issue to the John Randolph Club in the immediate wake of what he called the "race riots" in Los Angeles in 1992, which, he said, "had the effect of sharply radicalizing me rightward." "The response on all sides," he claimed, "was either to incite or approve of the rioting, or to hasten to appease the criminals by proposing massive new multibillions in subsidies and in special privileges." What if, he asked, they took this seriously as an insurrection? "If, in fact, we are in a revolutionary situation, then it seems to me that drastic crisis measures of massive counter-revolution may be in order." Among these were media problems. "Since most people get their view of reality from TV, the fact that the media systematically abuse their power to present a deliberately doctored view of reality, presents troubling questions to libertarians: e.g. should the media be allowed to get away with it? Is the new technological opening up of the media (cable TV, satellites, etc) enough of a countervailing force?"[83]

Just a few years later, the internet offered the very end-run around dominant channels of opinion creation that Rothbard was seeking. Attuned to this, Hoppe linked to the website Mises.org in an interview in 2002 and recommended that the Germans build up the equivalent of LewRockwell.com, the online presence of the ever-networking editor of the Ron Paul newsletters and founder of the Mises Institute.[84] Hoppe defended the importance of being online through the logic of wired vanguardism in an ignorant society. "The masses are always and everywhere indolent, dull, stupid, and incapable of developing their own (not preconceived) thoughts," he said in *EF*. "For revolutionary changes to happen, one needs at first only a few non-conformist people who think for themselves and outside the box (*Querdenker*).... If you can understand how to merge and motivate them into an ideological movement, then anything is possible. Especially in the age of the internet."[85]

Hoppe praised what was happening in Germany as part of "a blossoming, ever-growing international Mises movement."[86] He joined the *EF* board of advisors, no doubt seeing a chance to realize in the Germany of the early twenty-first century what failed in the United States of the late twentieth. Hoppe internationalized the paleo movement further after 2005, when, as mentioned in a previous chapter, he founded the Property and Freedom Society and began convening annual meetings in the gilded ballroom of the hotel on the Turkish Riviera owned by his wife, Gulcun. The years that followed featured talks by *EF* authors like Robert Grözinger, Philipp Bagus, and Rahim Taghizadegan, alongside other characters familiar from this book: Jared Taylor of American Renaissance, Doug Casey of *Crisis Investing* fame, Richard Lynn speaking on *The Global Bell Curve*, Peter Brimelow making "The Libertarian Case Against Open Immigration," and Richard Spencer introducing the "Alternative Right in America." *EF* celebrated the PFS in a 2008 cover story as the "anti-intellectual intellectuals."[87]

One person who took the podium at the first meeting of the PFS and again in 2014 was Jörg Guido Hülsmann. A fellow of the Mises Institute like Hoppe, Hülsmann was an *EF* stalwart and its chief in-house goldbug. In one of its first issues, he wrote that "paper money" led "inevitably to hyperinflation or collapse," recommending instead that the state abandon its monopoly on money production and allow for individuals to mint their own coins out of precious metals.[88] He translated Rothbard's 1963 book *What Has Government Done to Our Money?* in 2000, with an afterword describing the euro as the disastrous endpoint of the state monopoly of money.[89]

Hülsmann took the lead as *EF* began to turn more directly against the EU with the outbreak of the Global Financial Crisis. By 2007, Lichtschlag referred to the "European Union of Soviet Socialist Republics" (EUdSSR) and described the "EU Moloch" as the "preliminary stage to the desired world state"[90] The magazine published Cato Institute senior fellow Vladimir Bukovsky claiming he had seen secret documents outlining a plan to turn Europe into a socialist central state in cooperation with the Soviet Union.[91] As the crisis escalated, Hülsmann insisted that "long-term there is no alternative to a precious-metal-backed currency (*Edelmetallwährung*)."[92]

German paleos broke into mainstream politics in the fallout from the 2008 financial crisis. Speaking from the audience at Hoppe's PFS in 2017, the gold advisor Bandulet, who was also an EF columnist, noted that something new had happened recently in Germany.[93] There was a party, poised to become the third largest in the Bundestag, which was described as "populist" but also included libertarians and was led by a woman who "has lived in China, speaks fluently Mandarin, has worked for Goldman Sachs [who is] completely cosmopolitan, the same way I am, but she is against mass migration."[94] The party he was describing was the Alternative for Germany (AfD), an example of the paleo alliance in action with a vision of both monetary and moral order at its core.

The AfD was founded in 2013 by economics professors in protest against what they saw as Chancellor Angela Merkel's mishandling of the Eurozone crisis. Among them were Joachim Starbatty and Roland Vaubel, both members of the MPS and the Hayek Society. Starbatty helped found the BFB, which lodged a formal complaint in 1997 with the German Constitutional Court about the loss of national sovereignty involved in joining the Eurozone. Along with the AfD's first chair Bernd Lucke, he was also a key plaintiff in the case presented successfully to the Court in May 2020.[95] Scholarly and journalistic treatments of the AfD tend to focus on its anti-immigration policy, its Islamophobia, and its nativist pronatalism. Yet the original "alternative" they presented was not an alternative to nonwhite migration or "Islamification" but an alternative to the euro as a German currency. Some of its key leaders would later show a preference for what they saw as a "natural" foundation in precious metals. There is a story of the AfD that is written in gold.

The first act came in late 2014 after the AfD won seven of Germany's ninety-six seats in the European Parliament. To collect party financing from the state, the law required the AfD earn its own revenue. The conventional source was member contributions, but the AfD discovered a loophole. The revenue did not have to come from donations or dues. It could also come through sales. So they opened an online gold shop. Under the slogan, roughly translated, "the AfD is worth its weight in gold," they sold bars and coins, including the deutsche mark (reportedly the bestseller) but also four denominations of the South African Krugerrand.

Consumer demand was better than expected. As Melanie Amann and Martin Hesse reported for *Der Spiegel*, the AfD shop sold 1.6 million euros worth of gold in eleven days. Party leaders were forced to suspend their political activity to keep up with orders from their customers, many of whom were elderly. "We are the only party whose headquarters is also a profit center," the speaker for the AfD told a reporter proudly.[96] Inflated prices meant the party profited while also collecting matching funds from the state. The material effect of the sales was significant for a party with a small donor base. They ended up making two million euros in 2014 and 2015 before the law was changed.

More interesting than the profit was the symbolism. Drawing from the paleo playbook, the party sowed suspicion of fiat money and reaped the golden harvest. AfD leaders predicted the imminent collapse of the euro on the campaign trail, while the Gold Shop's website noted that "gold is fundamentally a product that many citizens perceive as a form of investment that is crisis-proof and future-oriented." Their pitch was direct: "Participation in the gold trade offers us the opportunity to provide a service to citizens, to point out the undesirable developments in the euro, to attract media attention and to increase our revenue through a very specific AfD service, rather than attracting stakeholder funds like other parties."[97] The party financing law, designed to encourage buy-in to the competition of parties within the democratic process was enabling citizens to purchase exit from the state-managed monetary system itself. Party sympathy was not expressed through the donation of current value but the promise of a future value. Party identification was transmuted into speculation in precious metals. Gold bars autographed by the party's leaders were sold at the party congress in 2015.[98]

A new dimension of the story broke in 2018 when journalists revealed that one of the most important early funders of the AfD was an eighty-eight-year-old German billionaire named August von Finck

Jr., who lived in a castle in Switzerland to escape taxes. Finck's father had run Merck Finck, one of the largest banks in Nazi Germany, and actively supported Hitler. This was the source of Finck fortune, which his son expanded into majority ownership in Mövenpick hotels, Löwenbrau beer, and other concerns. Through the 1980s and 1990s, Finck was involved in funding conservative and market-liberal parties, including Manfred Brunner and Bandulet's BFB, with a special focus on programs promoting lower taxes.[99]

In 2010, Finck acquired a firm with a tainted past—Degussa. A German firm of the same name had supplied death camps with Zyklon B through a subsidiary and had been directly responsible for melting down the gold teeth of the murdered. Rebooting this dubious heritage brand, Finck rode the wave of interest in gold and linked it directly to the AfD, supporting early events of the party. The gold sold in the AfD shop came from his company.[100] The links between the paleolibertarians, Finck, and the AfD were direct. Degussa's chief economist was Thorsten Polleit, who had been chief economist for Barclays in Germany for eleven years, appointed in 2012 as an honorary professor at the University of Bayreuth. A contributor to *EF*, Polleit became the founding president of the German branch of the Ludwig von Mises Institute in 2012, housed in the same building at Degussa. Hoppe, Hülsmann, and Bagus were on the advisory council.[101] Like its mother institute in Alabama, the German Mises Institute specialized in predicting the imminent collapse of the world economic system owing to the proliferation of unbacked paper money and the welfare programs it enabled. In early posts on their site, Hülsmann and Polleit called fiat money an "unorthodox road to serfdom" that led inevitably to "collective corruption," socialist collectivism, and economic downfall.[102] Another text recommended the return to a gold-backed deutsche mark.[103] In an earlier piece that thanked the Mises Institute for funding, Bagus turned the rhetoric a tick further, saying that "in a libertarian Nuremberg trial, banks would probably be sued for exploiting their monopoly and for financing the criminal activities of the state."[104]

At Hoppe's PFS gathering in Turkey in 2014, Polleit presented on "the new socialist destructionism" after Richard Lynn presented on "100 years of IQ research" and Carel Boshoff brought a report from the whites-only South African enclave of Orania. Writing for the Mises.de website, Polleit repeated Hoppe's case for closed-borders libertarianism, the difficulty if not impossibility of "multiculturalist democracy," and the need for the right to secession as a solution to undesirable immigration.[105] Speaking on stage with Thilo Sarrazin, Polleit condemned the EU's "open borders policies" and "bank rescue plans" as assaults on the twin pillars of hardwired culture and hard money.[106]

Even more prominent than Polleit was a fellow gold consultant who entered the Bundestag as the AfD's delegate from Munich in 2017: Peter Boehringer. Born in Munich in 1969, Boehringer held degrees in both business and communications. After working for the consulting firm Booz Allen Hamilton, he started a money management business and was one of three people who started the German Precious Metals Society in 2006, which stated as one of its aims the "remonetization of precious metals" with the "goal of the development and introduction of a precious metal-backed means of exchange parallel to the Euro." He also jointly ran a precious metals blog called Gold Pages (goldseiten.de). Boehringer was at home in paleo circles, joining the Hayek Society in 2012, winning its Roland Baader Award in 2013 and writing for *EF* beginning in 2012.[107] He was a classic goldbug, warning that "the unbacked paper money system is in a literal sense the tinder that will set the world on fire."[108] Following MPS member Roland Baader, he saw gold as the "natural money... for incontrovertible physical, historical and psychological reasons."[109]

Like catastrophe libertarians before him, Boehringer was adept at forecasting the crackup while making his own services indispensable when the time came. In 2012, he wrote that, though the timing could not be predicted with precision, "the citizens of the western world can count on a systemic collapse." Because all of those in power were complicit in reproducing the status quo, no experts could be trusted. The intuitions of the "pub regulars" (*Stammtisch*) were closer to reality than the "politically correct 'intelligentsia.'"[110] Boehringer preached that preparation for the coming crash had to be mental and emotional but also pecuniary. Gold was "the money that people have chosen through their free will for millennia," he wrote. The value of gold had been suppressed and manipulated by the "monetary monopolism of central banks," and even then "whenever even slight doubt about the ruling monetary system arises, many flee reflexively to gold." Boehringer reassured his readers to trust their gut. Money had to be tangible, not the rainbow paper of the EMU, introduced less than a generation earlier.

Where Boehringer showed his most impressive flare for public relations and a scent for the Zeitgeist was in a campaign he launched in March 2012 called "Repatriate our gold" (*Holt unser Gold heim*). Because of fears of Soviet invasion in the Cold War years, most of Germany's gold reserves were held in the Fed's vaults on Wall Street. There was no sign of this changing until Boehringer's campaign helped make it a public issue, leading to the repatriation of a large part of the gold, a small portion of was later put on display at the Bundesbank.[111] Boehringer found imitators for his gold repatriation campaigns on the Far Right in other countries, including Switzerland, Austria, Holland, and France, where it is led by Marine Le Pen.[112]

Explaining the decision for bringing the gold back, a Bundesbank board member told reporters, "we're doing this to show citizens that the gold bars are here, to show transparency," adding that they hoped to placate critics who had "questioned whether the gold holdings at home and abroad were real."[113] Yet literalizing the project through the display of the gold itself set up an impossible dynamic, a problem of fractional reserve optics. How could all the gold possibly be seen? Instead of direct democracy, where the mediating institution of the legislature is removed in favor of popular referendum, the gold display was a quixotic bid for "direct economy," where the citizen investor receives an unmediated encounter with what they (falsely) perceive as the final guarantor of value. Boehringer was predictably unimpressed by the Bundesbank's gesture. His own adaptation of the Marxist category of StaMoKap, or "state monopoly capitalism" to BaMoKap, or "bank monopoly capitalism," left little space for half measures. He questioned the provenance of the gold and asked why it did not bear the original stamps and had been recast into new forms, among other expression of suspicion. For him, the gold was the equivalent of Obama's birth certificate in parallel U.S. circles, a piece of evidence that could never rise to the level of persuasion. For the central bankers to cater to the skeptic's demand was only to lose the sovereignty of interpretation. By surrendering to the goldbugs, the central bankers likely only helped accelerate the erosion of confidence in their role.

Through theatrics and an effective online presence, Boehringer brought the previously marginal goldbugs toward the center of discussions in Germany. He also propagated his own form of resistance. The central act of what I call auripatriotism is the sale of paper assets for gold, an act that Boehringer dubbed "the sit-down strikes and Gandhian hunger strikes of our generation." It was only through such acts, Boehringer argued, that the AfD and its followers could defeat the "paper money totalitarians" of modern central banks.[114]

The goldbug fantasy has blind spots. For all his antagonism to fiat money, Boehringer focused exclusively on the activities of central banks and not on the private money creation carried out through a deregulated financial sector. The obvious role played by banks and states in guaranteeing the value of gold was either willfully repressed or genuinely ignored in statements like Boehringer's that gold is "the only money without power" and that "for 5,000 years, gold has required no institutional support as money."[115] Yet one of the lessons of reconstructing the trajectories of the new fusionists is the discovery that delusions can have serious effects. We see here that the "populism" of the German Far Right was also a monetary extremism, reliant on exits from the democratic control of money and appealing to a neo-naturalism that placed culture, morality, and currency in a single frame. As longtime member of the AfD federal board Dirk Driesang put it in 2014, "The fatal effects of fundamentally fake money (*Falschgeld*) on our society and politics, our family and our values, are destructive and undermine the fundamentals of our civilization as well as our western culture."[116] Boehringer put it pithily: "people make bad money, and that money makes bad people."[117]

To the paleos, fractional reserve banking and fiat money was a structure built on sand, designed to accelerate the purchase of political good will—and thus political power. "Fake money" was cloaked in what they saw as the fake morality of social justice, multiculturalism, diversity, and gender equality. This was all part of a regime of "monetary socialism" that began with the breakdown of Bretton Woods and rose ascendant in the EU after the fall of the Soviet bloc.[118] Their belief in metal morality was also a belief in the metal view of history.

Boehringer was not alone in the blend of ethnic alarmism and financial consulting. Another case in point was Walter Eichelburg, who contributed to *EF* and also ran the blog *Hartgeld*—"hard money"—combining apocalyptic prediction of currency collapse with the collapse of the social state through the "flood of asylum seekers." In the late 2010s, the preferred publisher for Far Right texts in Germany became Finanzbuch Verlag. Formerly specialized in investor advice manuals and introductions to Austrian economics, it took up a sideline in books like Thilo Sarrazin's *Enemy Takeover: How Islam Blocks Progress and Threatens Society*.[119]

The goldbug libertarianism of the AfD cannily tapped into not only rising anti-immigrant sentiment but also the decline in German confidence in paper assets in an era of financial crisis and zero-interest rates. The response of many average Germans was a flight to gold. The extent of this move is expressed in the remarkable fact that German private gold holdings went from "barely register[ing] on anyone's radar," in the words of *Forbes* magazine in 2008, to being the largest in the world, surpassing longtime champion India.[120] Bandulet wrote in *EF* of "gold's comeback."[121] Riding this golden wave helped the AfD to mainstream its paleo philosophy cultivated in the paleo alliances of the United States in the 1990s and the catastrophe libertarianism that stretches back to the 1970s.

THE WORLD VIRUS IS SOCIALISM

The year 2020 was what one journalist called the "hour of the crash prophets."[122] Bestsellers in Germany had titles that echoed the catastrophe libertarian classics of the 1970s, such as *The Greatest Crash of All Time: How You Can Still Protect Your Money*; *Powerquake: The World before the Greatest Economic Crisis of All Time*; *The Crash Is Here: What You Have to Do Now!*; *World System Crash: Crisis, Unrest, and the Birth of a New World Order*; and *The Crash Is the Solution: Why the Final Collapse Is Coming and How You Can Rescue Your Wealth*. True to the predictions of catastrophe libertarians, the gold price also shot up as volatility increased, rising over 36 percent by the end of 2020. New fusionists stepped in as Cassandras, posting YouTube videos that racked up hundreds of thousands of views in days as new tribunes of the collapse.

Among the most visible was a newcomer, Markus Krall, a rosy-cheeked man in a buzz cut in his late fifties who became the CEO in 2019 for Degussa after working as a risk management consultant for decades and launching a failed attempt to found a new credit rating agency.[123] Helming a new libertarian network called the Atlas Initiative and authoring a series of books attacking the euro and predicting monetary collapse, Krall became by 2020 what Bandulet called the "new spokesperson" of the "liberal, libertarian and conservative movement."[124]

"Corona[virus] will lead to the end of the euro," Krall told the Far Right *Compact* magazine in March 2020. The AfD's most right-wing leader, Björn Höcke, directed his readers to Krall for guidance.[125] "The collapse of the system is no longer only inevitable," Krall wrote in *Eigentumlich Frei*, "it is on our doorstep, here and now."[126] He described the "corona crash" as the "first domino of the Depression" and called for a return to the gold standard.[127] With paleo logic, Krall saw the economic crisis as the outcome of monetary socialism:

"The attack on freedom that the political class has been pursuing for years has entered a decisive, probably final phase with the outbreak of the Corona crisis." Efforts at containing the virus through lockdowns, masking, and social distancing were a pretense to perpetuate elite power for as long as possible. "Under the cloak of pandemic measures," he wrote, "politicians are using the situation to curtail freedom, no longer by inch by inch, but with a chainsaw."[128]

A quotation from Ayn Rand, "Money is the barometer of a society's virtue," opened Krall's book.[129] Alongside the gold standard, democracy had to be reformed and restricted to restore stability and balance. What he called a "bourgeois revolution" was necessary against the "long march of cultural Marxism through the institutions." Krall expanded on his proposal in a series of talks he gave for the Hayek Society and provincial gatherings of the AfD in 2020. Anyone who received government aid, Krall argued, whether a university student on a grant, a poor or disabled person on welfare, or a businessperson receiving subsidies, must forfeit the right to vote.[130] Democracy should not extend to those who lived in any way from the state. Forcing people to choose between a ballot and material support might drive people to real hardship but, to adapt an old expression, he was suggesting that real penury had never been tried. Krall saw the only hope in the return to a system, however punitive, based on property, family, and a Europe based on "Christian values."[131] His colleague, the head of Germany's Mises Institute, Thorsten Polleit, wrote in the midst of the pandemic that the real "world virus" was socialism; it was only by letting the world economy collapse and be rebuilt on sound money that the threat would be expunged.[132] Metal morality would translate into a new order out of the rubble.

As the Covid-19 outbreak began in the spring of 2020, Krall held forth on his ideas in one of Degussa's public relations gambits: the Frankfurt Gold Museum (Goldkammer), built less than a kilometer from the two-story symbol of the euro unveiled in 2001 described at the beginning of the chapter. Taking over from a kindergarten in

2019, the museum was housed in a neoclassical and baroque building from 1850 and fitted with a mine elevator to underground chambers holding gold artifacts. Krall was smiling as he spoke—and he had good reason to.[133] That same week he was quoted on the front page of the *Financial Times* reporting that consumer demand for gold was so high that Degussa could barely keep up with orders for gold bars and coins.[134] The collapse was making him a killing.

Walk into the money museum in Frankfurt, which sits below the Bundesbank itself. You walk past the usual artifacts of early barter and examples of currency. There is an old wood-burning stove with a circle glowing red. Inside you can see the bills spinning around, their value so degraded that they're useful only as tinder. Above the stove there are photographs of people in rooms wallpapered with currency, a jar of paste at its side. Interactive games teach you about the value of money. One brutally difficult one features a slender coin rolling through a desert landscape, maneuvering through the obstacles of "food prices," "inflation expectations" "oil prices," "real estate prices," "world economy," and "wages."

This is a classroom to learn about money, but it is also a church built to honor it. At the museum's center, the nave of the monetary cathedral, is a waist-high rectangular cube. The bottom two-thirds are backlit, showing high-resolution photographs of bars of gold individually numbered. The top third is encased in inch-thick safety glass within which sits a second glass cube. There is a circle cut into the outer cube, allowing you to insert and place your hand under the bar, lift it, let it sink down again with a satisfying padded thump, sense the haptic quality of high density that no goldbug text fails to mention. The imprint on the bar informs you of the donor: Degussa.

THE FREEDOM OF THE NETWORKED VAULT

Goldbugs claimed to be Ludwig von Mises's disciplines and his heirs. How close were they to the master? In fact, they were guilty of much of the same misplaced concreteness as the Hayek's bastards we have met in other chapters. From one perspective, Mises's writings gave plenty of ammunition to the goldbug. In his magnum opus *Human Action,* he wrote that "the struggle against gold... must not be looked upon as an isolated phenomenon. It is but one item in the gigantic process of destruction which is the mark of our time." But what he respected about gold was not its metaphysical or irreplaceable qualities but its ability to act as a brake on the tendency of democratic states to spend beyond their means. If there were some modern alchemy discovered by which the quantity of gold in the world could be infinitely expanded, he explained, then the foundation of money would not die, it would just migrate: "people will have to replace the gold standard by another standard."[135] "Gold is natural money" reads a recent post on the Mises Institute website, and "nature's money is gold."[136] But this was not the core of Mises's message. He was more pragmatic and never envisioned a return of mankind to a primal state of barter in precious metal.

What does gold do for the paleos? By focusing on gold as a means of acquiring individual monetary sovereignty supposedly outside of (and after) the state while simultaneously using it as a means of disciplining state stewardship of currency, we can understand how the project of the libertarian wing of the Far Right is more subtle and perhaps more radical than a simple entrenchment of national borders coupled with nativist pronatalism. Although paleos reject the slogan of "open borders," they offer, by definition, an ideology of open borders for gold. The nation nests within a golden globe where precious metals flow freely.

Far from rejecting globalization, in other words, their vision deepens it, subjecting the actions of the state to the continual audit of assetholders with the ability to move. With monetary policy, as with other political matters, the goldbugs were not actually a throwback to a supposedly autarkic past but creatures of their own moment. Even their demands for sovereignty and autonomy were uttered with one eye on the global picture. In the goldbug version of paleo ideology, the true opponent was not the itinerant migrant, who they saw as only a symptom of a larger problem. Rather their enemy was captured best in an image posted by Boehringer to his blog in 2010: Marx's head floating over Frankfurt, the icon of "monetary socialism" haunting the home of the European Central Bank.

Traveling with the goldbugs on the Far Right, we are far from simple "blood and soil" nationalism. The nation is reenvisioned as a platform, adopted insofar as it offers security for capital and a good return on investment. In the midst of the world crisis, the bastard offspring of Mises and Hayek preached a flight from democracy to safety: to gold, to family, to Christianity, a plea to divest from state money and into the metal that weighs heavy in the hand, the material for a self-minted coin, for exchange in a world stripped of the collective ties of obligation and care but still spanned by the webs of exchange: the call for a flight to the freedom of the networked vault. The first and overriding political imperative is to be ready for exit. As Boehringer wrote in 2012, "the citizens of the western world must reckon with a collapse of the system. Its exact moment cannot be seriously predicted... the transition as well as the time afterwards will, however, require both a violent mental reorientation for the great majority of people as well as private financial precautions with the greatest possible independence."[137] His advice for the coming apocalypse? Buy gold.

CONCLUSION

Rothbard's Mastiff

> Libertarians must short-circuit the dominant intellectual elites and address the masses directly to arouse their indignation and contempt for the ruling elites.
> —Hans-Hermann Hoppe

> Liberty, dammit!
> —Javier Milei at Davos

In 2023, one of Hayek's bastards took power in the second-largest country in Latin America. Javier Milei, a trained economist and newcomer to party politics, described himself as the most extreme form of libertarian, an anarcho-capitalist, who believed that states should be replaced entirely by private service providers. Clad in gold and yellow spandex, he appeared as "General Ancap" at comic conventions, promising to "kick Keynesians and collectivists in the ass."[1] After coming to power he declared a state of economic emergency and passed an omnibus bill of hundreds of articles. The measures were a chaotic mix: privatizing state-owned companies and lifting congressional approval to do so, deregulating credit cards and private health care, allowing employers to fire workers for participating in protests, limiting maternity leave, pardoning security forces for using violence. This was a mélange of economic shock therapy with social conservatism and authoritarianism. Someone wondering about the origin of this list could have looked no farther than Milei's mastiffs. There were five of them, four cloned from the original. One was named after a figure who recurs throughout the pages of this book, Murray Rothbard. Recall that Rothbard published his own plan for "paleopopulism" in 1992, combining the call to "unleash the cops," restore morality, and dismantle the redistributive state.[2] He would have approved of the name Milei gave to 2024: the "Year of the Defense of Life, Liberty, and Property." Philipp Bagus, renowned goldbug, *Eigentümlich Frei* author, and presenter at Hans-Hermann Hoppe's Property and Freedom Society, wrote on the website of Germany's Ludwig von Mises Institute that Milei was "one of us."[3] When rising Republican star Vivek Ramaswamy met Milei at the Conservative Political Action Conference in early 2024, he said "you're more of a von Mises guy, I'm a Hayek guy," to which Milei responded, "but one of the most wonderful thinkers of liberty was Murray Rothbard!"[4]

Milei is only the most prominent example of the politicians who have arisen in the last decade mixing combinations of the three "hards" identified in this book: hardwired culture, hard money, and hard borders. Even when they travel under new labels of "national conservative" or denounce neoliberalism themselves as Ramaswamy does, many continue to pay homage to the intellectual forefathers of the neoliberal tradition. In El Salvador, Nayib Bukele has combined an authoritarian crackdown and mass incarceration with a near-comical embrace of the "new gold" of cryptocurrency. Along with "Laissez faire!," one of the chants of the cadre in J. Neil Schulman's dystopian novel *Alongside Night* was "Mises over Marx!" During the protests against Dilma Rousseff in Brazil in 2014, signs began to appear reading "Less Marx, More Mises." Libertarian websites reported proudly in 2015 that Mises was the most-searched economist on Google.[5] By 2019, the Mises Institute in Brazil had 1.3 million monthly visitors to its website, half as many as the storied Heritage Foundation.[6]

Jair Bolsonaro's son Eduardo lists attendance at Mises Institute seminars on his CV, and Bolsonaro himself has been photographed holding editions of Mises's book published by the Mises Institute in São Paolo, whose leader reportedly helped place the Chicago-trained Paulo Guedes in the new cabinet.[7] The leader of Mises Brazil helped draft amendments to the constitutions on economic freedom, a libertarian influence on a regime characterized by persecution of minorities and accelerated ecological destruction.[8] Mises has become a cult figure in Brazil. After winning a lightweight bout in the Ultimate Fighting Championship in early 2024, a bloodied, bruised, and cauliflower-eared Renato Moicano shouted into the microphone: "I love private property, and let me tell you something, if you care about your country, read Ludwig von Mises and the six lessons of the Austrian economic school!"[9] Figures from speculative novels are walking off the page and onto the world stage.

Moments of global economic crisis allow for the breakthrough of eccentric and (for some) exhilaratingly novel forms of politics, but they do not appear from nowhere: they have their own intellectual lineages and material preconditions. We cannot understand the peculiar hybrids of extreme market ideology, Far Right authoritarianism, and social conservatism without familiarizing ourselves with the often-tangled genealogies traced in this book. Well-funded networks of think tanks, conferences, gatherings, and workshops, as well as investment forums, comments sections, and Reddit groups, offer nurseries for new adaptive ideological strains. Mises Institutes are a case in point. They proliferated globally in the twenty-first century, popping up in Romania in 2001, Poland in 2003, and Colombia in 2007. Funding for the original institute in Alabama rose after 2008, with IRS filings showing an annual revenue of between $3 million and $6 million.[10] By 2013 there were twenty-four Mises Institutes with active websites worldwide, arranging local meetings and making the writings of Mises, Rothbard, and Hoppe available in many languages.

What was once the world of niche magazines and newsletters has grown over time to news aggregator websites, blogs, video streams, and social media feeds. "TikTok and WhatsApp are to Milei what the radio was to FDR or to Getúlio Vargas in Brazil in the 1930s," writes the historian Ernesto Semán, "a way to connect directly with voters."[11] Common across the platforms and decades is a will to startle and an atmosphere of competitive speculation about the events of the near future. These are attention plays in an economy where attention is a scarce resource. Their strategy is to hit the same notes with a sledgehammer, the ones their consumers expected to hear: the crisis is around the corner. The crash is coming. The status quo is doomed. All assumptions must be undone. Taboos must shatter, the unspoken said aloud. Your liberty is at risk. Act now and act quickly. The centralizers are coming. The socialists are coming. The refugees are coming. The gold requisitioners are coming. The authorities are coming. The state is coming (even if we are the state). As the *New York Times* synopsis of a bestseller written by one right-wing libertarian read: "Buy gold, silver, Swiss francs, and a gun."[12] The alarmism is entrepreneurial. Newsletter subscriptions cost money, as do weekend seminars and conferences. The klaxon is a pitch. New fusionists are what libertarians began to call in the 1970s "ideological entrepreneurs." Praising the category in 1977, Murray Rothbard wrote that it was "the task of the entrepreneur... to be able to understand current conditions and to project the proper tactics for the near future." By definition, they are speculators, fiction writers for a possible unfolding of events that cannot be guaranteed but, through writing and speaking, one can make more or less likely.

James M. Buchanan has described interest in forms of collective life as a rational economic calculation. We devote, on average, little energy toward understanding ballot measures and local elections because we are aware of the tiny power of our ballot in the broader outcome. "Precisely the same logic may be extended to the emotional 'investment' in the totality of any collective enterprise," Buchanan wrote. "Any sense of effective participation is attenuated as numbers increase, and any assessment of collective action as self-selected is also lost."[13] The larger the polity, the less likely the investment will be worth it. Identity was literally the investment of assets, in this case of one's emotions.

One argument of this book is that we can think about the Far Right in terms of an investment strategy in a world of unequally distributed assets. It is an investment strategy not only in the sense that it appeals to people's material self-interest but also in that it offers ways to manage an unknowable future. It offers the prospect of secure assets in a time of uncertainty. A term from the pages of the financial press can be helpful. In times of crisis, investors often make what is called a "flight to safety" or a "flight to quality." They seek assets or commodities which are assumed to hold their value even at the risk of lower short-term yields. Classic examples would be capital leaving emerging markets or newer companies for U.S. Treasury bills or gold, out of stocks and into bonds. Such a move does not mean a withdrawal from the market, but rather what would be called in the jargon a "rebalancing of one's portfolio," changing the allocation of investments to decrease risk in a time of volatility. It is a shift in strategy, not a liquidation.

That safety has been defined in different terms. In this book we have read about the safety of racial homogeneity, not only as a shared psychological or emotional space but also as one open to quantification. The return of IQ racism can be explained by the desire to have a reliable benchmark of value comparable to stock valuation. We can also see the flight to safety in the much more standard form as the investment preference of the shiny yellow metal of gold. In one of the starker cases of the interweaving of symbolic and financial threads of right-wing libertarian ideology, gold for the last half century has been the nexus of an alternative morality, built on a claim that society and market have been "debauched" or "debased"—to use their own terminology—by the last half century of U.S.-led financial capitalism.

The era of quantitative easing that followed from 2008 until 2022 was a historically unique time. New laws of physics in the world economy seem to be emerging. No matter how far down central banks in the industrial countries pushed their interest rates, nothing resembling inflation seem to arise. Old preconceptions seemed destined for the dustbin of history. New ideas on the Left about modern monetary theory proposed that the laws had always been misunderstood. Maybe governments could indeed print as much money as they liked. It seemed especially true for the United States, which remained the issuer of the world's global reserve currency.

If there was a restlessness about what new order might transform the conditions of everyday life after 2008, these ideas spread like an algae bloom in the months of 2020. In an extraordinarily poorly timed decision, the head of the World Economic Forum, Klaus Schwab, long a lightning rod for justifiable discontent over globalization, chose July 2020 to roll out a new book that had been in preparation about what he called "the Great Reset."[14] While the book did little to build a new consensus among the world's elites, it did offer a new target of suspicion for many people on the Far Right and more conspiratorially minded Left. One of the earliest and most effective propagandists for the idea that the Covid-19 pandemic was part of a planned seizure of power from above was a denizen of one of the hard Right neoliberal think tanks most active in climate denial, the Heartland Institute. Justin Haskins wrote a series of articles denouncing the Great Reset and went on the talk show circuit, propagating the idea that lockdowns, vaccinations, and monetary policy to bail out ailing workers and businesses was part and parcel of a socialist coup from above. The very organization that appealed to bad science to deny the realities of climate change was now using appeals to bad science to oppose the utility of attempts to contain the pandemic.[15]

The Hoover Institution, a neoliberal think tank not known for its previous expertise in epidemiology, became a clearinghouse for bad facts on the virus. Most notable was longtime Mont Pelerin Society member and legal scholar Richard Epstein's prediction that the global Covid cases would peak at one million and the total deaths in the United States at fewer than fifty thousand.[16] As of this writing, he was off by approximately 699 million on the first figure, on the second by more than 1.5 million. In 2024, the Bradley Foundation, which funded Charles Murray as he wrote *The Bell Curve*, continued to fertilize the new fusionism when it granted its quarter-million dollar cash prize to two people: Samuel Gregg, holder of the Friedrich A. Hayek Chair in Economics and Economic History at the American Institute of Economic Research in Great Barrington, Massachusetts, and Jay Bhattacharya, a professor of health policy at Stanford University, senior fellow at the Hoover Institution, and coauthor of the Great Barrington Declaration, which opposed masking and lockdowns during the pandemic.[17]

Libertarian arguments draw ever more frequently from the arsenal of the hard sciences to ground their claims. One of the most fertile sites for the new fusionism has been Silicon Valley, where thinkers increasingly promote the idea that "traits like intelligence and work ethic... have a strong genetic basis." The author of that line is the American writer Richard Hanania. Hailed by his publisher, HarperCollins, as "one of the most talked-about writers in the nation," Hanania was exposed in 2023 as the pseudonymous author of openly racist articles for the website AlternativeRight.com, founded by the neo-Nazi and white supremacist Richard Spencer.[18] His articles included calls to forcibly sterilize everyone with an IQ under ninety and claimed that Hispanics "don't have the requisite IQ to be a productive part of a first world nation."[19] For Hanania, whose online guests have included high-profile intellectuals such as Steven Pinker and Tyler Cowen (whose Mercatus Center at George Mason University contributed $50,000 to him), high IQ in individuals and nations leads to success, libertarianism, and appreciation of markets.[20] Hanania frets about "dysgenic fertility" as measured in the decline of IQ rates in the American population and suggests that "the real source of class difference is traits like IQ and intellectual curiosity."[21]

Hanania is the intellectual heir of Richard J. Herrnstein and Charles Murray, but it is important to remember that *The Bell Curve* did not mean "cognitive elite" as a compliment. In later books Murray would even more pointedly criticize the cognitive elite for their literal and figurative aloofness from the rest of the population. But the moral charge was always ambiguous. The authors were themselves part of this elite. Both Herrnstein and Murray attended Harvard and lived in centers of wealth and privilege, greater Boston and greater Washington, DC. Wasn't membership in a cognitive elite being presented as an aspiration? The early 2000s saw what one journalist called "the revenge of the nerds" as the West Coast tech sector, far from the traditional centers of American power, began to emerge as the engine of the digital economy.[22] Seattle, a city known mostly for its rain, became the home of Amazon and the sleepy town of Portland the home of Intel. Farther south, the fruit-growing valley around Palo Alto, which had used by state defense contractors as a launchpad for many small companies, became the epicenter of a long-standing but newly hyped entity: the "startup."

In the process, the critical term "cognitive elite" became a self-congratulatory one. The apparent world historical inversion, whereby the smart kids were also the rich and most powerful ones, was celebrated on iconic blogs and listservs such as Slate Star Codex and Less Wrong (where users self-reported implausibly high IQ scores), as well as EconLib and Marginal Revolution. The latter were both run by libertarian GMU economics professors Bryan Caplan and Tyler Cowen, respectively. (Yet another GMU economist wrote a book on IQ called *Hive Mind* and defended gender differences in cognitive reasoning.)[23] Contributors and commenters on these sites reveled in arcane detail, the visual language of statistics and graphs, and the impression of academic rigor.

A high-profile member of this tech-adjacent strain of new fusionism was Curtis Yarvin, who blogged under the pseudonym Mencius Moldbug. As a teenager, Yarvin had been part of the Study of Mathematically Precocious Youth established by Johns Hopkins University psychology professor Julian Stanley to identify high-IQ youngsters.[24]

Still attached to the idea of the cognitive elite as an adult, he condemned democracy for spoiling coexistence between "high-IQ" and "low-IQ" individuals and proposed a "psychometric qualification" for voting in South Africa, disenfranchising everyone below an IQ of 120.[25] To followers of neo-reactionary ideology, the internet and its affiliated communities were offering an alternative public sphere where a new elite could arise by virtue of their brains, their genes, or frequently both.

In the runup to Donald Trump's election as U.S. president in 2016, the intelligence question emerged again in the ecosystem of what was now being called the alt-right. Charles Murray's work on the supposed "forbidden knowledge" of intelligence research served for another round of controversies, claims and counterclaims as the "intellectual dark web" earned hyperventilating profiles in the *New York Times*.[26] Trump himself seemed fixated on IQ, referring frequently to his allegedly high score.[27] The tone was captured well in a tweet from 2013 that read: "Sorry losers and haters, but my I.Q. is one of the highest—and you all know it! Please don't feel so stupid or insecure, it's not your fault."

This time around, the discourse was less about criticizing the detachment of the creative elite or praising new leaders of economic innovation. Instead, it had taken a graver turn toward the potential need to escape from the drag of surplus members of society or possibly even exclude them from equal status. The IQ-centric version of new fusionism was aided by considerable financial support from a few wealthy men including Harlan Crow, heir to a real estate fortune whose holding company had $19.6 billion under management in 2020. Murray, a regular guest at Crow's house along with Supreme Court Justice Clarence Thomas, dedicated his most recent two books on race science to him.[28] The kinship between the two men is captured in an unforgettable photorealistic portrait titled "Contemplation," showing the duo gazing into the distance together. Crow funds the Salem Center for Policy at the University of Texas at Austin, where Hanania was a fellow—not to be confused with the nonaccredited startup University of Austin, funded by Peter Thiel's partner Joe Lonsdale, where Hanania is also a lecturer in their "Forbidden Courses" summer program.[29]

Whereas Michael Young's 1958 dystopia portrayed a meritocracy working too well, the complaint of many of today's new fusionists is that it is not working well enough. Even after the Supreme Court ruling against affirmative action, a longtime goal of conservatives like Murray, they fear that admissions officers at top universities and hiring committees at top firms still assemble cohorts based on criteria rather than true ability. Lionel Shriver's novel *Mania* captured the anxiety of the libertarian–Far Right nexus in her depiction of an America where the high-IQ "brain-vain" are regarded as "cerebral supremacists" and campaigns of "Mental Parity" lower expectations for everyone and stigmatize achievement and excellence.[30] The opposition to so-called diversity, equity, and inclusion efforts is especially virulent. In his blurb to Hanania's 2023 book *The Origins of Woke: Civil Rights Law, Corporate America, and the Triumph of Identity Politics,* Peter Thiel uses violent rhetoric, writing "DEI will never *d-i-e* from words alone—Hanania shows we need the sticks and stones of government violence to exorcise the diversity demon."[31]

Declaring membership in the cognitive aristocracy could be harmless if it stayed in the comments section. But IQ fetishism has pernicious effects. It draws racial lines placing Caucasians, East Asians, and Ashkenazi Jews on one side of the line with other Asians, Hispanics, and people of African descent on the other. The IQ fetishists like to think they are living in a near future where they, the pure creative information workers imagined in the 1990s, have been elevated through their high intelligence and innate ability. They were not simply in the right place at the right time, bobbing along in a sea of liquidity in an era of zero interest rates. They were, like the staff at the Apple Store, *geniuses.*

Perhaps the darkest direction that new fusionist thinking could go was previewed by Yarvin in 2008. Speculating about the transformation of San Francisco into a private entity called "Friscorp," he wondered what could be done with the unproductive residents of the city that remained. After considering then dismissing the idea of pulping surplus "hominids" into biodiesel for city buses, he suggests that "the best humane alternative to genocide" was "not to liquidate the wards... but to *virtualize* them." He envisioned the incarceration of the knowledge economy's underclass in "permanent solitary confinement, waxed like a bee larva into a cell which is sealed except for emergencies." Against fears this would seed an insurrection, like that imagined by Michael Young a half-century earlier, he played the card of technology. The captive's cell would not be bare. It would include "an immersive virtual-reality interface which allows him to experience a rich, fulfilling life in a completely imaginary world."[32] May Day 2034 passes without notice.

Hayek's final book, *The Fatal Conceit*, famously proposes the circular argument that the proof of an ideology's adaptive capacity is the number of human lives it helps sustain. The new panic over fertility and birth rates promises a coming chaotic round of intellectual debates about how and if libertarian values can be adapted to continue to win the demographic race. Some of the leading figures have taken the drastic choice of restricting the bodily autonomy of women to make choices about their own reproduction. Among them are Ron Paul and the new Argentine president Javier Milei, who opposes the abortion that was legalized in the majority-Catholic country of Argentina only in 2020, after a successful decades-long mobilization. His argument blends a half-gesture to genetics with a stronger one to natural law. "It is true that the mother has the right over her body but not over the body of the child, which is a totally different body, it has a different DNA.... There is neither freedom nor property if you are not born."[33]

Milei cuts a bizarre figure in his AC/DC coiffure and meme-ready mugging for the camera, but in assessing the latest crop of Hayek's offspring, it is worth remembering the rapturous reception he received at that most mainstream of venues, the World Economic Forum at Davos. In his 2024 appearance Milei denounced the "radical feminist agenda," the "bloody abortion agenda," and the "Neo-Marxists [who] have managed to coopt the common sense of the Western world." He listed all the varieties of collectivism he opposed, including communists, fascists, social democrats, nationalists, national socialists, Nazis, Christian democrats, neo-Keynesians, progressives, populists, nationalists, and globalists. He reserved his praise for the wealthy gathered in the room. "You are the true protagonists of this story," he said, "you are heroes." Like Jair Bolsonaro, Sebastian Kurz, and Donald Trump, who had spoken from the same stage before him, Milei spoke less as a defector from the global capitalist order than its latest photogenic cheerleader. He posed for selfies with the managing director of the IMF after the show, just as he would pose later with Tim Cook, Mark Zuckerberg, and Elon Musk and take the stage at the Hoover Institution, introduced by its director, Condoleezza Rice. This book is a warning not to be taken in by false prophets, fooled by appearances or lazy media framing. Many supposed disruptors of the status quo are agents less of a backlash against global capitalism than a frontlash within it. Our genealogies of their ideas are X-rays that leave little doubt.

Acknowledgments

My list of debts for this book is long. I'd begin with John Ralston Saul, author of *Voltaire's Bastards*, the inspiration for the title, for writing serious nonfiction a searching teenager could read, and my parents for raising me to search. In the more recent years across which the book's writing stretched, I can thank Charlie Maier, Sven Beckert, and Sugata Bose at the Weatherhead Initiative on Global History at Harvard and Christy Thornton and Stuart Schrader who became close comrades there and then and have remained so. Mark Blyth supported me with a year at his Rhodes Center for International Economics at Brown University and continues to inspire me with his roving curiosity and intelligence. The writing of the book stretched through the pandemic and was interwoven with the writing of another one, *Crack-Up Capitalism*, for the now late and lamented Metropolitan Books, one of the only outposts for left-critical writing in the trade press world. Sara Bershtel and Grigory Tovbis were my shepherds there and much that was culled then is the fugitive flock here—I thank them for leaving me with these outcasts. Those who have thought with me through the ideas in this book include, in alphabetical order, Tim Barker, David Bebnowski, Melinda Cooper, Will Davies, Daniel Denvir, James Duesterberg, Katrina Forrester, Heinrich Geiselberger, Stefanos Geroulanos, Matt Goerzen, Ana Isabel Keilson, Hans Kundnani, Hari Kunzru, Boaz Levin, Jamie Martin, Thomas Meaney, Tom Penn,

Justin Reynolds, Thea Riofrancos, Pavlos Roufos, Ben Tarnoff, Alberto Toscano, Moira Weigel, and Kirsten Weld. I've profited from talking the ideas through with Daniel Bessner, Tom Clark, Richard Hames, Doug Henwood, Sarah Jaffe, November Kelly, Daniel McAteer, Chuck Mertz, Edward Ongweso, Riley Quinn, Jathan Sadowsky, Sam Seder, Emma Vigeland, and many others. My colleagues at Wellesley College and now Boston University have shown great hospitality to my eccentric interests. My thanks also to the Boston University Center for the Humanities for their contribution towards this book's production. Nawal Arjini, Carolyn Biltoft, Matthew Shen Goodman, Gav Jacobson, Chris Lehmann, Matt Lord, Kenneth Murphy, Vanessa Mobley, and others gave me the chance to try out ideas in print. Michel Feher and Meighan Gale make the small miracle of Zone Books possible and I am honored to be welcomed in their pages. A special thanks to Simon Denny for his inspiring work over the years and his contribution of the piece for the book jacket. Will Callison, Niklas Olsen, Dieter Plehwe, and Stuart Schrader were kindred spirits and co-authors. Melissa Flashman has been an accomplice. Hadji Bakara, Andrew Daily, and Ryan Jeffery remain lifelines from year to year, decade to decade. My two sisters have been inspirations, offering laughter in equal measure with reflection. And last, my most important two: Yann, my daily reminder of life's stream, and Michelle, my rudder, compass, blanket, and book. Let's find out what's beyond the next bend, I'm blessed to be with you in the drift.

Notes

INTRODUCTION

1. Charles Murray, "2006 Atlas Freedom Dinner Keynote Address," *Atlas Highlights* (Winter 2006–2007): p. 15.

2. Ibid., pp. 22, 23.

3. Charles Murray, "Changes over Time in the Black-White Difference on Mental Tests: Evidence from the Children of the 1979 Cohort of the National Longitudinal Survey of Youth," *Intelligence* 34 (2006): pp. 527–40.

4. Milford H. Wolpoff and Rachel Caspari, *Race and Human Evolution* (New York: Simon & Schuster, 1997), p. 164.

5. Charles Murray, "The Rediscovery of Human Nature and Human Diversity," Mont Pelerin Society Special Meeting, Galapagos Islands, Ecuador, June 22–29, 2013, http://darwinianconservatism.blogspot.com/2013/07/.

6. Ibid. For the attendance list see "Speakers," The Mont Pelerin Society Special Meeting June 22 to 29, 2013, University of San Francisco de Quito, https://www.usfq.edu.ec/en/events/mont-pelerin-society-special-meeting-june-22-29-2013.

7. There is a vast literature on the conservative movement. For the classic analysis, see George H. Nash, *The Conservative Intellectual Movement in America since 1945* (Wilmington, DE: ISI Books, 2006). For an illuminating inquiry, see Melinda Cooper, *Family Values: Between Neoliberalism and the New Social Conservatism* (New York: Zone Books, 2017). For a summary of the literature, see Kim Phillips-Fein, "Conservatism: A State of the Field," *Journal of American History* 98, no. 3 (December 2011): pp. 723–43. For the 1990s, see John Ganz,

When the Clock Broke: Con Men, Conspiracists, and How America Cracked up in the Early 1990s (New York: Farrar, Straus and Giroux, 2024); Nicole Hemmer, *Partisans: The Conservative Revolutionaries Who Remade American Politics in the 1990s* (New York: Basic Books, 2022).

8. Paul Gottfried, "Toward a New Fusionism?," *Policy Review* 42 (Fall 1987): p. 68; E. O. Wilson, *Sociobiology: The New Synthesis* (Cambridge, MA: Belknap Press of Harvard University Press, 1975), p. 562. For a learned study of what the author calls "neo-Darwinian conservatism," see Jon Anstein Olsen, "Neo-Darwinian Conservatism in the United States" (PhD diss., University of Oslo, 2013).

9. For a criticism of this literature from a different angle, see Quinn Slobodian, "The Backlash against Neoliberal Globalization from Above: Elite Origins of the Crisis of the New Constitutionalism," *Theory, Culture & Society* 38, no. 6 (2021): pp. 51–69.

10. In some cases they did. The Cato Institute planned in 1990 to present a bust of Hayek to the University of Moscow, and a bust of Mises cast in bronze by a foundry in Florida was presented to the University of Warsaw courtesy of the Ludwig von Mises Institute and the Institute for Humane Studies. The Mises bust was to sit in the library next to the Oskar Lange Memorial Room, a deliberate echo of the socialist calculation debate from the early century. George Koether to Gottfried Haberler, July 30, 1990. Stanford University, Hoover Institution Archives, Gottfried Haberler Papers Box 9, "Max Corden" Folder.

11. John Fund, "Hayek's Heirs Contemplate Greener Pastures," *Wall Street Journal*, September 19, 1991.

12. Fred L. Smith Jr., "The Bankruptcy of Collectivist Environmental Policy," MPS General Meeting Santiago 2000. Hoover Institution Archives, Mont Pelerin Society Papers Box 29, "2000 Meeting" folder (hereafter MPS Papers).

13. Peter Brimelow, "An Interview with Milton Friedman," *Forbes*, August 17, 1992.

14. Victoria Curzon-Price, "The Road to Freedom," presidential address at the MPS regional meeting in Reykjavik, August 21, 2005. *The Mont Pelerin Society Newsletter* (Fall 2005), p. 1. MPS Papers, Box 163.

15. General Meeting, Munich, Germany, September 2–8, 1990, *The Mont Pelerin Society Newsletter*, December 1990, p. 3. MPS Papers, Box 163.

16. Bruce N. Ames, "Misconceptions about Pollution and Cancer." MPS Papers, Box 143, "General Meeting 1990 Conference Papers Drafts" folder.

17. Victoria-Curzon Price, "Three Models of European Integration," in *Whose Europe? Competing Visions for 1992*, ed. Ralf Dahrendorf (London: Institute of Economic Affairs, 1989), p. 38. On the shifting opinions of organized neoliberals to Europe, see Quinn Slobodian and Dieter Plehwe, "Neoliberals against Europe," in *Mutant Neoliberalism: Market Rule and Political Ruptures*, eds. William Callison and Zachary Manfredi (New York: Fordham University Press, 2019), pp. 89–111; Roberto Ventresca, "Neoliberal Thinkers and European Integration in the 1980s and the Early 1990s," *Contemporary European History* 31, no. 1 (2022): pp. 31–47.

18. Quotes are from the published version: Gerard Radnitzky, "Towards a Europe of Free Societies: Evolutionary Competition or Constructivistic Design," *Ordo* 42 (1991): p. 150.

19. Ibid., p. 146.

20. Gary Becker, "Letter from the President," *The Mont Pelerin Society Newsletter*, December 1990, p. 2. MPS Papers, Box 163.

21. Michael S. Joyce, "The Present Political Crisis," MPS Special Gathering, April 10, 1997. MPS Papers, Box 143, "Papers presented at the 1997 Special Gathering 50th Anniversary" folder.

22. Ibid.

23. Charles Murray, "A Paper to be Presented for the Panel 'Markets and Morality: The Ethics of Liberty.'" MPS Papers, Box 113, "Regional Meeting Cape Town 10–13 Sep 95 (1)" folder. Though undated, the paper appears with Murrays name on the program for the Regional Mont Pelerin Society Meeting in Cancun, January 14–17, 1996. MPS Papers, Box 116, "Cancun Conference Materials" folder.

24. Herbert Spencer, *The Principles of Ethics* (New York: D. Appleton and Co., 1898), p. 394.

25. All quotes from Murray, "Paper for the panel 'Markets and Morality.'"

26. Henri LePage and Pascal Salin, "MPS Meetings—Board Role, Themes, Formats," MPS Papers, Box 107, "Special Board Meeting, 17–19 94 WDC" folder.

27. Murray, "Paper for 'Markets and Morality.'"

28. Emphasis in original. Radnitzky, "Towards a Europe of Free Societies," p. 151.

29. For an excellent scholarly contribution, see Naomi Beck, *Hayek and the Evolution of Capitalism* (Chicago: University of Chicago Press, 2018).

30. John Ralston Saul, *Voltaire's Bastards: The Dictatorship of Reason in the West* (New York: Vintage Books, 1993).

31. For a sample of the scholarship of those finding the origins of the current Right in neoliberalism, see William Callison and Zachary Manfredi, "Introduction: Theorizing Mutant Neoliberalism," in Callison and Manfredi, eds., *Mutant Neoliberalism*, pp. 1–38; Wendy Brown, *In the Ruins of Neoliberalism: The Rise of Antidemocratic Politics in the West* (New York: Columbia University Press, 2019), pp. 707–24; Melinda Cooper, "The Alt-Right: Neoliberalism, Libertarianism and the Fascist Temptation," *Theory, Culture & Society* 38, no. 6 (2021): pp. 29–50; Melinda Cooper, *Counterrevolution: Extravagance and Austerity in Public Finance* (New York: Zone Books, 2024); Neil Davidson and Richard Saull, "Neoliberalism and the Far-Right: A Contradictory Embrace," *Critical Sociology* 43, nos. 4–5 (2017): pp. 707–24; Henry A. Giroux, "Neoliberal Fascism as the Endpoint of Casino Capitalism," *Fast Capitalism* 16, no. 1 (2019): pp. 7–23; Daniel Martinez HoSang and Joseph E. Lowndes, *Producers, Parasites, Patriots: Race and the New Right-Wing Politics of Precarity* (Minneapolis: University of Minnesota Press, 2019); Ray Kiely, "Assessing Conservative Populism: A New Double Movement or Neoliberal Populism?," *Development and Change* 51, no. 2 (2020): pp. 398–417; Jo Littler, "Normcore Plutocrats in Gold Elevators," *Cultural Politics* 15, no. 1 (2019): pp. 15–28; Richard Saull, "Racism and Far Right Imaginaries Within Neo-liberal Political Economy," *New Political Economy* 23, no. 5 (2018): pp. 588–608.

32. See, as part of a large literature, Thomas Biebricher, *The Political Theory of Neoliberalism* (Stanford, CA: Stanford University Press, 2019); Philip Mirowski and Dieter Plehwe, eds., *The Road from Mont Pèlerin: The Making of the Neoliberal Thought Collective* (Cambridge, MA: Harvard University Press, 2009); Dieter Plehwe, Quinn Slobodian, and Philip Mirowski, eds., *Nine Lives of Neoliberalism* (New York: Verso, 2020); Quinn Slobodian, *Globalists: The End of Empire and the Birth of Neoliberalism* (Cambridge, MA: Harvard University Press, 2018).

33. "Steve Bannon's Full Speech in France," *Washington Post*, March 23, 2018.

34. Steve Bannon, interview by Roger Köppel for Weltwoche on the Road, Gotthard, Switzerland, March 5 and 6, 2018, posted March 5, 2018 by Weltwoche Daily, YouTube, https://www.youtube.com/watch?v=AeJaq599yh4.

35. "Alice Weidel zieht sich aus Hayek-Gesellschaft zurück," *Welt*, February 1, 2021.

36. Thomas D. Williams, "Exclusive Interview with German Populist AfD Leader Beatrix von Storch," Breitbar News Network, September 29, 2017, http://www.breitbart.com/london/2017/09/29/exclusive-interview-german-populist-afd-leader-beatrix-von-storch/.

37. "Koalitionsverhandlungen: Cluster-Sprecher stehen fest," kurier.at, October 28, 2017, https://kurier.at/politik/inland/schwarz-blaue-koalition-clustersprecher-fuer-verhandlungen-festgelegt/294.827.977.

38. Naomi Klein, *The Shock Doctrine: The Rise of Disaster Capitalism* (New York: Metropolitan Books, 2007).

39. John Williamson, "What Washington Means by Policy Reform," in *Latin American Adjustment: How Much Has Happened?*, ed. John Williamson (Washington, DC: Institute for International Economics, 1990), pp. 7–20.

40. This section draws on Quinn Slobodian, "The Law of the Sea of Ignorance: F. A. Hayek, Fritz Machlup, and Other Neoliberals Confront the Intellectual Property Problem," in Plehwe, Slobodian, and Mirowski, eds., *Nine Lives of Neoliberalism*, pp. 70–71.

41. Radnitzky, "Towards a Europe of Free Societies," p. 139.

42. Anthony de Jasay, *Against Politics: On Government, Anarchy, and Order* (London: Routledge, 1997), p. 3.

43. On internal conflicts, see Bernhard Walpen, *Die offenen Feinde und ihre Gesellschaft: Eine hegemonietheoretische Studie zur Mont Pelerin Society* (Hamburg: VSA-Verlag, 2004); Angus Burgin, *The Great Persuasion: Reinventing Free Markets since the Depression* (Cambridge, MA: Harvard University Press, 2012).

44. See Quinn Slobodian, "The World Economy and the Color Line: Wilhelm Röpke, Apartheid, and the White Atlantic," *German Historical Institute Bulletin Supplement* 10 (2014): pp. 61–87.

45. F. A. Hayek, *Our Moral Heritage* (Washington, DC: Heritage Foundation, 1983).

46. Emphasis added. F. A. Hayek, "Professor Friedrich Hayek's Closing Speech," speech to Mont Pelerin Society, March 3, 1984. Margaret Thatcher Foundation Archive, Hayek MSS (Hoover Institution) Box 109, http://www.margaretthatcher.org/document/117193.

47. Sebastian Friedrich and Gabriel Kuhn, "Between Capital and Volk," *Jacobin*, June 29, 2017, https://jacobin.com/2017/06/germany-afd-cdu-immigrants-merkel-xenophobia-neoliberalism.

48. Stephanie Mencimer, "Glenn Beck's Gold Gurus Charged with Fraud," *Mother Jones*, May 19, 2010, https://www.motherjones.com/politics/2010/05/glenn-beck-goldline-weiner/.

CHAPTER ONE: OF SAVANNAS AND SATELLITES

1. MPS Secretary's Report, September 1994. Stanford University, Hoover Institution Archives, Mont Pelerin Society Papers (hereafter MPS Papers), Box 107, "Misc Papers from Cannes General Meeting" folder.

2. See Victor L. Shammas, "Burying Mont Pèlerin: Milton Friedman and Neoliberal Vanguardism," *Constellations* 25, no. 1 (March 2018): pp. 117–32, https://onlinelibrary.wiley.com/doi/10.1111/1467-8675.12322.

3. MPS Notes to Financial Statements for the years ended March 31, 1994, and 1993, MPS Papers, Box 107, "Misc Papers from Cannes General Meeting" folder.

4. F. A. Hayek, *Rules and Order: A New Statement of the Liberal Principles of Justice and Political Economy* (London: Routledge & Kegan Paul, 1973), p. 74.

5. See Naomi Beck, *Hayek and the Evolution of Capitalism* (Chicago: University of Chicago Press, 2018).

6. F. A. Hayek, *The Mirage of Social Justice* (London: Routledge & Kegan Paul, 1976).

7. F. A. Hayek, "The Atavism of Social Justice," in *New Studies in Philosophy, Politics, Economics and the History of Ideas*, ed. F. A. Hayek (Chicago: University of Chicago Press, 1978), p. 67.

8. Ibid., p. 65. He would repeat these themes in F. A. Hayek, *The Fatal Conceit: The Errors of Socialism* (Chicago: University of Chicago Press, 1988).

9. Hayek, "Atavism of Social Justice," pp. 67–68.

10. F. A. Hayek, *The Constitution of Liberty* (Chicago: University of Chicago Press, 2011), pp. 519–33.

11. Ramon Diaz, "Why Hayek *Was* a Conservative," MPS General Meeting 1994, September 25–30, Cannes, France. MPS Papers, Box 107, "Misc Papers from Cannes General Meeting" folder.

12. Norman Barry, "Making Sense of Hayek: The Theory of Spontaneous Order," MPS General Meeting 1994. MPS Papers, Box 107, "Misc Papers from Cannes General Meeting" folder.

13. Victoria Curzon-Price, "Hayek's Extended Order," MPS General Meeting 1994. MPS Papers, Box 107, "Misc Papers from Cannes General Meeting" folder.

14. Gerard Radnitzky, "Selecting the Problem," MPS General Meeting 1994. MPS Papers, Box 107, "Misc Papers from Cannes General Meeting" folder.

15. Gerard Radnitzky, "An Economic Theory of the Rise of Civilization and Its Policy Implications: Hayek's Account Generalized," *Ordo* 38 (1987): p. 51.

16. Radnitzky, "Selecting the Problem."

17. Gerard Radnitzky, "The Image of Man as Basis and Metaphysics of the Sciences Humaines," *Science et métaphysique* 11 (1988): pp. 163–64.

18. Jean-Pierre Dupuy, "A Critique of Hayek," MPS General Meeting 1994. MPS Papers, Box 107, "Misc Papers from Cannes General Meeting" folder.

19. For a discussion of the teleocratic/nomocratic distinction, see Raymond Plant, *The Neo-liberal State* (Oxford: Oxford University Press, 2010), chap. 1.

20. Kenneth Minogue, "Hayek and Conservatism: Beatrice and Benedick?," Sydney Papers presented 1985. MPS Papers, Box 26, folder 4.

21. Ibid.

22. See Wendy Brown, *In the Ruins of Neoliberalism: The Rise of Antidemocratic Politics in the West* (New York: Columbia University Press, 2019); Jessica Whyte, *The Morals of the Market: Human Rights and the Rise of Neoliberalism* (New York: Verso, 2019).

23. "Professor Friedrich Hayek's Closing Speech," MPS Regional Conference, Paris, February 29–March 3, 1984. MPS Papers, Box 25, folder 6.

24. F. A. Hayek, *Our Moral Heritage* (Washington, DC: Heritage Foundation, 1983), p. 6.

25. Minogue, "Hayek and Conservatism: Beatrice and Benedick?" On Minogue see Sean Irving, "Competitiveness, Civilizationism, and the Anglosphere: Kenneth Minogue's Place in Conservative Thought," *Modern Intellectual History* (2024): pp. 1–20.

26. John Davenport, "Moral Agreement in a Free Society," MPS meeting, Cambridge 1984. MPS Papers, Box 25, folder 10.

27. Pedro Schwartz, "Comments on 'Obstacles to Restoring a Market Economy' by Profs Stubbletone and Smith," MPS Papers, Box 26, "Cambridge 1984 papers" folder.

28. See Melinda Cooper, *Family Values: Between Neoliberalism and the New Social Conservatism* (New York: Zone Books, 2017).

29. Ernest van den Haag, "Commentary on Shirley Robin Letwin's 'Moral Agreement in a Free Society,'" MPS Papers, Box 25, folder 10.

30. James M. Buchanan, "Transcending Genetic Limits," (working paper, Center for the Study of Public Choice, George Mason University, Fairfax, Virginia, 1997), https://web.archive.org/web/19990421193138/http://www.gmu.edu/departments/economics/working/wpe1/genetic.htm.

31. See Jo-Anne Pemberton, *Global Metaphors: Modernity and the Quest for One World* (London: Pluto Press, 2001); Ben Huf, Glenda Sluga, and Sabine Selchow, "Business and the Planetary History of International Environmental Governance in the 1970s," *Contemporary European History* 31, no. 4 (November 2022): pp. 553–69.

32. "Professor Friedrich Hayek's Closing Speech."

CHAPTER TWO: THE ROCK OF BIOLOGY

1. See Lars Cornelissen, "Neoliberal Imperialism," *Politics* (2023): pp. 1–17; Quinn Slobodian, *Globalists: The End of Empire and the Birth of Neoliberalism* (Cambridge, MA: Harvard University Press, 2018); Jessica Whyte, *The Morals of the Market: Human Rights and the Rise of Neoliberalism* (New York: Verso, 2019), chap. 3.

2. The literature is large. See, among others, Kathleen Belew, *Bring the War*

Home: The White Power Movement and Paramilitary America (Cambridge, MA: Harvard University Press, 2018); John Ganz, *When the Clock Broke: Con Men, Conspiracists, and How America Cracked Up in the Early 1990s* (New York: Farrar, Straus and Giroux, 2024); Daniel Geary, Camilla Schofield, and Jennifer Sutton, eds., *Global White Nationalism: From Apartheid to Trump* (Manchester: Manchester University Press, 2020); George Hawley, *Making Sense of the Alt-Right* (New York: Columbia University Press, 2017); Nicole Hemmer, *Partisans: The Conservative Revolutionaries Who Remade American Politics in the 1990s* (New York: Basic Books, 2022); John S. Huntington, *Far-Right Vanguard: The Radical Roots of Modern Conservatism* (Philadelphia: University of Pennsylvania Press, 2021); Talia Lavin, *Culture Warlords: My Journey into the Dark Web of White Supremacy* (New York: Hachette, 2020); Andrew Marantz, *Antisocial: How Online Extremists Broke America* (New York: Viking, 2019); Angela Nagle, *Kill All Normies: The Online Culture Wars from Tumblr and 4chan to the Alt-Right and Trump* (Winchester, UK: Zero Books, 2017); David Neiwert, *Alt-America: The Rise of the Radical Right in the Age of Trump* (New York: Verso, 2017); Alexander Minna Stern, *Proud Boys and the White Ethnostate: How the Alt-Right is Warping the American Imagination* (Boston: Beacon Press, 2019); David Austin Walsh, *Taking America Back: The Conservative Movement and the Far Right* (New Haven, CT: Yale University Press, 2024); Mike Wendling, *Alt-Right: From 4chan to the White House* (London: Pluto, 2018); Donna Zuckerberg, *Not All Dead White Men: Classics and Misogyny in the Digital Age* (Cambridge, MA: Harvard University Press, 2018).

3. Murray N. Rothbard, "Freedom, Inequality, Primitivism, and the Division of Labor," *Modern Age* (Summer 1971): pp. 233, 235, 244.

4. Ibid., 234, 242, 244. The quote is from Ludwig Mises, *Socialism: An Economic and Sociological Analysis (1922)* (Indianapolis, IN: Liberty Fund, 1981), p. 305. The book was first published in 1922.

5. Gustavo R. Velasco, "On Equality and Egalitarianism," *Modern Age* (Winter 1974): p. 23.

6. Louis Rougier, "Philosophical Origins of the Idea of Natural Equality," *Modern Age* (Winter 1974): p. 36.

7. Arthur Shenfield, "Equality before the Law," *Modern Age* (Spring 1973): pp. 118, 121.

8. Peter T. Bauer, "Economic Differences and Inequalities," *Modern Age* (Summer 1975): p. 302.

9. Peter T. Bauer, "Development Economics: The Spurious Consensus and Its Background," in *Roads to Freedom: Essays in Honour of Friedrich A. von Hayek*, ed. Erich W. Streissler (London: Routledge & Kegan Paul, 1969), pp. 29–30.

10. Arthur Shenfield, "The Ideological War against Western Society," *Modern Age* 14, no. 2 (Spring 1970): p. 161. For more on neoliberals and empire, see Cornelissen, "Neoliberal Imperialism," pp. 1–17.

11. Nathaniel Weyl, "Envy and Aristocide in Underdeveloped Countries," *Modern Age* (Winter 1974): p. 42.

12. Murray Rothbard, "Egalitarianism as a Revolt against Nature," Modern Age (Fall 1973): pp. 355, 357.

13. For an inside account, see John Blundell, "IHS and the Rebirth of Austrian Economics: Some Reflections on 1974–1976," *Quarterly Journal of Austrian Economics* 17, no. 1 (Spring 2014): pp. 92–107.

14. Janek Wasserman, *Marginal Revolutionaries: How Austrian Economics Fought the War of Ideas* (New Haven, CT: Yale University Press, 2019), p. 237.

15. Ibid., p. 258. The center began at Rutgers University before moving to George Mason University. It shares a building with the Koch-funded Institute for Humane Studies. For details see Jane Mayer, *Dark Money: The Hidden History of the Billionaires Behind the Rise of the Radical Right* (New York: Doubleday, 2016).

16. Don Lavoie, "Austrian Models? Possibilities of Evolutionary Computation," in *The Elgar Companion to Austrian Economics*, ed. Peter J. Boettke (Aldershot, UK: Edward Elgar, 1994), p. 551.

17. Ludwig M. Lachmann, "Austrian Economics: A Hermeneutic Approach," in *Economics and Hermeneutics*, ed. Don Lavoie (London: Routledge, 1990), p. 140. See also Joshua Lee Harris, "Gadamer, Lavoie, and Their Critics: The Hermeneutics Debate Revisited," *Journal of Markets & Morality* 19, no. 1 (Spring 2016): pp. 61–78.

18. Richard Ebeling, "Toward a Hermeneutical Economics: Expectations, Prices, and the Role of Interpretation in a Theory of the Market Process," in *Subjectivism, Intelligibility and Economic Understanding*, ed. Israel M. Kirzner (Basingstoke, UK: Macmillan, 1986), pp. 40, 47–48.

19. Nicos Poulantzas, "The Problem of the Capitalist State," *New Left Review* (November–December 1969): p. 68; Stuart Hall, "Cultural Studies and the Centre: Some Problematics and Problems," in *Culture, Media, Language: Working Papers in Cultural Studies, 1972–79*, ed. Stuart Hall et al. (London: Routledge, 1980), p. 23; Johanna Brenner and Maria Ramas, "Rethinking Women's Oppression," *New Left Review* (March–April 1984): p. 34. See also Ernesto Laclau and Chantal Mouffe, *Hegemony and Socialist Strategy: Towards a Radical Democratic Politics*, 2nd ed. (New York: Verso, 1985).

20. Lachmann, "Austrian Economics," p. 133.

21. Peter J. Boettke, "The Theory of Spontaneous Order and Cultural Evolution in the Social Theory of F. A. Hayek," *Cultural Dynamics* 3, no. 1 (1990): p. 62.

22. Don Lavoie, "The Market as a Procedure for Discovery and Conveyance of Inarticulate Knowledge," *Comparative Economic Studies* 28 (Spring 1986): pp. 5–9.

23. Boettke, "Theory of Spontaneous Order," p. 70.

24. For a rare flirtation with the use of computers see Lavoie, "Austrian Models?" For a wing of libertarianism that was much closer to computing see Erik Baker, "The Ultimate Think Tank: The Rise of the Santa Fe Institute Libertarian," *History of the Human Sciences* 35, nos. 3–4 (2022): pp. 32–57. See also Philip Mirowski and Edward Nik-Khah, *The Knowledge We Have Lost in Information: The History of Information in Modern Economics* (Oxford: Oxford University Press, 2017); Orit Halpern, "The Future Will Not Be Calculated: Neural Nets, Neoliberalism, and Reactionary Politics," *Critical Inquiry* 48, no. 2 (Winter 2022): pp. 334–59.

25. Peter J. Boettke, "Where Did Economics Go Wrong?: Modern Economics as a Flight from Reality," *Critical Review* 11, no. 1 (Winter 1997): p. 43.

26. F. A. Hayek, "Nature v. Nurture Once Again," in *New Studies in Philosophy, Politics, Economics and the History of Ideas*, ed. F. A. Hayek (Chicago: University of Chicago Press, 1978), p. 293; Edward Feser, "Hayek on Tradition,"

Journal of Libertarian Studies 17, no. 2 (Winter 2003): p. 24; Ulrich Witt, "Evolutionary Economics," in Boettke, ed., *The Elgar Companion to Austrian Economics*, p. 547.

27. For details on the Austrian split, see Quinn Slobodian, "Anti-68ers and the Racist-Libertarian Alliance: How a Schism among Austrian School Neoliberals Helped Spawn the Alt Right," *Cultural Politics* 15, no. 3 (2019): pp. 372–86.

28. Lew Rockwell, CV. Hoover Institution Archives, Center for Libertarian Studies Papers, Box 1, Folder 2.

29. David Gordon, "Hermeneutics Versus Austrian Economics (1986)," Mises Institute, April 9, 2015, https://mises.org/library/hermeneutics-versus-austrian-economics. He repeated many of the same criticisms in a review in the inaugural issue of a new journal under his editorship, the *Mises Review*. See David Gordon, "What Should Anti-Economists Do? Review of *The Market Process: Essays in Contemporary Austrian Economics*, by Peter Boettke and David Prychitko," *The Mises Review* 1, no. 1 (Spring 1995), https://mises.org/mises-review/market-process-essays-contemporary-austrian-economics-peter-boettke-and-david-prychitko. For further criticism of the "self-styled radical subjectivists," see David Gordon, "Lost in the Move?: Review of *Austrian Economics in America: The Migration of a Tradition*, by Karen Vaughn," *The Mises Review* 1, no. 3 (Fall 1995), https://mises.org/mises-review/austrian-economics-america-migration-tradition-karen-vaughn.

30. Murray N. Rothbard, "The Hermeneutical Invasion of Philosophy and Economics," *Review of Austrian Economics* 3, no. 1 (Winter 1989): pp. 56, 46.

31. Hans-Hermann Hoppe, "In Defense of Extreme Rationalism: Thoughts on Donald McCloskey's *The Rhetoric of Economics*," *Review of Austrian Economics* 3, no. 1 (Winter 1989): p. 179.

32. Hoppe's dissertation was published as Hans-Hermann Hoppe, *Handeln und Erkennen: Zur Kritik des Empirismus am Beispiel der Philosophie David Humes* (Bern: Peter Lang, 1976). He also finished his habilitation at Frankfurt. Hans-Hermann Hoppe, *Kritik der kausalwissenschaftlichen Sozialforschung* (Opladen: Westdeutscher Verlag, 1983).

33. Hans-Hermann Hoppe, *A Theory of Socialism and Capitalism: Economics, Politics, and Ethics* (Boston: Kluwer, 1989).

34. Hans-Hermann Hoppe, "Vom Konzept der Wohlfahrtsmessung der Theorie der Gerechtigkeit—zur Begründung einer analytischen Theorie der sozialen Wohlfahrt," *Zeitschrift für Politik* 29, no. 4 (November 1982): pp. 403–28.

35. Ludwig Mises, *Socialism: An Economic and Sociological Analysis* (Indianapolis, IN: Liberty Fund, 1981), pp. 325–26.

36. Ibid., p. 327.

37. "The innate inequality of various individuals does not break up the zoological uniformity and homogeneity of the species man, to such an extent as to divide the supply of labor into disconnected sections." Ludwig Mises, *Human Action: A Treatise on Economics* (Auburn, AL: Ludwig Von Mises Institute, 1998), pp. 5, 134, 165. He also devotes a section of an earlier book to polylogism in its various forms, including racial. See Ludwig Mises, *Omnipotent Government: The Rise of the Total State and Total War* (New Haven, CT: Yale University Press, 1944), pp. 143–47.

38. Mises, *Omnipotent Government*, p. 107.

39. Ludwig Mises, *Nationalökonomie: Theorie des Handelns und Wirtschaftens* (Geneva: Editions Union Genf, 1940), pp. 157–58.

40. See David Roth Singerman, "Keynesian Eugenics and the Goodness of the World," *Journal of British Studies* 55 (July 2016): pp. 538–65.

41. Mises, *Human Action*, p. 168.

42. Jacob Siegel, "The Alt-Right's Jewish Godfather," *Tablet*, November 29, 2016, http://www.tabletmag.com/jewish-news-and-politics/218712/spencer-gottfried-alt-right.

43. The meeting included, among others, Paul Gottfried, the *Washington Times* columnist Samuel Francis, Jeffrey Tucker of the Mises Institute, *National Review* author Joseph Sobran, Burton Blumert, and George Resch of the Center for Libertarian Studies. See the photograph in Ben Harrison, "Reconciliation on the Right," *The Free Market* 8, no. 4 (April 1990): p. 7.

44. After the meeting, Rothbard wrote to the main JRC organizers: "Tom [Fleming]'s phrase from the podium of the 'new fusionism' is inspired and I think should now be used to describe our new ideology." Rothbard to Fleming,

Carlson, Warder, Rockwell, and Blumert, December 9, 1990. Northern Illinois University Archives, Howard Center for Family, Religion and Society Collection, Allan Carlson Papers (hereafter Carlson Papers), Box 173.

45. Llewellyn H. Rockwell, *Liberty, Property, and the Austrian School of Economics: Ten Years of the Ludwig Von Mises Institute* (Auburn, AL: Ludwig von Mises Institute, 1992), p. 3.

46. Paul Gottfried, "The Decline and Rise of the Alternative Right," *American Renaissance* (November 21, 2008), https://www.amren.com/news/2016/08/the-decline-and-rise-of-the-alternative-right/.

47. Llewellyn H. Rockwell, "The Case for Paleo-Libertarianism," *Liberty* 3, no. 3 (January 1990), pp. 35, 37.

48. This section expands on chapter 5 of Quinn Slobodian, *Crack-Up Capitalism: Market Radicals and the Dream of a World without Democracy* (New York: Metropolitan, 2023).

49. Transcript of John Randolph Club Meeting, December 1, 1990. Northern Illinois University Archives, Howard Center for Family, Religion and Society Collection, Allan Carlson Papers (hereafter Carlson Papers), Box 173, Folder 13.

50. Ibid.

51. Murray N. Rothbard, "The 'New Fusionism': A Movement for Our Time," *Rothbard-Rockwell Report* 2, no. 1 (January 1991): p. 8.

52. Murray N. Rothbard, "Nations by Consent: Decomposing the Nation-State," *Journal of Libertarian Studies* 11, no. 1 (Fall 1994): p. 9.

53. Transcript of John Randolph Club Meeting, December 1, 1990.

54. Rothbard, "Nations by Consent," p. 10.

55. Rothbard, "New Fusionism," p. 8.

56. Transcript of John Randolph Club Meeting, December 1, 1990.

57. "Who Speaks For Us?," *American Renaissance* 1, no. 1 (November 1990), https://www.amren.com/archives/back-issues/november-1990/#cover.

58. Michael Levin, "Why Race Matters: A Preview," *Journal of Libertarian Studies* 12, no. 2 (Fall 1996): pp. 295–321.

59. Murray N. Rothbard, "Race! That Murray Book," *Rothbard-Rockwell Report* 5, no. 12 (December 1994): p. 9.

60. Cover of *The New Republic*, October 31, 1994.

61. Samuel Francis, "Up from the Ice Age," *Chronicles*, March 1995, p. 29.

62. Samuel Francis, "Why Race Matters," *American Renaissance* (September 1994), https://www.amren.com/news/2017/04/why-race-matters-white-identity-sam-t-francis.

63. See, e.g., Samuel T. Francis, "Rhodesia in Transition," *Heritage Foundation Backgrounder* 62 (August 9, 1978); Samuel T. Francis, "The Rhodesian Elections and the Sanctions Issue," *Heritage Foundation Backgrounder* 84 (May 17, 1979).

64. "Who Speaks For Us?"

65. Sam Francis quoted in Dinesh D'Souza, "Racism: It's a White (and Black) Thing," *Washington Post*, September 24, 1995.

66. Paul Craig Roberts, "I Resign From the Mont Pelerin Society," LewRockwell.com, August 21, 2008, https://www.lewrockwell.com/2008/08/paul-craig-roberts/i-resign-from-the-mont-pelerin-society/. See Paul Craig Roberts, "Sandy Hook Puzzles," March 1, 2016, https://www.paulcraigroberts.org/2016/03/01/sandy-hook-puzzles/; Paul Craig Roberts, "Orlando Shooting—Paul Craig Roberts," June 13, 2016, https://www.paulcraigroberts.org/2016/06/13/orlando-shooting-paul-craig-roberts/.

67. Hans-Hermann Hoppe, "Nationalism and Secession," *Chronicles*, November 1993, pp. 22–25.

68. Hans-Hermann Hoppe, "Free Immigration or Forced Integration?," *Chronicles*, July 1995, pp. 25–27.

69. William H. Tucker, *The Funding of Scientific Racism: Wickliffe Draper and the Pioneer Fund* (Urbana: University of Illinois Press, 2002), p. 179.

70. Murray N. Rothbard, "The Vital Importance of Separation," *Rothbard-Rockwell Report* 5, no. 4 (April 1994): p. 5. This was followed by a conspiracy theory article about the death of Vincent Foster.

71. "JRC Member List, 1/19/93," Carlson Papers, Box 173; James Robbins and Patrick Buchanan, "The Liberty Interview: Patrick J. Buchanan," *Liberty* 5, no. 4 (March 1992): p. 19.

72. Murray N. Rothbard and Llewellyn H. Rockwell, "For President: Pat Buchanan," *Rothbard-Rockwell Report* (January 1992): p. 5. For criticism see, e.g., an article by Bill Bradford, founding coeditor of the *Journal of Ayn*

Rand Studies, published under his pseudonym Chester Alan Arthur, "Inside Pat Buchanan," *Liberty* 5, no. 4 (March 1992): pp. 21–28.

73. *The Daily Reporter* (Martinville, IN), February 18, 1992; Robbins and Buchanan, "Liberty Interview," p. 19.

74. Murray N. Rothbard, "Toward a Strategy for Libertarian Social Change," unpublished manuscript, April 1977, pp. 1, 11, 12, https://archive.org/details/Rothbard1977TowardAStrategyForLibertarianSocialChange.

75. Murray N. Rothbard, "1996! The Morning Line," *Rothbard-Rockwell Report*, February 1995, p. 12.

76. Murray N. Rothbard, "A Strategy for the Right," *Rothbard-Rockwell Report*, March 1992, p. 8.

77. Murray N. Rothbard, "Right-Wing Populism: A Strategy for the Paleo Movement," *Rothbard-Rockwell Report*, January 1992, pp. 5–6. See also John Ganz, "The Year the Clock Broke," *Baffler*, November 2018, https://thebaffler.com/salvos/the-year-the-clock-broke-ganz.

78. Melinda Cooper, *Counterrevolution: Extravagance and Austerity in Public Finance* (New York: Zone Books, 2024), p. 155.

79. Rothbard, "Right-Wing Populism," p. 7.

80. Ibid., pp. 7, 8, 12, 13.

81. Rothbard, "A Strategy for the Right," p. 9.

82. John Ganz, "The Forgotten Man," *Baffler*, December 15, 2017, https://thebaffler.com/latest/the-forgotten-man-ganz.

83. Rothbard, "1996! The Morning Line," p. 12.

84. Hans-Hermann Hoppe, "The Property and Freedom Society—Reflections after Five Years," *The Libertarian Standard*, June 10, 2010, http://libertarianstandard.com/articles/hans-hermann-hoppe/the-property-and-freedom-society-reflections-after-5-years/.

85. Hans-Hermann Hoppe, "The Economic and Political Rationale for European Secessionism," in *Secession, State, and Liberty*, ed. David Gordon (New Brunswick, NJ: Transaction, 1998), p. 219.

86. Reproduced in N. Stephan Kinsella, "History and Principles," *Property and Freedom Society*, July 20, 2009, http://propertyandfreedom.org/about/.

87. Richard Spencer, "The ''Alternative Right' in America," lecture given at the Property and Freedom Society Meeting 2010, posted February 21, 2018, by Property and Freedom Society, YouTube, https://www.youtube.com/watch?v=XgPNVNE8C6M.

88. "PFP051 | Hoppe, Spencer, Bassani, Gottfried, Lynn, Discussion, Q&A (PFS 2010)," Property and Freedom Society Meeting 2010, posted Feburary 21, 2018 by Property and Freedom Society, YouTube, https://www.youtube.com/watch?v=upr_FtwWYq8.https://www.youtube.com/watch?v=upr_FtwWYq8.

89. Hans-Hermann Hoppe, *A Short History of Man: Progress and Decline* (Auburn, AL: Mises Institute, 2015).

90. Spencer, "The 'Alternative Right' in America."

91. Jeff Deist, "For a New Libertarian," Mises Institute, July 28, 2017, https://mises.org/blog/new-libertarian.

92. Jeff Deist, "Rothbard on Libertarian Populism," LewRockwell.com, December 5, 2015, https://www.lewrockwell.com/2015/12/jeff-deist/populism-path-liberty/; Jeff Deist, "Self-Determination, Not Universalism, Is the Goal," Mises Institute, May 29, 2017, https://mises.org/blog/self-determination-not-universalism-goal.

93. Jeff Deist, "The 2016 Election's Silver Lining," LewRockwell.com, November 9, 2016, https://www.lewrockwell.com/2016/11/jeff-deist/time-rebrand-libertarianism/.

94. Murray N. Rothbard, "The Nationalities Question (August 1990)," in *The Irrepressible Rothbard*, ed. Llewellyn H. Rockwell (Burlingame, CA: Center for Libertarian Studies, 2000), p. 234.

95. Hoppe, *A Short History of Man*.

96. Hans-Hermann Hoppe, "Libertarianism and the Alt-Right: In Search of a Libertarian Strategy for Social Change," Ludwig von Mises Centre (UK), October 20, 2017, https://misesuk.org/2017/10/20/libertarianism-and-the-alt-right-hoppe-speech-2017/.

97. Ibid.

98. Chase Rachels, *White, Right, and Libertarian* (Seattle: Createspace, 2018).

CHAPTER THREE: ETHNO-ECONOMY

1. Neal Stephenson, *Snow Crash* (New York: Del Rey, 1992), pp. 319, 325.

2. Steve Sailer, "Snow Crash and the Camp of the Saints," *iSteve*, May 27, 2006, https://isteve.blogspot.com/2006/05/snow-crash-and-camp-of-saints.html.

3. Sara Diamond, "Right-Wing Politics and the Anti-Immigration Cause," *Social Justice* 23, no. 3 (Fall 1996): p. 158.

4. Samuel Francis, "Illegal Immigration Pressure," *Washington Times*, December 31, 1991.

5. Aristide R. Zolberg, *A Nation by Design: Immigration Policy in the Fashioning of America* (Cambridge, MA: Harvard University Press, 2008), pp. 384–85.

6. C.K. Tyler, "'Disadvantaged' May Pay New Tax," *Washington Times*, July 18, 1993.

7. Jean Raspail, *The Camp of the Saints* (Petosky, MI: Social Contract Press, 1994).

8. John Tanton, "The Camp of the Saints Revisited," *The Social Contract* (Winter 1994–95): p. 83.

9. Jared Taylor, "Fairest Things Have Fleetest Endings," *American Renaissance*, June 1995, https://www.amren.com/news/2017/03/camp-of-the-saints-jean-raspail-muslim-immigration-european-suicide/.

10. Rockwell: "When I was working at Arlington House in the Conservative Book Club, I had something to do with getting that publicized." Transcript of John Randolph Club Meeting, December 1, 1990. Northern Illinois University Archives, Howard Center for Family, Religion and Society Collection, Allan Carlson Papers (hereafter Carlson Papers), Box 173, Folder 13.

11. Murray N. Rothbard, "Nations by Consent: Decomposing the Nation-State," *Journal of Libertarian Studies* 11, no. 1 (Fall 1994): p. 7.

12. "Bosnia, USA: Ethnic Conflict at Home and Abroad," JRC Meeting, Chicago, December 11–12, 1992. Carlson Papers, Box 196, folder 1.

13. John Ganz, "The Year the Clock Broke," *The Baffler*, November 2018, https://thebaffler.com/salvos/the-year-the-clock-broke-ganz.

14. Peter Brimelow, "Time to Rethink Immigration?," *National Review*, June 22, 1992, pp. 30–46.

15. Peter Brimelow, *Alien Nation: Common Sense about America's Immigration Disaster* (New York: Random House, 1995); Jesse E. Todd Jr., "The Horror of Immigration," *Daily Press* (Newport News, VA), July 9, 1995.

16. Zolberg, *A Nation by Design*, p. 396.

17. David G. Gutiérrez and Pierrette Hondagneu-Sotelo, "Introduction: Nation and Migration," *American Quarterly* 60, no. 3 (September 2008): p. 511.

18. David Frum, "Immigration Needs Reform, Not Abolition," *Financial Post*, April 22, 1995.

19. Peter Brimelow, "I Believe I Will Be At Least Exempted From 'The Curses Of Those Who Come After'—Peter Brimelow's Foreword to the 2013 Kindle Edition of Alien Nation," VDARE.com, August 5, 2013, https://web.archive.org/web/20181011184645/https://vdare.com/articles/i-believe-i-will-be-at-least-exempted-from-the-curses-of-those-who-come-after-peter-brimelow-s-foreword-to-the-2013-kindle-edition-of-alien-nation; Robert Costa, "At Birthday Party, Kudlow Hosted a Publisher of White Nationalists," *Washington Post*, August 22, 2018.

20. See VDARE.com. See also Jeff Tischauser and Kevin Musgrave, "Far-Right Media as Imitated Counterpublicity: A Discourse Analysis on Racial Meaning and Identity on Vdare.com," *Howard Journal of Communications* 31, no. 3 (2020): pp. 282–96.

21. Nicholas Confessore, "How Tucker Carlson Reshaped Fox News—and Became Trump's Heir," *New York Times*, April 30, 2022.

22. See Ashley Jardina, *White Identity Politics* (Cambridge: Cambridge University Press, 2019); Timothy Snyder, *The Road to Unfreedom: Russia, Europe, America* (New York: Tim Duggan Books, 2018); Benjamin R. Teitelbaum, *War for Eternity: Inside Bannon's Far-Right Circle of Global Power Brokers* (New York: Dey Street Books, 2020).

23. Jonathon Catlin, "The Authoritarian Personality and Its Discontents," *Journal of the History of Ideas Blog*, January 10, 2018, https://jhiblog.org/2018/01/10/the-authoritarian-personality-and-its-discontents/.

24. See Cas Mudde, *The Far Right Today* (Cambridge: Polity, 2019).

25. One mention in Kathleen Belew, *Bring the War Home: The White Power Movement and Paramilitary America* (Cambridge, MA: Harvard University

Press, 2018). One mention in a quote in David Neiwert, *Alt-America: The Rise of the Radical Right in the Age of Trump* (New York: Verso, 2017). Two mentions in Mike Wendling, *Alt-Right: From 4chan to the White House* (London: Pluto, 2018). Three mentions in Alexander Minna Stern, *Proud Boys and the White Ethnostate: How the Alt-Right is Warping the American Imagination* (Boston: Beacon Press, 2019). For the last see George Hawley, *Making Sense of the Alt-Right* (New York: Columbia University Press, 2017), p. 113.

26. Daniel Denvir, *All-American Nativism* (New York: Verso, 2020), p. 160; George Hawley, *Right-Wing Critics of American Conservatism* (Lawrence: University Press of Kansas, 2016), p. 188; Patrik Hermansson et al., *The International Alt-Right: Fascism for the 21st Century?* (New York: Routledge, 2020), p. 37.

27. Peter Brimelow, "'Immigration Is the Viagra of the State': A Libertarian Case against Immigration," VDARE.com, June 4, 2008, https://vdare.com/articles/immigration-is-the-viagra-of-the-state-a-libertarian-case-against-immigration. For the latter see Peter Brimelow, "Julian Simon and Me," *Forbes*, April 20, 1998.

28. On said networks see Philip Mirowski and Dieter Plehwe, eds., *The Road from Mont Pèlerin: The Making of the Neoliberal Thought Collective* (Cambridge, MA: Harvard University Press, 2009).

29. List of Participants, MPS Regional Meeting, Vancouver 1983, The Howard Center for Family Religion and Society, Rockford Illinois Records in the Regional History Center (hereafter Rockford Records), Northern Illinois University. John Howard Papers, Box 94, folder 3.

30. Peter Brimelow and Thomas Sowell, "Human Capital," *Forbes*, July 6, 1988; Peter Brimelow, "A Man Alone," *Forbes*, August 24, 1987; Peter Brimelow and Peter Bauer, "Let Them Work Out Their Own Problems," *Forbes*, February 22, 1988; Peter Brimelow and Milton Friedman, "Milton Friedman at 85," *Forbes*, December 29, 1997; Peter Brimelow and Milton Friedman, "Beware the Funny Money," *Forbes*, May 3, 1999; Peter Brimelow, "'No Water' Economics," *Forbes*, March 6, 1989.

31. "Privilege-Seeking?," *Forbes*, September 22, 1997; Peter Brimelow and Edwin S. Rubenstein, "L Is for Layoffs," *Forbes*, August 20, 2001; Peter

Brimelow, "Do You Want to Be Paid in Rockefellers? In Wristons? Or How About a Hayek?," *Forbes*, May 30, 1988.

32. Peter Brimelow, "The Lively Lives of Two Famous Devotees of the 'Dismal Science,'" *Washington Times*, June 14, 1998.

33. Jennifer M. Miller, "Neoconservatives and Neo-Confucians: East Asian Growth and the Celebration of Tradition," *Modern Intellectual History* 18, no. 3 (September 2021): pp. 806–32.

34. Peter Brimelow, "Freedom Pays," *Forbes*, June 16, 1997.

35. See, e.g., Francis Fukuyama, *Trust: The Social Virtues and the Creation of Prosperity* (New York: Free Press, 1995), pp. 16–33; Robert D. Putnam, "Bowling Alone: America's Declining Social Capital," *Journal of Democracy* 6, no. 1 (1995): pp. 223–34.

36. See Zsófia Barta and Alison Johnston, *Rating Politics: Sovereign Credit Ratings and Democratic Choice in Prosperous Developed Countries* (Oxford: Oxford University Press, 2023); Tore Fougner, "Neoliberal Governance of States: The Role of Competitiveness Indexing and Country Benchmarking," *Millennium: Journal of International Studies* 37, no. 2 (2008): pp. 303–26; Quinn Slobodian, "World Maps for the Debt Paradigm: Risk Ranking the Poorer Nations in the 1970s," *Critical Historical Studies* 8, no. 1 (Spring 2021): pp. 1–22.

37. Gerald F. Davis, *Managed by the Markets: How Finance Reshaped America* (New York: Oxford University Press, 2009), p. 85.

38. Peter Brimelow, *The Wall Street Gurus: How You Can Profit from Investment Newsletters* (New York: Random House, 1986); Joseph Granville, *The Warning: The Coming Great Crash in the Stock Market* (New York: Freundlich Press, 1985); John C. Boland, *Wall Street Insiders: How You Can Watch Them and Profit* (New York: William Morrow, 1985).

39. See Rita Abrahamsen et al., "Confronting the International Political Sociology of the New Right," *International Political Sociology* 14, no. 1 (2020): pp. 94–107; Jean-François Drolet and Michael C. Williams, "Radical Conservatism and Global Order: International Theory and the New Right," *International Theory* 10, no. 3 (2018): pp. 285–313; Christopher Vials, "Empire after Liberalism: The Transatlantic Right and Identitarian War," *Journal of American Studies* 56, no. 1 (2022): pp. 87–112; Rodrigo Duque Estrada Campos, "The

International Turn in Far-Right Studies: A Critical Assessment," *Millennium* 51, no. 3 (2023): pp. 892–919; Pablo de Orellana and Nicholas Michelsen, "Reactionary Internationalism: The Philosophy of the New Right," *Review of International Studies* 45, no. 5 (2019): pp. 748–67.

40. Brimelow, *Alien Nation*, p. 34.

41. Nicholas Lemann, "Too Many Foreigners," *New York Times*, April 16, 1995.

42. Wilmot Robertson, *The Ethnostate* (Cape Canaveral, FL: Howard Allen, 1993).

43. "Welcome Back, Peter," *Financial Post*, March 11, 1978.

44. Peter Brimelow, "Letters from the South: 'God Won't Abandon Us,'" *Financial Post*, December 1, 1973; Peter Brimelow, "Business Schools: Inside View," *Financial Post*, May 25, 1974.

45. Peter Brimelow, "Can You Beat Market? Some Say Yes, Some No," *Financial Post*, July 5, 1975; Peter Brimelow, "Why the Blacks Have Declared War on Jews," *Financial Post*, October 6, 1979.

46. Peter Brimelow, "Ian Smith's Rhodesia Is Worth Remembering," *Human Events*, May 26, 1979, pp. 8–9; Peter Brimelow, "Support Grows for Flat-Rate Income Tax Levy," *Human Events*, October 17, 1981, pp. 12, 20.

47. Peter Brimelow, "Summer in the Big Apple Far from Rosy," *Financial Post*, August 19, 1978.

48. See Peter Brimelow, *The Patriot Game: Canada and the Canadian Question Revisited* (Stanford, CA: Hoover Institution Press, 1987). See, e.g., Peter Brimelow, "The Case Against Immigration as We Know It," *Hoover Digest*, April 30, 1998. https://www.hoover.org/research/case-against-immigration-we-know-it. For recent intellectual histories of neoliberalism in Canada, see Mack Penner, "Modes of Influence: The Making of the Calgary School" (PhD diss., McMaster University, 2024); Joshua F. Rossetti, "The Fraser Institute: British Columbia, Canada, and the Neoliberal Thought Collective" (MA thesis, Freie Universität Berlin, 2024); Troy Vettese, "Limits and Cornucopianism: A History of Neo-Liberal Environmental Thought, 1920–2007" (PhD diss., New York University, 2019).

49. Peter Brimelow, "Immigration Shifts Political Loyalties," *Financial Post*, April 5, 1988.

50. Philip Mathias, "Just What Is an Anglo-Saxon?," *Financial Post*, May 11, 1989.

51. Peter Brimelow, "We're Consistently Wrong on the Soviet Union," *Financial Post*, December 5, 1989.

52. Peter Brimelow, "A Green Face Instead of a Red Face?," *Forbes*, December 11, 1989.

53. Ludwig Mises, "Vom Ziel der Handelspolitik," *Archiv für Sozialwissenschaft und Sozialpolitik* 42, no. 2 (1916): p. 566.

54. Ludwig Mises, *Nation, State, and Economy* (New York: New York University Press, 1983), p. 92. His vision had similarities to the visions of some Austrian socialists. See Natasha Wheatley, *The Life and Death of States: Central Europe and the Transformation of Modern Sovereignty* (Princeton, NJ: Princeton University Press, 2023).

55. Ludwig Mises, *Omnipotent Government: The Rise of the Total State and Total War* (New Haven, CT: Yale University Press, 1944), p. 106.

56. Ibid., p. 107.

57. F. A. Hayek, "The Politics of Race and Immigration," *Times* (London), February 11, 1978.

58. On Enoch Powell, see Robbie Shilliam, "Enoch Powell: Britain's First Neoliberal Politician," *New Political Economy* 26, no. 2 (2021): pp. 239–49.

59. John O'Sullivan, "Migration to Utopia," Proceedings 1978 Papers. Stanford University, Hoover Institution Archives, Friedrich A. Hayek Papers, Box 87, Folder 11.

60. Arthur Shenfield, "The Nation in Classical Liberal Thought," MPS Meeting Paris, 1984. Stanford University, Hoover Institution Archives, Mont Pelerin Society Papers (hereafter MPS Papers) Box 25, Folder 6.

61. Brimelow and Bauer, "Let Them Work Out Their Own Problems."

62. Peter T. Bauer, "Development Economics: The Spurious Consensus and Its Background," in *Roads to Freedom: Essays in Honour of Friedrich A. von Hayek*, ed. Erich W. Streissler (London: Routledge & Kegan Paul, 1969), p. 10.

63. Peter T. Bauer, "Economic Differences and Inequalities," *Modern Age* (Summer 1975): p. 302.

64. Peter T. Bauer, "Foreign Aid, Forever?," *Encounter*, March 1974, p. 17.

65. See Peter T. Bauer, *Dissent on Development* (Cambridge, MA: Harvard University Press, 1976). For the first publication, see Peter T. Bauer, *Dissent on Development* (London: Weidenfeld and Nicolson, 1971).

66. Brimelow and Bauer, "Let Them Work Out Their Own Problems."

67. Peter Brimelow, "Peter Bauer and the Emperor," (keynote at conference How Does Development Happen?: A Tribute to Peter Bauer, Princeton University, May 6, 2004), https://mediacentral.princeton.edu/media/How+Does+Development+HappenF+A+Tribute+to+Peter+Bauer+++Peter+Bauer+and+The+Emperor/1_1ekvb7fq.

68. "In Praise of Huddled Masses," *Wall Street Journal*, July 3, 1984.

69. "The Rekindled Flame," *Wall Street Journal*, July 3, 1986. It ran again the next year: "Simpson-Volstead-Mazzoli," *Wall Street Journal*, July 3, 1987, and under the title "The Rekindled Flame" on July 3, 1989, and July 3, 1990.

70. "The Simpson Curtain," *Wall Street Journal*, February 1, 1990.

71. "The Rekindled Flame," 1986

72. "In Praise of Huddled Masses."

73. See Julian Simon, The Economic Consequences of Immigration into the United States (1989), http://www.juliansimon.com/writings/Immigration/. Originally published as Julian Simon, *The Economic Consequences of Immigration* (Cambridge, MA: Blackwell, 1989).

74. William McGurn, "Let 'Em In: The Argument for Immigrants," *Wall Street Journal*, November 10, 1989.

75. Julian Simon, *The Ultimate Resource* (Princeton, NJ: Princeton University Press, 1981).

76. Tom Wolfe, "1988 Wriston Lecture: Fact and Fiction in the New York of the Eighties," Manhattan Institute, https://www.manhattan-institute.org/html/1988-wriston-lecture-fact-and-fiction-new-york-eighties-6392.html.

77. Peter Brimelow, "Politics in Command of Learning," *Financial Post*, June 28, 1988.

78. Brimelow, *Alien Nation*, pp. 139–40.

79. Quinn Slobodian, *Globalists: The End of Empire and the Birth of Neoliberalism* (Cambridge, MA: Harvard University Press, 2018), p. 50.

80. Brimelow, *Alien Nation*, pp. 140–41.

81. Peter Brimelow, "Julian Simon and Me," *Forbes*, April 20, 1998.

82. Simon, "The Economic Consequences of Immigration."

83. Julian Simon, "Auctioning Immigration Visas: Doing Well While Doing Good," MPS Meeting 1986, Saint-Vincent, Italy, MPS Papers, Box 26; The Mont Pelerin Society Membership Directory, 1993. MPS Papers, Box 67.

84. Sayo Kaji, "A Comment on 'Auctioning Immigrant Visas,'" MPS Meeting 1986. MPS Papers, Box 26.

85. Emphasis in the original. Brimelow, *Alien Nation*, p. 175.

86. Brimelow, "Julian Simon and Me."

87. See, e.g., MPS member since 1978 (and later president) Pedro Schwartz, "The Market and the Metamarket: A Review of the Contributions of the Economic Theory of Property Rights," in *Socialism: Institutional, Philosophical and Economic Issues*, ed. Svetozar Pejovich (Dordrecht: Kluwer Academic, 1987), pp. 11–32.

88. Peter Brimelow, "Why Liberalism Is Now Obsolete: An Interview with Nobel Laureate Milton Friedman," *Forbes*, December 12, 1988.

89. Peter Brimelow, "Free Markets May Need Cultural Prerequisites," *Financial Post*, February 21, 1989.

90. Ibid. For more on Friedman's opinions of Hong Kong, see Quinn Slobodian, *Crack-Up Capitalism: Market Radicals and the Dream of a World Without Democracy* (New York: Metropolitan Books, 2023), chap. 1.

91. Peter Brimelow, "Words of Wisdom from the Cutting Room Floor," *Financial Post*, August 1, 1989.

92. Brimelow, *Alien Nation*, p. 176.

93. Ibid.

94. Peter Brimelow, "Does the Nation-State Exist?," *The Social Contract* 3, no. 4 (Summer 1993): p. 232.

95. Gregory P. Pavlik, "Review of Peter Brimelow, *Alien Nation*," *The Freeman*, December 1995, p. 794.

96. Brimelow, *Alien Nation*, p. xvii. See, e.g., Peter Brimelow, "Refugees Stir Emotion—But Are Cause and Effect Yet Understood?," *Financial Post*, August 25, 1979.

97. Brimelow, *Alien Nation*, p. xxi.

98. Ibid., pp. 237, 119.

99. Ibid., p. 230.

100. Ibid., pp. 219, 161.

101. Charles Taylor, "The Politics of Recognition," in *Multiculturalism and the Politics of Recognition*, ed. Amy Gutmann (Princeton, NJ: Princeton University Press, 1992), pp. 25–74.

102. Brimelow, *Alien Nation*, pp. 217, 219.

103. Garrett Hardin, "Lifeboat Ethics: The Case against Helping the Poor," *Psychology Today* (September 1974), pp. 800–12.

104. Brimelow, *Alien Nation*, pp. 245, 249.

105. Ibid., p. 245.

106. "Soviets' 500 Day Plan Debated at Cato Round Table," *Cato Policy Report* 1 (January–February 1991): p. 4.

107. Paul Craig Roberts, "Alien Future," *Chronicles*, July 1995, p. 29.

108. Samuel Francis, "The Democrats Take the Lead on Stopping Immigration," *Washington Times*, June 9, 1995.

109. E. J. Dionne, "Buchanan Says Bush Forsakes His Conservative Principles," *Indianapolis News*, December 9, 1991.

110. Paul A. Gigot, "Potomac Watch: Pat Buchanan Puts Conservatism Back in a Pup Tent," *Wall Street Journal*, December 13, 1991.

111. William F. Buckley, "Brits, Zulus, Buchanan and Politics," *Detroit Free Press*, February 23, 1992.

112. Brimelow, *Alien Nation*, p. 108.

113. Margo Hammond, "Race Issue Sours a Needed Debate on Immigration," *Tampa Bay Times*, April 23, 1995.

114. Francis Fukuyama, "Immigrants and Family Values," *Commentary*, May 1993, p. 31.

115. See Ben J. Wattenberg, *The First Universal Nation: Leading Indicators and Ideas about the Surge of America in the 1990s* (New York: Free Press, 1992).

CHAPTER FOUR: NEUROCASTES

1. Michael Young, *The Rise of the Meritocracy, 1870–2033* (London: Penguin Books, 1958), p. 11. The description of the narrator as an "imaginary Michael Young" comes from Michael Young, *The Rise of the Meritocracy, 1870–2033*, 2nd ed. (New Brunswick, NJ: Transaction Publishers, 1994), p. xiv.

2. Young, *Rise of the Meritocracy*, p. 133.

3. Daniel Seligman, "Foretelling the Bell Curve," *National Review*, December 19, 1994.

4. Daniel Seligman and William Sheeline, "Brainstorms," *Fortune*, August 3, 1987.

5. Robert B. Reich, "Secession of the Successful," *New York Times*, January 20, 1991.

6. William Gibson, *Neuromancer* (New York: Ace Science Fiction, 1984).

7. Bruce Sterling, *Islands in the Net* (New York: Ace Books, 1988), p. 201.

8. Christopher Lasch, *Revolt of the Elites and the Betrayal of Democracy* (New York: W. W. Norton, 1994), p. 20.

9. Steven Rose, "The Rise of Neurogenetic Determinism," *Nature* 373 (February 2, 1995): pp. 380–82.

10. Daniel Seligman, "A Substantial Inheritance," *National Review*, October 10, 1994.

11. Samuel Francis, "Up From the Ice Age," *Chronicles*, March 1995.

12. Peter Brimelow, "Social Engineers Take Refuge in Human Rights," *Financial Post*, September 14, 1988.

13. William F. Buckley and Charles Murray, *The IQ Controversy: What's Going On? Part 2, Firing Line* transcript, November 29, 1994, Hoover Institution Library & Archives, https://digitalcollections.hoover.org/objects/7228.

14. Stephen Jay Gould, *The Mismeasure of Man*, rev. ed. (New York: W. W. Norton, 1996), p. 367; Bob Herbert, "Throwing a Curve," *New York Times*, October 26, 1994.

15. Jason DeParle, "Daring Research or 'Social Science Pornography'?: Charles Murray," *New York Times*, October 9, 1994; "Is Charles Murray Now 'the Most Dangerous Conservative'?," Conservative Book Club advertisement, Richard J. Herrnstein Papers, Harvard University Archives (hereafter

Herrnstein Papers), Box 12, "The Bell Curve—publisher, agent. 1 of 4" folder.

16. See the special issue of the *New Republic*, October 31, 1994, and, among others, Bernie Devlin, *Intelligence, Genes, and Success: Scientists Respond to The Bell Curve* (New York: Springer, 1997); Steve Fraser, *The Bell Curve Wars: Race, Intelligence, and the Future of America* (New York: Basic Books, 1995); Russell Jacoby, Naomi Glauberman, and Richard J. Herrnstein, *The Bell Curve Debate: History, Documents, Opinions* (New York: Times Books, 1995); Joe L. Kincheloe, Shirley R. Steinberg, and Aaron David Gresson, *Measured Lies: The Bell Curve Examined* (New York: St. Martin's Press, 1996); and Peter Knapp et al., *The Assault on Equality* (Westport, CT: Praeger, 1996). For the task force report see Ulric Neisser et al., "Intelligence: Knowns and Unknowns," *American Psychologist* 51, no. 2 (February 1996): pp. 77–101.

17. Knapp, *The Assault on Equality*, p. 25.

18. Richard J. Herrnstein and Charles Murray, *The Bell Curve: Intelligence and Class Structure in American Life* (New York: Free Press, 1994), p. 201.

19. Ibid., pp. 341, 549.

20. Dick [Herrnstein] to Binky [Urban], June 15, 1994. Herrnstein Papers, Box 12, "The Bell Curve—publisher, agent. 1 of 4" folder.

21. Herrnstein and Murray, *The Bell Curve*, pp. 340, 323.

22. Ibid., p. 551.

23. Robyn L. Cohen, "Prisoners in 1990," *Bureau of Justice Statistics Bulletin* (1991): p. 2; Allen J. Beck and Paige M. Harrison, "Prisoners in 2000," *Bureau of Justice Statistics Bulletin* (August 2001): p. 1.

24. Herrnstein and Murray, *The Bell Curve*, pp. 91, 416.

25. Quoted in Henry A. Giroux and Susan Searls, "Race Talk and the Bell Curve Debate: The Crisis of Democratic Vision," *Cultural Critique* 34 (Fall 1996): p. 20.

26. Among the most foundational critiques were those by people sympathetic to the authors. See James J. Heckman, "Lessons from the Bell Curve," *Journal of Political Economy* 103, no. 5 (October 1995): pp. 1091–120; Thomas Sowell, "Ethnicity and IQ," *American Spectator*, February 1995.

27. Charles Lane, "The Tainted Sources of 'The Bell Curve,'" *New York Review of Books*, December 1, 1994.

28. For the authoritative treatment, see William Tucker, *The Funding of Scientific Racism: Wickliffe Draper and the Pioneer Fund* (Urbana: University of Illinois Press, 2002).

29. Graham Richards, *"Race," Racism and Psychology: Towards a Reflexive History* (London: Routledge, 1997), p. 260.

30. Rogers Brubaker, *Grounds for Difference* (Cambridge, MA: Harvard University Press, 2015), p. 20.

31. For introductions to this vast topic, see Sheldon Krimsky and Kathleen Sloan, eds., *Race and the Genetic Revolution: Science, Myth, and Culture* (New York: Columbia University Press, 2011); Angela Saini, *Superior: The Return of Race Science* (Boston: Beacon Press, 2019); Alondra Nelson, *The Social Life of DNA: Race, Reparations, and Reconciliation after the Genome* (Boston: Beacon Press, 2016); Catherine Bliss, *Race Decoded: The Genomic Fight for Social Justice* (Stanford, CA: Stanford University Press, 2012).

32. Milton Friedman in Michael A. Walker, ed., *Freedom, Democracy and Economic Welfare: Proceedings of an International Symposium* (Vancouver: Fraser Institute, 1988), p. 135.

33. See Thomas Biebricher, "Neoliberalism and Democracy," *Constellations* 22, no. 2 (2015): pp. 255–66.

34. See Niklas Olsen, *The Sovereign Consumer: A New Intellectual History of Neoliberalism* (Cham, Switzerland: Palgrave Macmillan, 2019).

35. Malcolm Harris, *Palo Alto: A History of California, Capitalism, and the World* (New York: Little, Brown, 2023), pp. 64–115.

36. Wolfgang Saxon, "Stefan T. Possony, 82, a Scholar of International Security Affairs," *New York Times*, May 2, 1995.

37. Martin Walker, "Dark Dreamer of Star Wars," *The Guardian*, May 5, 1995.

38. Quoted in Ryan M. Irwin, "Apartheid on Trial: South West Africa and the International Court of Justice, 1960–66," *International History Review* 32, no. 4 (2010): pp. 619–42.

39. Brian Doherty, *Radicals for Capitalism: A Freewheeling History of the Modern American Libertarian Movement* (New York: Public Affairs, 2007), pp. 287, 289.

40. F.A. Harper, "Liberty: A Path to Its Recovery (1949)," in *The Writings of F.A. Harper* (Menlo Park, CA: Institute for Humane Studies, 1978), p. 318.

41. John H. Jackson, "Baldy Harper and the Racist Right," *Fardels Bear: A History of the Alt-Right*, October 4, 2017, https://altrightorigins.com/2017/10/04/harper-racist-right/. See Harper, "Liberty," p. 317.

42. The figures are for 2022. "Institute for Humane Studies," ProPublica Nonprofit Explorer, https://projects.propublica.org/nonprofits/organizations/941623852.

43. Harper to Weyl, May 4, 1972. Stanford University, Hoover Institution Library & Archives. Nathaniel Weyl Papers (hereafter Weyl Papers), Box 6 Folder 25.

44. Michael G. Kenny, "John R. Baker on Eugenics, Race, and the Public Role of the Scientist," *Isis* 95 (2004): pp. 408–18.

45. Stefan Kühl, *For the Betterment of the Race: The Rise and Fall of the International Movement for Eugenics and Racial Hygiene* (New York: Palgrave Macmillan, 2013), pp. 160–76.

46. See John R. Baker, *Race* (New York: Oxford University Press, 1974); John P. Jackson, *Science for Segregation: Race, Law, and the Case against Brown v. Board of Education* (New York: New York University Press, 2005), p. 198.

47. Kenny, "Baker on Eugenics," p. 395.

48. Weyl to Harper, November 5, 1972. Weyl Papers, Box 6, Folder 25.

49. Doherty, *Radicals for Capitalism*, p. 287.

50. Weyl to Meyer, September 5, 1967, Weyl Papers, Box 10, Folder 8.

51. Resch to Weyl, December 8, 1971, Weyl Papers, Box 6, Folder 25.

52. Weyl to Resch, December 21, 1971. Weyl Papers, Box 6, Folder 25.

53. Regnery to Weyl, May 16, 1967. Weyl Papers, Box 6, Folder 26.

54. Aram Roston and Joel Anderson, "This Man Used His Inherited Fortune to Fund the Racist Right," *Buzzfeed News*, July 23, 2017, https://www.buzzfeednews.com/article/aramroston/hes-spent-almost-20-years-funding-the-racist-right-it.

55. Robert A. Schadler, National Director, ISI to Weyl, April 30, 1971. Weyl Papers, Box 6, Folder 26.

56. ISI Eastern/Southern Summer School, American University, DC, August 22–28, 1971. Weyl Papers, Box 6, Folder 26.

57. See Nathaniel Weyl, *Traitors' End: The Rise and Fall of the Communist Movement in Southern Africa* (New Rochelle, NY: Arlington House, 1970).

58. Weyl to Morris B. Schnapper, editor Public Affairs Press, March 27, 1966. Weyl Papers, Box 11, Folder 6.

59. Rockwell to Weyl, July 29, 1970. Weyl Papers, Box 3, Folder 6.

60. Robert Gayre, "Review: Traitors End by Nathaniel Weyl," *Mankind Quarterly*, October 1971, p. 120.

61. Rockwell to Weyl, December 2, 1969. Weyl Papers, Box 3, Folder 6.

62. Rockwell to Weyl, February 11, 1970. Weyl Papers, Box 34, Folder 8.

63. Unpublished draft MS of "Integration." Weyl Papers, Box 34, Folder 8.

64. Herrnstein to Weyl, October 8, 1991. Herrnstein Papers, Box 11, "Wb-Willie 1982- correspondence" Folder.

65. Nathaniel Weyl and Stefan Possony, *The Geography of Intellect* (Chicago: Henry Regnery, 1963), p. ix. On Regnery Press, see Nicole Hemmer, *Messengers of the Right: Conservative Media and the Transformation of American Politics* (Philadelphia: University of Pennsylvania Press, 2016).

66. Weyl and Possony, *Geography of Intellect*, p. 288.

67. Weyl to Gayre, June 11, 1964. Weyl Papers, Box 8, Folder 10.

68. Weyl to Gayre, April 2, 1964. Weyl Papers, Box 8, Folder 10.

69. Weyl and Possony, *Geography of Intellect*, p. x.

70. Weyl to Buckley, January 27, 1962. Weyl Papers, Box 10, Folder 7.

71. Ibid.

72. Weyl and Possony, *Geography of Intellect*, pp. 245–46.

73. Weyl to Lynn, May 16, 1975. Weyl Papers, Box 8, Folder 3.

74. Lynn was specifically attacked for having fudged data to attribute especially low IQ scores to Black children in South Africa. For details see Leon Kamin, "Scientific American Debunks," *Scientific American* 272, no. 2 (February 1995): pp. 99–103.

75. John Connolly, "Of Race and Right," *Irish Times*, December 6, 1994.

76. See the overviews published three years before *The Bell Curve*: Richard Lynn, "Race Differences in Intelligence: A Global Perspective," *Mankind*

Quarterly 31, no. 3 (Spring 1991): pp. 255–96; Richard Lynn, "The Evolution of Racial Differences in Intelligence," *Mankind Quarterly* 32, no. 1 (Fall 1991): pp. 99–121.

77. For the frequently used phrase, see, e.g. Edwin J. Feulner, "Waging and Winning the War of Ideas," *The Heritage Lectures* 84 (Washington, DC: The Heritage Foundation, 1986).

78. Christopher Muller, "The Institute of Economic Affairs: Undermining the Post-War Consensus," in *Ideas and Think Tanks in Contemporary Britain*, ed. Michael David Kandiah and Anthony Seldon (London: Frank Cass, 1996), p. 92.

79. Richard Lynn, "National Planning and Industrial Frustration," in *Growth through Industry*, ed. John Jewkes et al. (London: Institute of Economic Affairs, 1967), p. 147.

80. Ibid., pp. 148, 154.

81. Geoffrey K. Fry, *The Politics of the Thatcher Revolution* (New York: Palgrave Macmillan, 2008), p. 127; Richard Cockett, "The New Right and the 1960s: The Dialectics of Liberation," in *New Left, New Right and Beyond: Taking the Sixties Seriously*, eds. Geoff Andrews et al. (Houndmills, UK: Macmillan, 1999), p. 100; David E. Cooper, *Illusions of Equality* (London: Routledge, 1980), p. ix.

82. Richard Lynn, "Streaming: Standards or Equality?," *Critical Survey* 5, no. 1 (Winter 1970): pp. 26–29.

83. Richard Lynn, "Genetic Implications of the Brain Drain," *New Scientist* (March 20, 1969), pp. 622–24.

84. "A Climate of Anxiety," *New Society* 16 (December 1971): p. 1190.

85. "Anxiety and Economic Growth," *Nature* 219 (August 17, 1968): pp. 765–66; "Low Arousal Makes British Poor, Professor Says," *The Times* (London), September 9, 1969.

86. Richard Herrnstein, "I.Q.," *The Atlantic* Monthly, September 1971, pp. 43–64.

87. Lynn to Herrnstein, January 27, 1972, Herrnstein Papers, Box 8, "Lf-Lz 1982-correspondence" folder.

88. Harris to Lynn, May 12, 1970, Stanford University, Hoover Institution

Library & Archives, Institute of Economic Affairs Papers (hereafter IEA Papers), Box 297, Folder 11.

89. Lynn to Harris, July 2, 1970. IEA Papers, Box 297, Folder 11.

90. Ibid.; Galton Institute for Social Research (proposal). IEA Papers, Box 297, Folder 11; John O'Sullivan, "V-Dare," *National Review*, April 17, 2012, https://www.nationalreview.com/corner/v-dare-john-osullivan/.

91. Lynn to Harris, n.d., and Lynn to Harris, March 3, 1972. IEA Papers, Box 297, Folder 12.

92. Vinson to Harris, January 1, 1971. IEA Papers, Box 306, Folder 8.

93. Cahal Milmo, "Multi-Millionaire Backers of Climate Change Denial Think-Tank Revealed," *The Independent*, September 2, 2014.

94. See Rüdiger Graf, "Human Behavior as a Limit to and a Means of State Intervention: Günter Schmölders and Behavioral Social Science," in *Nine Lives of Neoliberalism*, ed. Dieter Plehwe, Quinn Slobodian, and Philip Mirowski (London: Verso, 2020), pp. 143–65.

95. See Dieter Plehwe, "Schumpeter Revival?: How Neoliberals Revised the Image of the Entrepreneur," in Plehwe, Slobodian, and Mirowski, eds., *Nine Lives of Neoliberalism*, pp. 120–42.

96. Richard Lynn, ed., *The Entrepreneur: Eight Case Studies* (London: George Allen & Unwin, 1974), p. 12.

97. See Marie-Laure Djelic and Reza Mousavi, "How the Neoliberal Think Tank Went Global: The Atlas Network, 1981 to Present," in Plehwe, Slobodian, and Mirowski, eds., *Nine Lives of Neoliberalism*, pp. 257–82.

98. See Lynn to Weyher, November 16, 1987. The source and reference were provided by William Tucker from his research materials.

99. Ibid.

100. Schedule H, Part XVI, Line 3a (IRS 990 form for year ending December 31, 1990). The reference was also generously provided by Tucker from his research materials. The Atlas grant to Lynn is mentioned in Tucker, *The Funding of Scientific Racism*, p. 214.

101. See Lynn, "Race Differences in Intelligence" and "The Evolution of Racial Differences in Intelligence."

102. "Individual Differences and Public Policy," proposal for a book by

Richard J. Herrnstein and Charles Murray, n.d., Herrnstein Papers, Box 12, "The Bell Curve 5. Correspondence between RJH and CAM" folder. They received $146,000 from the Carthage Foundation and $50,000 from the Smith Richardson Foundation. Herrnstein to Frank Miele [de Tocqueville] October 4, 1990, "The Bell Curve—general. 2 of 4" folder.

103. Herrnstein to Murray, September 1, 1992, "The Bell Curve 5" folder.

104. Charles Murray, *Safety Nets and the Truly Needy: Rethinking the Social Welfare System* (Washington, DC: Heritage Foundation, 1982); Charles Murray, *Losing Ground: American Social Policy 1950–1980* (New York: Basic Books, 1984); Doherty, *Radicals for Capitalism*, p. 478.

105. The latter is reflected in the subtitle of Murray's doctoral dissertation, "Investment and Tithing in Thai Villages: A Behavioral Study of Rural Modernization" (PhD diss., Massachusetts Institute of Technology, 1974).

106. Murray, *Losing Ground*, pp. 179, 284, 278, 285; Matt McIntosh, "10 Questions for Charles Murray," *Gene Expression*, July 25, 2006, http://www.gnxp.com/blog/2006/07/10-questions-for-charles-murray.php.

107. Charles Murray, "Right Questions and Wrong Answers," *AEI Lecture*, January 8, 2018, posted by American Enterprise Institute, YouTube, https://www.youtube.com/watch?v=DDSWxumrGAY&t=1s.

108. W. M. Baum, "Richard J. Herrnstein: A Memoir," *Behavior Analyst* 17, no. 2 (1994): p. 202. For the pigeonman anecdote, see Richard J. Herrnstein, *IQ in the Meritocracy* (Boston: Little, Brown, 1974), p. 20.

109. Herrnstein, "IQ," p. 64. For a similar statement see Murray, *Losing Ground*, p. 154.

110. Herrnstein, *IQ in the Meritocracy*, p. 7.

111. Ibid.

112. Charles Murray, "The Rediscovery of Human Nature and Human Diversity," Mont Pelerin Society Special Meeting, Galapagos Islands, Ecuador, June 22–29, 2013, http://darwinianconservatism.blogspot.com/2013/07/.

113. Herrnstein and Murray, *The Bell Curve*, pp. 8–9.

114. McIntosh, "10 Questions for Charles Murray."

115. R. B. Cattell, *A New Morality from Science: Beyondism* (New York:

Pergamon Press, 1972). On Cattell, see William H. Tucker, *The Cattell Controversy: Race, Science, and Ideology* (Urbana: University of Illinois Press, 2009).

116. Howard Wainer and Daniel H. Robinson, "Profiles in Research: Linda S. Gottfredson," *Journal of Educational and Behavioral Statistics* 34, no. 3 (September 2009): p. 406.

117. Colleen Cordes, "'IQ Gap' Linked to Job Lags, Crime," *APA Monitor* 18, no. 2 (February 1987): p. 20; Linda Gottfredson, "The Practical Significance of Black-White Differences in Intelligence," *Behavioral and Brain Sciences* 10, no. 3 (1987): p. 512.

118. Robert Gordon, "SES versus IQ in the Race-IQ-Delinquency Model," *International Journal of Sociology and Social Policy* 7, no. 3 (1987): pp. 30–96.

119. Herrnstein and Murray to Alice E. Mayhew, VP and editorial director, Simon & Schuster, February 23, 1990, Herrnstein Papers, Box 12, "The Bell Curve—publisher, agent. 1 of 4" folder.

120. Herrnstein and Murray, *Bell Curve*, p. 480.

121. Linda Gottfredson, "Egalitarian Fiction and Collective Fraud," *Society* 31, no. 3 (March–April 1994): pp. 53–59; Charles Murray, "Deeper into the Brain," *National Review* (January 24, 2000): p. 48.

122. Undated fax, Herrnstein Papers, Box 12, "The Bell Curve 5. Correspondence between RJH and CAM" folder.

123. Herrnstein and Murray, *The Bell Curve*, p. 508.

124. Untitled entry, February 26, 1982, Herrnstein Papers, Box 12, "Notebooks with misc notes by RJH" folder.

125. Charles Murray, "Changes over Time in the Black-White Difference on Mental Tests: Evidence from the Children of the 1979 Cohort of the National Longitudinal Survey of Youth," *Intelligence* 34 (2006): pp. 527–40; Charles Murray, "The Magnitude and Components of Change in the Black-White IQ Difference from 1920 to 1991: A Birth Cohort Analysis of the Woodcock-Johnson Standardizations," *Intelligence* 35 (2007): pp. 305–18.

126. Herrnstein and Murray, *The Bell Curve*, p. 342.

127. See Charles Murray, *Human Diversity: The Biology of Gender, Race, and Class* (New York: Twelve, 2020).

128. Herrnstein to CMC [C. Michael Curtis, *The Atlantic Monthly*], November 17, 1967. Herrnstein Papers, Box 6. "C 1958-67" folder.

129. Charles Murray, *Income Inequality and IQ* (Washington, DC: AEI Press, 1998), p. 44.

130. Herrnstein and Murray, *The Bell Curve*, p. 551.

131. Murray, "2006 Atlas Freedom Dinner Keynote Address," p. 22.

132. Charles Murray, "Underclass: A Disaster in the Making," *Sunday Times Magazine*, November 26, 1989; Charles Murray, "Underclass: The Crisis Deepens," *Sunday Times*, May 29, 1994; Charles Murray, *The Emerging British Underclass* (London: IEA Health and Welfare Unit, 1990); Charles Murray, *Underclass: The Crisis Deepens* (London: IEA Health and Welfare Unit, 1994). These pieces were anthologized with commentaries in Charles Murray, *Charles Murray and the Underclass: The Developing Debate* (London: IEA, 1996).

133. Andrew Denham, *Think Tanks of the New Right* (Aldershot, UK: Dartmouth, 1996), pp. 61, 70.

134. Digby Anderson, ed., *This Will Hurt: The Restoration of Virtue and Civic Order* (London: Social Affairs Unit, 1995), and *The Loss of Virtue: Moral Confusion and Social Disorder in Britain and America* (London: Social Affairs Unit, 1992).

135. Richard Lynn, "Self-Control: The Family as the Source of 'Conscience,'" in Anderson, *Loss of Virtue*, p. 132.

136. Lynn to Herrnstein, January 31, 1991, Herrnstein Papers, Box 8, "Lf-Lz 1982-correspondence" folder. His effort at rehabilitating eugenics was realized in two volumes: Richard Lynn, *Dysgenics: Genetic Deterioration in Modern Populations* (Westport, CT: Praeger, 1996), and *Eugenics: A Reassessment* (Westport, CT: Praeger, 2001).

137. Herrnstein to Lynn, April 8, 1991; Lynn to Herrnstein, September 9, 1993; Herrnstein to Lynn, December 17, 1993, all in "Lf-Lz 1982-correspondence" folder.

138. Lynn to Herrnstein, October 1, 1990, "Lf-Lz 1982-correspondence" folder.

139. Murray quoted in Jane Mayer, *Dark Money: The Hidden History of the*

Billionaires Behind the Rise of the Radical Right (New York: Doubleday, 2016), p. 221.

140. "AEI Establishes W. H. Brady Program in Culture and Freedom," *AEI Newsletter*, June 1, 2003, https://www.aei.org/articles/aei-establishes-w-h-brady-program-in-culture-and-freedom/.

141. Murray, *Human Diversity*.

142. Richard Lynn, review of Jared Taylor, *White Identity: Racial Consciousness in the 21st Century* (Oakton, VA: New Century Books: 2011), https://store.amren.com/product/white-identity. Lynn has also been cited over 400 times on VDARE.com. Dan Samorodnitsky et al., "Journals That Published Richard Lynn's Racist 'Research' Articles Should Retract Them," *Stat*, June 20, 2024, https://www.statnews.com/2024/06/20/richard-lynn-racist-research-articles-journals-retractions/.

143. See Richard Lynn, *Race Differences in Intelligence: An Evolutionary Analysis* (Augusta, GA: Washington Summit Publishers, 2006); Richard Lynn and Tatu Vanhanen, *IQ and Global Inequality* (Augusta, GA: Washington Summit Publishers, 2006); Richard Lynn, *The Global Bell Curve: Race, IQ, and Inequality Worldwide* (Augusta, GA: Washington Summit Publishers, 2008); Richard Lynn, *The Chosen People: A Study of Jewish Intelligence and Achievement* (Augusta, GA: Washington Summit Publishers, 2011).

144. See Lynn, *Global Bell Curve*.

145. Richard Lynn, "On Human Diversity: The Global Bell Curve—Updates and Critical Replies," *Property and Freedom Society*, June 3–7, 2010, posted by Alt Right Media, August 2, 2013, YouTube, https://www.youtube.com/watch?v=4EWBvUuioSk.

146. Lynn, *Eugenics*, p. vii. On IQ, see Eli Cook, "Naturalizing Inequality: The Problem of Economic Fatalism in the Age of Piketty," *Capitalism: A Journal of History and Economics* 1, no. 2 (Spring 2020): pp. 364–65. For a critique of Lynn from within the profession see Jelte M. Wicherts et al., "Another Failure to Replicate Lynn's Estimate of the Average IQ of Sub-Saharan Africans," *Learning and Individual Differences* 20, no. 3 (June 2010): pp. 155–57.

147. See Charles Murray, *What It Means to Be a Libertarian: A Personal Interpretation* (New York: Broadway Books, 1996).

148. John Derbyshire, "Charles Murray on Immigration," *National Review*, December 12, 2006, https://www.nationalreview.com/corner/charles-murray-immigration-john-derbyshire/#:~:text=Regarding%20legal%20immigration%3A-,1.,used%20to%20apply%20to%20everyone.

149. Thilo Sarrazin, *Deutschland schafft sich ab* (Munich: Deutsche Verlags Anstalt, 2010).

150. On Thilo Sarrazin, see Sander Gilman, "Thilo Sarrazin and the Politics of Race in the Twenty-First Century," *New German Critique* 39, no. 3 (Fall 2012): pp. 47–59; Michael Meng, "Silences about Sarrazin's Racism in Contemporary Germany," *Journal of Modern History* 87 (March 2015): pp. 102–35.

151. For the reference see Frank Schirrmacher, "Thilo Sarrazin im Streitgespräch," *Frankfurter Allgemeine Zeitung*, October 1, 2010; Heiner Rindermann, Oasis Kodila-Tedika, and Gregory Christainsen, "Cognitive Capital, Good Governance, and the Wealth of Nations," *Intelligence* 51 (2015): pp. 98–108. See also Andrew S. Winston, "Neoliberalism and IQ: Naturalizing Economic and Racial Inequality," *Theory & Psychology* 28, no. 5 (2018): p. 609.

152. Erich Weede and Sebastian Kämpf, "The Impact of Intelligence and Institutional Improvements on Economic Growth," *Kyklos* 55, no. 3 (2002): p. 376.

153. Erich Weede, "Welche Art der Einwanderung braucht unser Land?," (Forum Freiheit 2017 "Die Zukunft der Freiheit," November 7, 2017), https://hayek.de/wp-content/uploads/2017/10/Weede-Welche-Einwandg.-braucht-unser-Land.pdf.

154. "Freiheit und Sicherheit u.a. T. Sarrazin, Prof. Weede, Prof. Habermann," Forum Freiheit, Berlin, October 2017, posted by Friedrich August von Hayek-Gesellschaft, November 7, 2017, YouTube, https://www.youtube.com/watch?v=gj96MnZ9rsk.

155. Erich Weede, "Mass Immigration: Cost or Benefit?," *Hungarian Review* 6 (June 2015): pp. 12–13.

156. Weede, "Welche Art?"

157. Erich Weede, "Ungleichheit als Schicksal und Notwendigkeit," in

Soziologie der sozialen Ungleichheit, eds. Bernhard Giesen and Hans Haferkamp (Opladen: Westdeutscher Verlag, 1987), p. 200.

158. Erich Weede, "Vertragen die alternden europäischen Sozialstaaten die Massenzuwanderung, die wir haben?," June 30, 2016, https://www.ludwig-erhard.de/vertragen-die-alternden-europaeischen-sozialstaaten-die-massenzuwanderung-die-wir-haben. See Gary Becker and Richard Posner, *Uncommon Sense: Economic Insights, from Marriage to Terrorism* (Chicago: University of Chicago Press, 2009), p. 56.

159. See Daniel Pick, *Faces of Degeneration: A European Disorder, c. 1848–c. 1918* (New York: Cambridge University Press, 1989).

160. See Anson Rabinbach, *The Human Motor: Energy, Fatigue, and the Origins of Modernity* (New York: Basic Books, 1990).

161. See David Sessions, "Man, Machines, and Modernity: Inventing 'Industrial Society' in French Social Science, 1930–1975" (PhD diss., Boston College, 2021).

162. Fritz Machlup, *The Production and Distribution of Knowledge in the United States* (Princeton, NJ: Princeton University Press, 1962). For details, see Quinn Slobodian, "The Law of the Sea of Ignorance: F. A. Hayek, Fritz Machlup, and Other Neoliberals Confront the Intellectual Property Problem," in Plehwe, Slobodian, and Mirowski, eds., *Nine Lives of Neoliberalism*, pp. 79–83.

163. See, e.g., Hans-Hermann Hoppe, "Time Preference, Government, and the Process of De-Civilization: From Monarchy to Democracy," *Journal des économistes et des études humaines* 5, nos. 2–3 (June–September 1994): pp. 319–51.

164. See also Paul Nadal, "How Neoliberalism Remade the Model Minority Myth," *Representations* 163 (2023): pp. 79–99.

165. Young, *The Rise of the Meritocracy*, p. 29. See Barry Sautman, "Theories of East Asian Intellectual and Behavioral Superiority and Discourses on 'Race Differences,'" *positions* 4, no. 3 (Winter 1996): pp. 519–67.

166. Murray, "The Rediscovery of Human Nature and Human Diversity."

167. Denis Dutton, "Building Political Structures with the Crooked Timber of Humanity," MPS Meeting Sydney 2010. MPS Papers, Box 151, "MPS Meeting Sydney 2010" folder (1 of 2).

CHAPTER FIVE: GOLDBUGS

1. For the full debates, see Matthias Schmelzer, *Freiheit für Wechselkurse und Kapital: Die Ursprünge neoliberaler Währungspolitik und die Mont Pèlerin Society* (Marburg: Metropolis, 2010).

2. See J. Neil Schulman, *Alongside Night* (New York: Avon, 1987).

3. See Melinda Cooper, *Counterrevolution: Extravagance and Austerity in Public Finance* (New York: Zone Books, 2024).

4. Bruce Ramsey, "Don't Default on Me," *Liberty*, October 2010, pp. 24, 38.

5. Samuel Edward Konkin III, afterword in J. Neil Shulman, *Alongside Night*, 30th anniversary edition (Pahrump, NV: Pulpless, 2009), p. 274.

6. Harry Browne, *How to Profit from the Coming Devaluation* (New Rochelle, NY: Arlington House, 1970).

7. Harry Browne and Terry Coxon, *Inflation-Proofing Your Investments* (New York: William Morrow, 1981).

8. Shulman, *Alongside Night*, 30th anniversary edition, p. 266.

9. Mark Skousen, "Murray Rothbard as Investment Advisor," in *Man, Economy, and Liberty: Essays in Honor of Murray N. Rothbard*, ed. Walter Block and Llewellyn H. Rockwell (Auburn, AL: Ludwig von Mises Institute, 1988), p. 9.

10. See *Libertarian Review*, January–February 1976, p. 11.

11. For an overview, see Barry Eichengreen, *Globalizing Capital: A History of the International Monetary System* (Princeton, NJ: Princeton University Press, 2008).

12. See Roland Baader, *Geldsozialismus: Die wirklichen Ursachen der neuen globalen Depression* (Gräfelfing: Resch Verlag, 2010).

13. Browne, *How to Profit from the Coming Devaluation*, p. 70.

14. This argument was made most clearly by the so-called neoconservatives. See Melinda Cooper, *Family Values: Between Neoliberalism and the New Social Conservatism* (New York: Zone Books, 2017), pp. 53–64.

15. See Howard Ruff, *How to Prosper During the Coming Bad Years* (New York: Harper & Row, 1979); Douglas E. Casey, *Crisis Investing: Opportunities and Profits in the Coming Great Depression* (New York: HarperCollins, 1979); Harry Schultz, *Panics & Crashes and How You Can Make Money Out of Them* (New Rochelle, NY: Arlington House, 1972).

16. See Harry Browne, *You Can Profit from a Monetary Crisis* (New York: Macmillan, 1974).

17. On the political influence of the direct mail strategies of Richard Viguerie, see Rick Perlstein, *Reaganland: America's Right Turn, 1976–1980* (New York: Simon & Schuster, 2020).

18. See Peter Brimelow, *The Wall Street Gurus: How You Can Profit from Investment Newsletters* (New York: Random House, 1986).

19. Browne, *How to Profit from the Coming Devaluation*, pp. 150, 160, 175–76.

20. Gary Allen and Larry Abraham, *None Dare Call It Conspiracy* (Cutchogue, NY: Buccaneer Books, 1976).

21. Ron Paul, Tribute to Burt Blumert, 155 Cong Rec E 882 (April 2, 2009).

22. Gary North, "It All Began with Fred Schwarz," in *I Chose Liberty: Autobiographies of Contemporary Libertarians*, ed. Walter Block (Auburn, AL: Ludwig von Mises Institute, 2010), pp. 239–47.

23. For a discussion of North, see Cooper, *Counterrevolution*, pp. 351–55.

24. Gary North, *How You Can Profit from the Coming Price Controls* (Durham, NC: American Bureau of Economic Research, 1978).

25. See, e.g., Murray N. Rothbard, "Deflation Or More Inflation?," *Inflation Survival Letter*, June 17, 1974; Murray N. Rothbard, "Inflation or Deflation," *Inflation Survival Letter*, June 4, 1975; Murray N. Rothbard, "Inflation: Its Cause and Cure," *Inflation Survival Letter*, May 19, 1976.

26. James Kirchik, "Angry White Man," *New Republic*, January 7, 2008; Julian Sanchez and David Weigel, "Who Wrote Ron Paul's Newsletters?," *Reason*, January 16, 2008.

27. "Inflation, Gold, and Gold Shares," *Ron Paul Investment Letter*, January 15, 1988.

28. "Say Yes to Gary Allen," *Ron Paul Investment Letter*, September 15, 1988.

29. Hans-Hermann Hoppe, "The European Central Bank and the Coming World State," *Ron Paul Investment Letter*, November 15, 1988; "The Bankster Push for World Government," *Ron Paul Investment Letter*, September 15, 1988; "The Coming World Monetary Order," *Ron Paul Investment Letter*, May 15, 1988.

30. "The Coming World Monetary Order."

31. "The Bankster Push for World Government."

32. "Could It Happen Here?," *Ron Paul Investment Letter,* April 15, 1989.

33. "Beware the Phoenix," *Ron Paul Investment Letter,* February 15, 1988.

34. "What to Expect from the 1990s," *Ron Paul Investment Letter,* December 15, 1989.

35. "We Will Survive, and Prosper!," *Ron Paul Investment Letter,* December 15, 1992.

36. "Surviving the 1990s," *Ron Paul Survival Report,* September 15, 1993.

37. "Haitians for Clinton," *Ron Paul Survival Report,* January 15, 1993.

38. "The Somalian Question," *Ron Paul Survival Report,* January 15, 1993.

39. Jean-Pierre Louvet, *The Coming Investment War-How to Win It* (Gainesville, GA: New Classics Library, 1989).

40. James B. Powell, "How to Protect Yourself Against Urban Violence," *Ron Paul Strategy Guide* (1993), p. 2. This was published as an insert with the *Ron Paul Survival Report.*

41. Ibid., pp. 2, 3, 7.

42. "The Ron Paul Strategy Guide." *Ron Paul Survival Report,* February 15, 1993.

43. "How to Store Your Gold at Home," *Ron Paul Investment Letter,* March 15, 1988.

44. "Foreign Passports, Please," *Ron Paul Survival Report,* June 15, 1993.

45. "Government by Emergency," *Ron Paul Investment Letter,* February 15, 1992.

46. "Don't Trade Your Krugerrands," *Ron Paul Investment Letter,* July 15, 1992.

47. "Using Gold During Chaos," *Ron Paul Survival Report,* September 15, 1994.

48. "A Giant at 65," *Ron Paul Survival Report,* March 15, 1994.

49. "Don't Trade Your Krugerrands."

50. "Blood Sport," *Ron Paul Survival Report,* April 15, 1996.

51. "Racial Central Planning," *Ron Paul Survival Report,* October 15, 1993.

52. "Race Trouble," *Ron Paul Survival Report,* May 15, 1993.

53. "Real Racism," *Ron Paul Survival Report,* March 15, 1993.

54. "Beware the Phoenix."

55. "The Return of the Gold Standard," *Ron Paul Survival Report*, September 15, 1996.

56. "Thank you!" *Ron Paul Survival Report*, December 15, 1996.

57. Sterling, *Islands in the Net*, p. 77; Bruce Sterling, *A Good Old-Fashioned Future* (New York: Bantam Spectra, 1999), p. 148.

58. Stephenson, *Snow Crash*, p. 287.

59. Lionel Shriver, *The Mandibles: A Family, 2029–2047* (New York: Harper Perennial, 2016), p. 234.

60. Jerry Pournelle, *The Mercenary* (New York: Pocket Books, 1977), p. 86.

61. "EuroSham," *Ron Paul Survival Report*, July 15, 1993.

62. "The Bankster Push for World Government."

63. For details see Quinn Slobodian and Dieter Plehwe, "Neoliberals against Europe," in *Mutant Neoliberalism: Market Rule and Political Ruptures*, eds. William Callison and Zachary Manfredi (New York: Fordham University Press, 2019), pp. 89–111.

64. Gerard Radnitzky, "Requiem für die D-Mark," *Eigentümlich Frei* 20 (2001): pp. 18–21.

65. Gerard Radnitzky, "European Integration: Evolutionary Competition against Constructivistic Design," Mont Pelerin Society Meeting, 1990. MPS Papers, Box 143, "General meeting 1990 Conference Papers Drafts" folder.

66. Bruno Bandulet, "Der Todfeind des erfolgreichen Investierens ist die Ideologie," in *20 Jahre eigentümlich frei: Das Buch*, ed. André F. Lichtschlag (Grevenbroich: Lichtschlag Verlag, 2017), p. 34. The www.bandulet.de website includes links to Radnitzky's site, described as "Einer der großen liberalen Denker."

67. See "Germany—2024 State Election Results," Politico, July 2024, https://www.politico.eu/europe-poll-of-polls/germany/.68. André F. Lichtschlag, "Die Libertären und der 'Libertarianism,'" *Eigentümlich Frei* 1 (1998): p. 16.

69. See Murray N. Rothbard, *Eine neue Freiheit: Das libertäre Manifest* (Berlin: Stefan P. Kopp Verlag, 1999); Murray N. Rothbard, *Die Ethik der Freiheit* (Sankt Augustin: Academia Verlag, 1999).

70. André F. Lichtschlag, “Hilfe—die Libertären kommen!,” *Eigentümlich Frei* 10 (2000): p. 35.

71. Gerard Radnitzky, “‘Demokratie’ eine Begriffsanalyse,” *Eigentümlich Frei* 3 (1998): p. 72.

72. Lichtschlag, “Hilfe,” p. 35.

73. Hayek, *The Constitution of Liberty* (Chicago: University of Chicago Press, 2011), p. 169. Hayek also noted that at the time in Switzerland women had no right to vote, “apparently with the approval of the majority of them,” and that a suffrage limited to landowners would be effective in “primitive conditions.”

74. André F. Lichtschlag, “Entzieht den Nettostaatsprofiteuren das Wahlrecht!,” *Die Welt*, September 19, 2006, https://www.welt.de/print-welt/article153823/Entzieht-den-Nettostaatsprofiteuren-das-Wahlrecht.html.

75. On the German New Right, see Volker Weiß, *Die autoritäre Revolte: Die neue Rechte und der Untergang des Abendlandes* (Stuttgart: Klett-Cotta, 2017).

76. Reinhard Stiebler, “‘1. Berliner Kolleg’ des Instituts für Staatspolitik,” *Eigentümlich Frei* 12 (2000): p. 416.

77. André F. Lichtschlag, “Für die libertär-konservative Sezession,” *Sezession* 3 (October 2003): pp. 39–40.

78. Hans-Hermann Hoppe, *Demokratie: Der Gott, der keiner ist* (Leipzig: Manuscriptum, 2003).

79. Hans-Hermann Hoppe, “Demokratie—Der Gott, der keiner ist,” *Sezession* 4 (January 2004): pp. 20–23; Hans-Hermann Hoppe, “Wacht auf, Etatisten!,” *Junge Freiheit*, May 27, 2005.

80. André F. Lichtschlag, “Die ‘17. Libertarian World Convention’ in Berlin,” *Eigentümlich Frei* 4 (1998): p. 135.

81. André F. Lichtschlag, “Autorengespräch: Der Antidemokrat Interview mit Hans-Hermann Hoppe,” *Eigentümlich Frei* 41 (2004): p. 38.

82. Hans-Hermann Hoppe, “Der Staat und die Zuwanderung,” *Eigentümlich Frei* 58 (2005–2006): pp. 16–20. Quotes are from the English original in Hans-Hermann Hoppe, “Natural Order, the State, and the Immigration Problem,” *Journal of Libertarian Studies* 16, no. 1 (Winter 2002): pp. 75–97.

83. Murray [Rothbard] to Fleming, Carlson, Warder, Rockwell Blumert, June 26, 1992. Howard Papers, Box 95, folder 3.

84. Hans-Hermann Hoppe, "Sezessionsbestrebungen als Chance für die Freiheit," *Eigentümlich Frei* 21 (2002), pp. 4–5.

85. Lichtschlag, "Autorengespräch," p. 40.

86. Hans-Hermann Hoppe, "Von der Unmöglichkeit des Sozialismus," *Junge Freiheit*, October 17, 2003.

87. *Eigentümlich Frei* 84 (2008), cover.

88. Jörg Guido Hülsmann, "Liberale Währungreform: Ein Entwurf," *Eigentümlich Frei* 4 (1998): pp. 110–12.

89. See Murray N. Rothbard, *Das Schein-Geld-System* (Gräfelfing: Resch Verlag, 2000); Detmar Doering, "Zurück zum Gold," *Eigentümlich Frei* 12 (2000): p. 429.

90. André F. Lichtschlag, "Editorial," *Eigentümlich Frei* 69 (2007): p. 4.

91. Wladimir Bukowski, "Die EU-Verschwörung," *Eigentümlich Frei* 69 (2007), p. 24. See also his Vladimir Bukovsky and Pavel Stroilov, *EUSSR: The Soviet Roots of European Integration* (Worcester Park, UK: Sovereignty Publications, 2004).

92. Jörg Guido Hülsmann, "Lagebericht vom Schlachtfeld der Ideen," *Eigentümlich Frei* 87 (2008): p. 23.

93. Bandulet, "Der Todfeind," p. 34.

94. "PFP184 | Dürr, Hoppe, Daniels, Kinsella, Discussion, Q&A (PFS 2017)," 2017 Annual Meeting of the Property and Freedom Society, Bodrum, Turkey, 14–19 September, 2017, posted November 1, 2017, by Property and Freedom Society, YouTube, https://www.youtube.com/watch?v=T4-negu-EoE.

95. See Nik De Boer and Jens Van't Klooster, "The ECB, the Courts and the Issue of Democratic Legitimacy after Weiss," *Common Market Law Review* 57, no. 6 (2020): pp. 1689–724.

96. Melanie Amann and Martin Hesse, "Herbstgold," *Der Spiegel*, November 3, 2014.

97. https://web.archive.org/web/20141214184411/https://www.afd-gold.de/aktion.html.

98. Paul Starzmann, "Goldrausch bei der Neuen Rechten," *Zeit Online*, February 8, 2016, https://blog.zeit.de/stoerungsmelder/2016/02/08/goldrausch-bei-der-neuen-rechten_21218.

99. David Bebnowski and Lisa Julika Förster, "Wettbewerbspopulismus: Die Alternative für Deutschland und die Rolle der Ökonomen," *OBS-Arbeitspapier* 14 (2014): p. 8.

100. See Anna Jikhareva, January Jirát, and Kaspar Surber, "Eine schrecklich rechte Familie," *Die Wochenzeitung*, November 29, 2018; Melanie Amann, Sven Becker, and Sven Röbel, "A Billionaire Backer and the Murky Finances of the AfD," *Der Spiegel*, November 30, 2018. https://www.spiegel.de/international/germany/billionaire-backing-may-have-helped-launch-afd-a-1241029.html.

101. "Liberale gründen deutsches Mises-Institut," *Junge Freiheit*, October 26, 2012; Degussa Goldhandel, "Degussa mit Thorsten Polleit als Chefvolkswirt," April 24, 2012, https://www.presseportal.ch/de/pm/100051852/100717017. See, e.g., Thorsten Polleit, "Inflation voraus: Die Botschaft der 'Kreditkrise,'" *Eigentümlich Frei* 103 (2010): pp. 34–36.

102. Jörg Guido Hülsmann, "Ein unorthodoxer Weg zur Knechtschaft," *Ludwig von Mises Institut Deutschland*, October 5, 2012, http://www.misesde.org/?p=2982; Thorsten Polleit, "Die Geldschöpfung 'aus dem Nichts' führt in die Krise," *Ludwig von Mises Institut Deutschland*, September 24, 2012, http://www.misesde.org/?p=2925; Jörg Guido Hülsmann, "Wirtschaft und Ethik: Ein unorthodoxer Weg zur Knechtschaft," *Eigentümlich Frei* 115 (2011); Thorsten Polleit, "Fiat-Geld zerstört die Marktwirtschaft," *Ludwig von Mises Institut Deutschland*, December 19, 2012, http://www.misesde.org/?p=3844.

103. Godfrey Bloom and Patrick Barron, "Eine deutsche Goldmark ist der Schlüssel zur Beendigung der Papiergeld-Inflation," *Ludwig von Mises Institut Deutschland*, December 5, 2012, http://www.misesde.org/?p=3719.

104. Philipp Bagus, "Monetary Reform: The Case for Button-Pushing," *New Perspectives on Political Economy* 5, no. 2 (2009): p. 117.

105. Thorsten Polleit, "Großer Staat entsteht—großer Staat vergeht," Mises.de, November 10, 2017, https://www.misesde.org/2017/11/groser-staat-entsteht-groser-staat-vergeht/.

106. "Politik zwischen Wirklichkeit und Utopie: Zuschauerfragen," Ludwig von Mises Institut Conference 2018, September 15, 2018, posted October 22,

2018, by misesde, YouTube,https://www.youtube.com/watch?v=a3059UtBN5k&list=PLT5CrkVpGB_bMw4m3gIcsmj55K4rWUCTg&index=6.

107. Peter Boehringer, "Roland Baader und das Gold: Materialisierte Freiheit," *Eigentümlich Frei* 120 (2012): p. 36; Peter Boehringer, "Der real existierende Islam," *Eigentümlich Frei* 130 (2013): pp. 52–54 ; "Die Ratio und eine Videokamera im Gepäck," *Eigentümlich Frei* 138 (2013), p. 74.

108. Peter Boehringer, "Wollt ihr den totalen Euro?," *Peter Boehringer Blog*, May 8, 2010, http://www.pboehringer.com/post/wollt-ihr-den-totalen-euro/.

109. Boehringer, "Roland Baader und das Gold," p. 36

110. Peter Boehringer, "Die geistige Vorbereitung," in *Der private Rettungsschirm: Weil ihnen Staat und Banken im Krisenfall nicht helfen werden*, ed. Simone Boehringer (Munich: FinanzBuch Verlag, 2012).

111. Claire Jones, "How Germany Got Its Gold Back," *Financial Times*, November 10, 2017.

112. See Peter Boehringer, *Holt unser Gold heim: Der Kampf um das deutsche Staatsgold* (Munich: FinanzBuch Verlag, 2015).

113. AFP, "Finally Home, Bundesbank's Gold Goes on Show," *The Local Germany*, April 22, 2018, https://www.thelocal.de/20180422/finally-home-bundesbanks-gold-goes-on-show.

114. Peter Boehringer, "Volksbelehrung und Umerziehung: Wir müssen die EU lieben," *Peter Boehringer Blog*, March 30, 2010. http://www.pboehringer.com/post/volksbelehrung-und-umerziehung-wir-muess/.

115. Boehringer, "Roland Baader und das Gold," p. 36.

116. Bewerbung Dirk Driesang, October 3, 2014. Site neither active nor archived. Original is available from author upon request.

117. Boehringer, *Holt unser Gold heim*, p. 27.

118. See Boehringer's "favorite book" by his mentor, Baader, *Geldsozialismus*.

119. See Thilo Sarrazin, *Feindliche Übernahme: Wie der Islam den Fortschritt behindert und die Gesellschaft bedroht* (Munich: Finanzbuch Verlag, 2018).

120. Frank Holmes, "Germans Have Quietly Become the World's Biggest Buyers of Gold," *Forbes*, October 11, 2017.

121. Bruno Bandulet, "DeutschlandBrief: Das Comeback des Goldes," *Eigentümlich Frei* 196 (2019): p. 8.

122. Carsten Korfmacher, "Die Stunde der Crash-Propheten," *Nordkurier*, May 21, 2020, https://www.nordkurier.de/politik-und-wirtschaft/die-stunde-der-crash-propheten-2139440705.html.

123. Jakob Blume, "Degussa-Chef Markus Krall: Provokateur mit Kalkül," *Handelsblatt*, January 16, 2020, https://www.handelsblatt.com/finanzen/maerkte/devisen-rohstoffe/goldhandel-degussa-chef-markus-krall-provokateur-mit-kalkuel/25407060.html; Allan Hall, "The European Commission Is . . . ," *Times* (London), July 12, 2011.

124. Bruno Bandulet, "Review: Krall, Die bürgerliche Revolution," *Eigentümlich Frei* 202 (2020): p. 56. He also published under the pseudonym Diogenes Rant. See Markus Krall, *Verzockte Freiheit: Wehrt euch! Politiker und Finanz-Eliten setzen unsere Zukunft aufs Spiel* (Munich: Finanzbuch Verlag, 2014); *Der Draghi Crash: Warum uns die entfesselte Geldpolitik in die finanzielle Katastrophe führt* (Munich: Finanzbuch Verlag, 2017); and *Die bürgerliche Revolution: Wie wir unsere Freiheit und unseren Wohlstand erhalten* (Stuttgart: Langenmüller, 2020).

125. Markus Krall, " 'Corona wird zu einem Ende des Euro führen': Markus Krall im Interview," interview by Martin Müller-Mertens for CompactTV, March 21, 2020, posted March 21, 2020, by CompactTV, YouTube, https://www.youtube.com/watch?v=8OVQCCE1F8E;Björn Höcke, "Dr. Markus Krall kann als ein wirklicher Kenner des europäischen Bankensektors gelten," Facebook, April 6, 2020, https://www.facebook.com/Bjoern.Hoecke.AfD/photos/a.1424703574437591/2607134486194488/.

126. Markus Krall, "Politik als Pandemie: Großangriff auf die Freiheit," *Eigentümlich Frei* 202 (2020): pp. 24–27.

127. Mathias Pellack, "Markus Krall: 'Der Euro wird nicht mehr akzeptiert werden,'" *Junge Freiheit*, November 9, 2020, https://jungefreiheit.de/debatte/interview/2020/der-euro-wird-nicht-mehr-akzeptiert-werden/; "Markus Krall im JF-Interview: 'Corona ist der erste Dominostein zur Depression,'" *Junge Freiheit*, March 20, 2020, https://jungefreiheit.de/pressemitteilung/2020markus-krall-im-jf-interview-corona-ist-der-erste-dominostein-zur-depression/.

128. Krall, "Politik als Pandemie," p. 25.

129. See Krall, *Die Bürgerliche Revolution.*

130. See Blume, "Degussa-Chef Markus Krall"; Roland Tichy and Markus Krall, "Die bürgerliche Revolution: notwendige Reform unserer Gesellschaft," *Tichys Einblick,* March 22, 2020, https://www.tichyseinblick.de/feuilleton/buecher/die-buergerliche-revolution-notwendige-reform-unserer-gesellschaft/.

131. Dr. Markus Krall, "Gedanken zur Krise," Atlas-Initiative.de, April 4, 2020).

132. Thorsten Polleit, "EinBlick: Weltvirus Sozialismus," *Eigentümlich Frei* 202 (2020): p. 44.

133. "Markus Krall und Max Otte im Gespräch: Was passiert mit unserem Geld?," conversation between Dr. Markus Krall and Dr. Max Otte moderated by Roland Tichy, Goldkammer, Frankfurt, Germany, posted March 22, 2020, by Tichys Einblick, YouTube, https://www.youtube.com/watch?v=px5gXOkwvEY.

134. Henry Sanderson, "Gold Bars in Short Supply Due to Coronavirus Disruption," *Financial Times,* March 23, 2020.

135. Ludwig Mises, *Human Action: A Treatise on Economics* (Auburn, AL: Ludwig Von Mises Institute, 1998), p. 473.

136. James Turk, "Gold as Natural Money," Mises Institute, October 4, 2022, https://mises.org/wire/gold-natural-money.

137. Boehringer, "Die geistige Vorbereitung," p. 22.

CONCLUSION: ROTHBARD'S MASTIFF

1. "No me pises: Argentina's Libertarians," *The Economist,* October 9, 2021.

2. For the same observation, see Ernesto Semán, "Argentina: Into the Abyss," *New York Review of Books,* March 15, 2024.

3. Philipp Bagus, "Rechtspopulismus als erfolgreiche Strategie: Javier Milei," Ludwig von Mises Institut Deutschland, September 8, 2023, https://www.misesde.org/2023/09/rechter-populismus-als-erfolgreiche-strategie-javier-milei/. See also William Callison, "Milei's Chainsaw," *Sidecar,* October 5, 2023, https://newleftreview.org/sidecar/posts/mileis-chainsaw; Tony Wood, "Javier Milei's Agenda," *London Review of Books,* December 14, 2023; Quinn Slobodian, "Monster of the Mainstream," *New Statesman,* November 20, 2023,

https://www.newstatesman.com/ideas/2023/11/javier-milei-argentina-president-monster-mainstream.

4. Vivek Ramaswamy (@VivekGRamaswamy), "Ask yourself what our Founding Fathers would say today & act accordingly," X, February 24, 2024, 5:04 p.m., https://x.com/VivekGRamaswamy/status/1761436837288001622/.

5. Tho Bishop, "Ludwig Von Mises Is the Most Searched Economist in Brazil," *Mises Wire*, Mises Institute, December 15, 2015, https://mises.org/wire/ludwig-von-mises-most-searched-economist-brazil.

6. Alejandro Chafuen, "The 2019 Ranking of Free-Market Think Tanks Measured by Social Media Impact," *Forbes*, April 10, 2019.

7. Jim Epstein, "Libertarians Forged an Alliance with Brazilian President Jair Bolsonaro: Was It a Deal with the Devil?," *Reason*, July 2019.

8. Rafael Ribeiro, "Brazil Pivots toward Economic Freedom," Foundation for Economic Education, May 10, 2019, https://fee.org/articles/brazil-pivots-toward-economic-freedom/. On libertarianism in Brazil, see Jimmy Casas Klausen and Paulo Chamon, "Neoliberalism Out of Place: The Rise of Brazilian Ultraliberalism," in *Market Civilizations: Neoliberals East and South*, eds. Quinn Slobodian and Dieter Plehwe (New York: Zone Books, 2022), pp. 221–48.

9. David Shortell, "Why a Brazilian UFC Star is Championing a Dead Austrian Economist," *CNN*, April 28, 2024, https://www.cnn.com/2024/04/28/americas/analysis-mises-ufc-moicano-economy-intl-latam/index.html. The preceding paragraphs draw from Niklas Olsen and Quinn Slobodian, "Locating Ludwig von Mises: Introduction," *Journal of the History of Ideas* 83, no. 2 (Apr 2022): pp. 260–61.

10. Dieter Plehwe et al., "The Mises Network and Climate Policy. 9 Findings," *Climate Social Science Network*, July 2021, p. 10. https://cssn.org/wp-content/uploads/2021/07/CSSN-Mises-Research-Report.pdf.

11. Semán, "Argentina."

12. Melvin Maddocks, "Fathoming Inflation's an Impossible Feat," *Baltimore Sun*, July 14, 1974.

13. James M. Buchanan, "Transcending Genetic Limits," (working paper, Center for the Study of Public Choice, George Mason University, Fairfax, Vir-

ginia, 1997), https://web.archive.org/web/19990421193138/http://www.gmu.edu/departments/economics/working/wpe1/genetic.htm.

14. Klaus Schwab and Thierry Malleret, *COVID-19: The Great Reset* (Davos: World Economic Forum, 2020).

15. See Quinn Slobodian, "How the 'Great Reset' of Capitalism became an Anti-Lockdown Conspiracy," *Guardian*, December 4, 2020.

16. Isaac Chotiner, "The Contrarian Coronavirus Theory That Informed the Trump Administration," *New Yorker*, March 29, 2020.

17. WisBusiness, "The Bradley Foundation: Announces Dr. Samuel Gregg as a 2024 Bradley Prize Winner," press release, March 27, 2024, https://www.wisbusiness.com/2024/the-bradley-foundation-announces-dr-samuel-gregg-as-a-2024-bradley-prize-winner; "The Bradley Foundation: Announces Dr. Jay Bhattacharya as a 2024 Bradley Prize Winner," press release, April 10, 2024, https://www.wisbusiness.com/2024the-bradley-foundation-announces-dr-jay-bhattacharya-as-a-2024-bradley-prize-winner/.

18. Christopher Mathias, "Richard Hanania, Rising Right-Wing Star, Wrote for White Supremacist Sites under Pseudonym," *Huffpost*, August 4, 2023, https://www.huffpost.com/entry/richard-hanania-white-supremacist-pseudonym-richard-hoste_n_64c93928e4b021e2f295e817.

19. Jeet Heer, "Why Does This Racist Keep Getting Silicon Valley Money?," *The Nation*, August 11, 2023.

20. Mercatus Center, Inc., Form 990 Schedule 1, for fiscal year ending August 2021, https://projects.propublica.org/nonprofits/organizations/541436224/202230409349300513/IRS990ScheduleI.

21. Richard Hanania, "A Psychological Theory of the Culture War," *Richard Hanania's Newsletter*, October 22, 2022, https://www.richardhanania.com/p/a-psychological-theory-of-the-culture.

22. Steven Lagerfeld, "The Revenge of the Nerds," *Wilson Quarterly*, Summer 2004, pp. 28–34.

23. See Garrett Jones, *Hive Mind: How Your Nation's IQ Matters So Much More Than Your Own* (Stanford, CA: Stanford University Press, 2015); Arnold Kling, "Garett Jones on Ultramasculine Economics," *EconLog*, April 12, 2011, https://www.econlib.org/archives/2011/04/garett_jones_on.html.

24. Jacob Siegel, "The Red-Pill Prince," *Tablet*, March 30, 2022, https://www.tabletmag.com/sections/news/articles/red-pill-prince-curtis-yarvin.

25. Curtis Yarvin, "Why I Am Not a White Nationalist," *Unqualified Reservations*, November 22, 2007, https://www.unqualified-reservations.org/2007/11/why-i-am-not-white-nationalist/; Curtis Yarvin, "South Africa: The Solution," *Unqualified Reservations*, October 21, 2009, https://www.unqualified-reservations.org/2009/10/south-africa-solution/.

26. Sam Harris, "Episode 73: Forbidden Knowledge: A Conversation with Charles Murray," *Sam Harris Podcast*, April 22, 2017, https://www.samharris.org/podcasts/making-sense-episodes/73-forbidden-knowledge; Bari Weiss, "Meet the Renegades of the Intellectual Dark Web," *New York Times*, May 8, 2018.

27. Andrew Restuccia, "Trump Fixates on IQ as a Measure of Self-Worth," *Politico*, May 30, 2019, https://www.politico.com/story/2019/05/30/donald-trump-iq-intelligence-1347149.

28. See Charles Murray, *Human Accomplishment: The Pursuit of Excellence in the Arts and Sciences, 800 B.C. to 1950* (New York: Harper Perennial, 2004); Charles Murray, *Human Diversity: The Biology of Gender, Race, and Class* (New York: Twelve, 2020).

29. Jamelle Bouie, "Why an Unremarkable Racist Enjoyed the Backing of Billionaires," *New York Times*, August 12, 2023.

30. See Lionel Shriver, *Mania* (New York: HarperCollins, 2024).

31. *The Origins of Woke* product page, https://www.harpercollins.com/products/the-origins-of-woke-richard-hanania.

32. Curtis Yarvin, "Patchwork: A Political System for the 21st Century (Chapter Two: Profit Strategies for Our New Corporate Overlords)," *Unqualified Reservations*, November 13, 2008, https://www.unqualified-reservations.org/2008/11/patchwork-2-profit-strategies-for-our/.

33. "An Interview with Javier Milei," *The Economist*, September 7, 2023.

Bibliography

Abrahamsen, Rita, Jean-François Drolet, Alexandra Gheciu, Karin Narita, Srdjan Vucetic, and Michael Williams. "Confronting the International Political Sociology of the New Right." *International Political Sociology* 14, no. 1 (2020): pp. 94–107.

"Alice Weidel zieht sich aus Hayek-Gesellschaft zurück." *Welt*, February 1, 2021. https://www.welt.de/politik/deutschland/article225497211/Streit-ueber-AfDler-in-der-Hayek-Gesellschaft-Alice-Weidel-zieht-sich-zurueck.html.

Allen, Gary, and Larry Abraham. *None Dare Call It Conspiracy*. Cutchogue, NY: Buccaneer Books, 1976.

Amann, Melanie, Sven Becker, and Sven Röbel. "A Billionaire Backer and the Murky Finances of the Afd." *Spiegel Online*, November 30, 2018.

Amman, Melanie, and Martin Hesse. "Herbstgold." *Der Spiegel*, November 3, 2014.

Anderson, Digby, ed. *The Loss of Virtue: Moral Confusion and Social Disorder in Britain and America*. London: Social Affairs Unit, 1992.

———. *This Will Hurt: The Restoration of Virtue and Civic Order*. London: Social Affairs Unit, 1995.

Arthur, Chester Alan. "Inside Pat Buchanan." *Liberty*, March 1992, pp. 21–28.

Baader, Roland. *Geldsozialismus: Die wirklichen Ursachen der neuen globalen Depression*. Gräfelfing: Resch Verlag, 2010.

Bagus, Philipp. "Monetary Reform: The Case for Button-Pushing." *New Perspectives on Political Economy* 5, no. 2 (2009): pp. 111–28.

———. "Rechtspopulismus als erfolgreiche Strategie: Javier Milei." September 8,

2023. Ludwig von Mises Institut Deutschland. https://www.misesde.org/2023/09/rechter-populismus-als-erfolgreiche-strategie-javier-milei/.
Baker, Erik. "The Ultimate Think Tank: The Rise of the Santa Fe Institute Libertarian." *History of the Human Sciences* 35, nos. 3–4 (2022): pp. 32–57.
Baker, John R. *Race.* New York: Oxford University Press, 1974.
Bandulet, Bruno. "Der Todfeind des erfolgreichen Investierens ist die Ideologie." In *20 Jahre Eigentümlich Frei: Das Buch,* ed. André F. Lichtschlag, pp. 30–47. Grevenbroich: Lichtschlag Verlag, 2017.
———. "Deutschlandbrief: Das Comeback des Goldes." *Eigentümlich Frei* 196 (2019): pp. 8–10.
———. "Review: Krall, *Die bürgerliche Revolution.*" *Eigentümlich Frei* 202 (2020): p. 56.
"Bankster Push for World Government, The." *Ron Paul Investment Letter,* September 15, 1988.
Bannon, Steve. Interview by Roger Köppel for Weltwoche on the Road, Gotthard, Switzerland, March 5 and 6, 2018. Posted March 5, 2018 by Weltwoche Daily. YouTube. https://www.youtube.com/watch?v=AeJaq599yh4.
Barta Zsófia and Johnston, Alison. Rating Politics: Sovereign Credit Ratings and Democratic Choice in Prosperous Developed Countries. Oxford: Oxford University Press, 2023. Bauer, Peter T. "Development Economics: The Spurious Consensus and Its Background." In *Roads to Freedom: Essays in Honour of Friedrich A. Von Hayek,* ed. Erich W. Streissler, pp. 5–46. London: Routledge & Kegan Paul, 1969.
———. *Dissent on Development.* London: Weidenfeld and Nicolson, 1971.
———. *Dissent on Development.* Cambridge, MA: Harvard University Press, 1976.
———. "Economic Differences and Inequalities." *Modern Age* 19, no. 3 (Summer 1975): pp. 295–306.
———. "Foreign Aid, Forever?" *Encounter,* March 1974, pp. 15–28.
Baum, W. M. "Richard J. Herrnstein: A Memoir." The Behavior Analyst 17, no. 2 (1994): p. 202.
Bebnowski, David, and Lisa Julika Förster. "Wettbewerbspopulismus: Die Alternative für Deutschland und die Rolle der Ökonomen." *OBS-Arbeitspapier* 14 (2014): pp. 1–18.

Beck, Allen J., and Paige M. Harrison. "Prisoners in 2000." *Bureau of Justice Statistics Bulletin*, August 2001, pp. 1–15.

Beck, Naomi. *Hayek and the Evolution of Capitalism*. Chicago: University of Chicago Press, 2018.

Becker, Gary, and Richard Posner. *Uncommon Sense: Economic Insights, from Marriage to Terrorism*. Chicago: University of Chicago Press, 2009.

Belew, Kathleen. *Bring the War Home: The White Power Movement and Paramilitary America*. Cambridge, MA: Harvard University Press, 2018.

"Beware the Phoenix." *Ron Paul Investment Letter*, February 15, 1988.

Biebricher, Thomas. "Neoliberalism and Democracy." *Constellations* 22, no. 2 (2015): pp. 255–66.

———. *The Political Theory of Neoliberalism*. Stanford, CA: Stanford University Press, 2019.

Bishop, Tho. "Ludwig Von Mises Is the Most Searched Economist in Brazil." *Mises Wire*, Mises Institute, December 15, 2015. https://mises.org/wire/ludwig-von-mises-most-searched-economist-brazil.

Bliss, Catherine. *Race Decoded: The Genomic Fight for Social Justice*. Stanford, CA: Stanford University Press, 2012.

"Blood Sport." Ron Paul Survival Report, April 15, 1996.

Bloom, Godfrey, and Patrick Barron. "Eine deutsche Goldmark ist der Schlüssel zur Beendigung der Papiergeld-Inflation." Ludwig von Mises Institut Deutschland, December 5, 2012. http://www.misesde.org/?p=3719.

Blume, Jakob. "Degussa-Chef Markus Krall: Provokateur mit Kalkül." *Handelsblatt*, January 16, 2020. https://www.handelsblatt.com/finanzen/maerkte/devisen-rohstoffe/goldhandel-degussa-chef-markus-krall-provokateur-mit-kalkuel/25407060.html.

Blundell, John. "IHS and the Rebirth of Austrian Economics: Some Reflections on 1974–1976." *Quarterly Journal of Austrian Economics* 17, no. 1 (Spring 2014): pp. 92–107.

Boehringer, Peter. "Die geistige Vorbereitung." In *Der private Rettungsschirm: Weil ihnen Staat und Banken im Krisenfall nicht helfen werden*, ed. Simone Boehringer, pp. 21–94. Munich: FinanzBuch Verlag, 2012.

———. *"Die Ratio und eine Videokamera im Gepäck." Eigentümlich Frei* 138 (2013): p. 74.

———. "Der real existierende Islam." *Eigentümlich Frei* 130 (2013): pp. 52–54.

———. *Holt unser Gold heim: Der Kampf um das deutsche Staatsgold*. Munich: FinanzBuch Verlag, 2015.

———. "Roland Baader und das Gold: Materialisierte Freiheit." *Eigentümlich Frei* 120 (2012): p. 36.

———. "Volksbelehrung und Umerziehung: Wir müssen die EU lieben." *Peter Boehringer Blog*, March 30, 2010. http://www.pboehringer.com/post/volksbelehrung-und-umerziehung-wir-muess/.

———. "Wollt ihr den totalen Euro?" *Peter Boehringer Blog*, May 8, 2010. http://www.pboehringer.com/post/wollt-ihr-den-totalen-euro/.

Boettke, Peter J. "The Theory of Spontaneous Order and Cultural Evolution in the Social Theory of F. A. Hayek." *Cultural Dynamics* 3, no. 1 (1990): pp. 61–83.

———. "Where Did Economics Go Wrong?: Modern Economics as a Flight from Reality." *Critical Review* 11, no. 1 (Winter 1997): pp. 11–64.

Boland, John C. *Wall Street Insiders: How You Can Watch Them and Profit*. New York: William Morrow, 1985.

Bouie, Jamelle. "Why an Unremarkable Racist Enjoyed the Backing of Billionaires." *New York Times*, August 12, 2023.

"Bradley Foundation: Announces Dr. Samuel Gregg as a 2024 Bradley Prize Winner, The." WisBusiness. https://www.wisbusiness.com/2024/the-bradley-foundation-announces-dr-samuel-gregg-as-a-2024-bradley-prize-winner.

Brenner, Johanna, and Maria Ramas. "Rethinking Women's Oppression." *New Left Review*, March–April 1984, pp. 33–71.

Brimelow, Peter. *Alien Nation: Common Sense about America's Immigration Disaster*. New York: Random House, 1995.

———. "Business Schools: Inside View." *Financial Post*, May 25, 1974.

———. "Can You Beat Market? Some Say Yes, Some No." *Financial Post*, July 5, 1975.

———. "The Case against Immigration as We Know It." *Hoover Digest*, April 30,

1998. https://www.hoover.org/researchcase-against-immigration -we-know-it.
———. "Do You Want to Be Paid in Rockefellers? In Wristons? Or How About a Hayek?" *Forbes*, May 30, 1988.
———. "Does the Nation-State Exist?" *The Social Contract*, Summer 1993, pp. 229–34.
———. "Free Markets May Need Cultural Prerequisites." *Financial Post*, February 21, 1989.
———. "Freedom Pays." *Forbes*, June 16, 1997.
———. "I Believe I Will Be At Least Exempted From 'The Curses Of Those Who Come After'—Peter Brimelow's Foreword to the 2013 Kindle Edition of Alien Nation." VDARE.com, August 5, 2013. https://web.archive.org/web/20181011184645/https://vdare.com/articles/i-believe-i-will-be-at-least -exempted-from-the-curses-of-those-who-come-after-peter-brimelow-s -foreword-to-the-2013-kindle-edition-of-alien-nation.
———. "A Green Face Instead of a Red Face?" *Forbes*, December 11, 1989.
———. "Ian Smith's Rhodesia Is Worth Remembering." *Human Events*, May 26, 1979, pp. 8–9.
———. "'Immigration Is the Viagra of the State': A Libertarian Case against Immigration." VDARE.com, June 4, 2008. https://vdare.com/articles immigration-is-the-viagra-of-the-state-a-libertarian-case-against -immigration.
———. "Immigration Shifts Political Loyalties." *Financial Post*, April 5, 1988.
———. "An Interview with Milton Friedman." *Forbes*, August 17, 1992.
———. "Julian Simon and Me." *Forbes*, April 20, 1998.
———. "Letters from the South: 'God Won't Abandon Us.'" *Financial Post*, December 1, 1973.
———. "The Lively Lives of Two Famous Devotees of the 'Dismal Science.'" *Washington Times*, June 14, 1998.
———. "A Man Alone." *Forbes*, August 24, 1987.
———. "'No Water' Economics." *Forbes*, March 6, 1989.
———. *The Patriot Game: Canada and the Canadian Question Revisited.* Stanford, CA: Hoover Institution Press, 1987.

———. "Peter Bauer and the Emperor." Keynote at conference How Does Development Happen?: A Tribute to Peter Bauer, Princeton University, May 6, 2004. https://mediacentral.princeton.edu/media/How+Does+Development+HappenF+A+Tribute+to+Peter+Bauer+++Peter+Bauer+and+The+Emperor/1_1ekvb7fq.

———. "Politics in Command of Learning." *Financial Post*, June 28, 1988.

———. "Privilege-Seeking?" *Forbes*, September 22, 1997.

———. "Refugees Stir Emotion—But Are Cause and Effect Yet Understood?" *Financial Post*, August 25, 1979.

———. "Social Engineers Take Refuge in Human Rights." *Financial Post*, September 14, 1988.

———. "Summer in the Big Apple Far from Rosy." *Financial Post*, August 19, 1978.

———. "Support Grows for Flat-Rate Income Tax Levy." *Human Events*, October 17, 1981.

———. "Time to Rethink Immigration?" *National Review*, June 22, 1992.

———. *The Wall Street Gurus: How You Can Profit from Investment Newsletters*. New York: Random House, 1986.

———. "We're Consistently Wrong on the Soviet Union." *Financial Post*, December 5, 1989.

———. "Why Liberalism Is Now Obsolete: An Interview with Nobel Laureate Milton Friedman." *Forbes*, December 12, 1988.

———. "Why the Blacks Have Declared War on Jews." *Financial Post*, October 6, 1979.

———. "Words of Wisdom from the Cutting Room Floor." *Financial Post*, August 1, 1989.

Brimelow, Peter, and Peter Bauer. "Let Them Work Out Their Own Problems." *Forbes*, February 22, 1988.

Brimelow, Peter, and Milton Friedman. "Beware the Funny Money." *Forbes*, May 3, 1999.

———. "Milton Friedman at 85." *Forbes*, December 29, 1997.

Brimelow Peter and Edwin S. Rubenstein. "L Is for Layoffs." *Forbes*, August 20, 2001.

Brimelow, Peter, and Thomas Sowell. "Human Capital." *Forbes*, July 6, 1988.

Brown, Wendy. *In the Ruins of Neoliberalism: The Rise of Antidemocratic Politics in the West*. New York: Columbia University Press, 2019.

Browne, Harry. *How to Profit from the Coming Devaluation*. New Rochelle, NY: Arlington House, 1970.

———. *You Can Profit from a Monetary Crisis*. New York: Macmillan, 1974.

Browne, Harry, and Terry Coxon. *Inflation-Proofing Your Investments*. New York: William Morrow, 1981.

Brubaker, Rogers. *Grounds for Difference*. Cambridge, MA: Harvard University Press, 2015.

Buchanan, James M. "Transcending Genetic Limits." Working Paper. Center for the Study of Public Choice, George Mason University, Fairfax, Virginia, 1997. https://web.archive.org/web/19990421193138/http://www.gmu.edu/departments/economics/working/wpe1/genetic.htm

Buckley, William F. "Brits, Zulus, Buchanan and Politics." *Detroit Free Press*, February 12, 1992.

Buckley, William F., and Charles Murray. "The IQ Controversy: What's Going On? Part 2." *Firing Line* Transcript, November 29, 1994. Hoover Institution Library & Archives, https://digitalcollections.hoover.org/objects/7228.

Bukovsky, Vladimir, and Pavel Stroilov. *EUSSR: The Soviet Roots of European Integration*. Worcester Park, UK: Sovereignty Publications, 2004.

Bukowski, Wladimir. "Die EU-Verschwörung." *Eigentümlich Frei* 69 (2007): pp. 24–26.

Burgin, Angus. *The Great Persuasion: Reinventing Free Markets since the Depression*. Cambridge, MA: Harvard University Press, 2012.

Callison, William. "Milei's Chainsaw." *Sidecar*, October 5, 2023. https://newleftreview.org/sidecar/posts/mileis-chainsaw.

Callison, William, and Zachary Manfredi. "Introduction: Theorizing Mutant Neoliberalism." In *Mutant Neoliberalism: Market Rule and Political Ruptures*, eds. William Callison and Zachary Manfredi, pp. 1–38. New York: Fordham University Press, 2019.

Campos, Rodrigo Duque Estrada. "The International Turn in Far-Right Studies: A Critical Assessment." *Millennium* 51, no. 3 (2023): pp. 892–919.

Casey, Douglas E. *Crisis Investing: Opportunities and Profits in the Coming Great Depression*. New York: HarperCollins, 1979.

Catlin, Jonathon. "The Authoritarian Personality and Its Discontents." *Journal of the History of Ideas Blog*, January 10, 2018. https://jhiblog.org/2018/01/10/the-authoritarian-personality-and-its-discontents/.

Cattell, R. B. *A New Morality from Science: Beyondism*. New York: Pergamon Press, 1972.

Chafuen, Alejandro. "The 2019 Ranking of Free-Market Think Tanks Measured by Social Media Impact." *Forbes*, April 10, 2019.

Chotiner, Isaac. "The Contrarian Coronavirus Theory That Informed the Trump Administration." *New Yorker*, March 29, 2020.

"A Climate of Anxiety." *New Society* 16 (December 1971): p. 1190.

Cockett, Richard. "The New Right and the 1960s: The Dialectics of Liberation." In New Left, New Right and Beyond: Taking the Sixties Seriously, edited by Geoff Andrews et al. Houndmills, UK: Macmillan, 1999.

Cohen, Robyn L. "Prisoners in 1990." *Bureau of Justice Statistics Bulletin* (1991): p. 2.

Confessore, Nicholas. "How Tucker Carlson Reshaped Fox News—and Became Trump's Heir." *New York Times*. April 30, 2022.

Cook, Eli. "Naturalizing Inequality: The Problem of Economic Fatalism in the Age of Piketty." *Capitalism: A Journal of History and Economics* 1, no. 2 (Spring 2020): pp. 338–78.

Connolly, John. "Of Race and Right." *Irish Times*, December 6, 1994.

"Coming World Monetary Order, The." *Ron Paul Investment Letter*, May 15, 1988.

Cooper, David E. *Illusions of Equality*. London: Routledge, 1980.

Cooper, Melinda. "The Alt-Right: Neoliberalism, Libertarianism and the Fascist Temptation." *Theory, Culture & Society* 38, no. 6 (2021): pp. 29–50.

———. *Counterrevolution: Extravagance and Austerity in Public Finance*. New York: Zone Books, 2024.

———. *Family Values: Between Neoliberalism and the New Social Conservatism*. New York: Zone Books, 2017.

Cordes, Colleen. "'IQ Gap' Linked to Job Lags, Crime." *APA Monitor* 18, no. 2 (February 1987): pp. 20, 22.

Cornelissen, Lars. "Neoliberal Imperialism." *Politics* 4 (2023): pp. 1–17.
Costa, Robert. "At Birthday Party, Kudlow Hosted a Publisher of White Nationalists." *Washington Post*, August 22, 2018.
"Could It Happen Here?." *Ron Paul Investment Letter*, April 15, 1989.
Curzon-Price, Victoria. "Three Models of European Integration." In *Whose Europe? Competing Visions for 1992*, ed. Ralf Dahrendorf, pp. 23–38. London: Institute of Economic Affairs, 1989.
D'Souza, Dinesh. "Racism: It's a White (and Black) Thing." *Washington Post*, September 24, 1995.
The Daily Reporter (Martinville, IN), February 18, 1992.
Davidson, Neil, and Richard Saull. "Neoliberalism and the Far-Right: A Contradictory Embrace." *Critical Sociology* 43, nos. 4–5 (2017): pp. 707–24.
Davis, Gerald F. *Managed by the Markets: How Finance Reshaped America*. New York: Oxford University Press, 2009.
De Boer, Nik, and Jens Van't Klooster. "The ECB, the Courts and the Issue of Democratic Legitimacy after Weiss." *Common Market Law Review* 57, no. 6 (2020): pp. 1689–724.
de Jasay, Anthony. *Against Politics: On Government, Anarchy, and Order*. London: Routledge, 1997.
Degussa Goldhandel. "Degussa mit Thorsten Polleit als Chefvolkswirt," April 24, 2012. https://www.presseportal.ch/de/pm/100051852/100717017.
Deist, Jeff. "The 2016 Election's Silver Lining." LewRockwell.com, November 9, 2016. https://www.lewrockwell.com/2016/11/jeff-deist/time-rebrand-libertarianism/.
———. "For a New Libertarian." Mises Institute, July 28, 2017. https://mises.org/blog/new-libertarian.
———. "Rothbard on Libertarian Populism." LewRockwell.com, December 5, 2015. https://www.lewrockwell.com/2015/12/jeff-deist/populism-path-liberty/.
———. "Self-Determination, Not Universalism, Is the Goal." Mises Institute, May 29, 2017. https://mises.org/blog/self-determination-not-universalism-goal.
Denham, Andrew. *Think Tanks of the New Right*. Aldershot, UK: Dartmouth, 1996.

Denvir, Daniel. *All-American Nativism*. New York: Verso, 2020.
de Orellana, Pablo, and Nicholas Michelsen. "Reactionary Internationalism: The Philosophy of the New Right." *Review of International Studies* 45, no. 5 (2019): pp. 748–67.
DeParle, Jason. "Daring Research or 'Social Science Pornography'?: Charles Murray." *New York Times*, October 9, 1994.
Derbyshire, John. "Charles Murray on Immigration." *National Review*, December 12, 2006. https://www.nationalreview.com/corner/charles-murrayimmigration-john-derbyshire/#:~:text=Regarding%20legal%20immigration%3A-,1.,used%20to%20apply%20to%20everyone.
Devlin, Bernie. *Intelligence, Genes, and Success: Scientists Respond to the Bell Curve*. New York: Springer, 1997.
Diamond, Sara. "Right-Wing Politics and the Anti-Immigration Cause." *Social Justice* 23, no. 3 (Fall 1996): pp. 154–68.
Dionne, E. J. "Buchanan Says Bush Forsakes His Conservative Principles." *Indianapolis News*, December 9, 1991.
Djelic, Marie-Laure, and Reza Mousavi. "How the Neoliberal Think Tank Went Global: The Atlas Network, 1981 to Present." In *Nine Lives of Neoliberalism*, eds. Dieter Plehwe, Quinn Slobodian, and Philip Mirowski, pp. 257–82. New York: Verso, 2020.
Doering, Detmar. "Zurück zum Gold." *Eigentümlich Frei* 12 (2000): p. 429.
Doherty, Brian. *Radicals for Capitalism: A Freewheeling History of the Modern American Libertarian Movement*. New York: Public Affairs, 2007.
"Don't Trade Your Krugerrands." *Ron Paul Investment Letter*, July 15, 1992.
Drolet, Jean-François, and Michael C. Williams. "Radical Conservatism and Global Order: International Theory and the New Right." *International Theory* 10, no. 3 (2018): pp. 285–313.
Ebeling, Richard. "Toward a Hermeneutical Economics: Expectations, Prices, and the Role of Interpretation in a Theory of the Market Process." In *Subjectivism, Intelligibility and Economic Understanding*, ed. Israel M. Kirzner, pp. 39–55. Basingstoke, UK: Macmillan, 1986.
Eichengreen, Barry. *Globalizing Capital: A History of the International Monetary System*. Princeton, NJ: Princeton University Press, 2008.

Eigentümlich Frei 84 (2008).
Epstein, Jim. "Libertarians Forged an Alliance with Brazilian President Jair Bolsonaro: Was It a Deal with the Devil?." *Reason*, July 2019.
"EuroSham." *Ron Paul Survival Report*, July 15, 1993.
Ferguson, Tim W. "The Sleeper Issue of the 1990s Awakens." *Wall Street Journal*, June 23, 1992.
Feser, Edward. "Hayek on Tradition." *Journal of Libertarian Studies* 17, no. 2 (Winter 2003): pp. 17–56.
Feulner, Edwin J. "Waging and Winning the War of Ideas." *The Heritage Lectures* 84. Washington, DC: The Heritage Foundation, 1986.
"Foreign Passports, Please." *Ron Paul Survival Report*, June 15, 1993.
Fougner, Tore. "Neoliberal Governance of States: The Role of Competitiveness Indexing and Country Benchmarking." *Millennium: Journal of International Studies* 37, no. 2 (2008): pp. 303–26.
Francis, Samuel. "The Democrats Take the Lead on Stopping Immigration." *Washington Times*, June 9, 1995.
———. "Illegal Immigration Pressure." *Washington Times*, December 31, 1991.
———. "Rhodesia in Transition." *Heritage Foundation Backgrounder* 62 (August 9, 1978).
———. "The Rhodesian Elections and the Sanctions Issue." *Heritage Foundation Backgrounder* 84 (May 17, 1979).
———. "Up from the Ice Age." *Chronicles*, March 1995, pp. 28–31.
———. "Why Race Matters." *American Renaissance*, September 1994. https://www.amren.com/news/2017/04/why-race-matters-white-identity-sam-t-francis.
Fraser, Steve. *The Bell Curve Wars: Race, Intelligence, and the Future of America*. New York: Basic Books, 1995.
Friedrich, Sebastian, and Gabriel Kuhn. "Between Capital and Volk." *Jacobin*, June 29, 2017. https://jacobin.com/2017/06/germany-afd-cdu-immigrants-merkel-xenophobia-neoliberalism.
Frum, David. "Immigration Needs Reform, Not Abolition." *Financial Post*, April 22, 1995.

Fukuyama, Francis. "Immigrants and Family Values." *Commentary*, May 1993, pp. 26–32.

———. *Trust: The Social Virtues and the Creation of Prosperity*. New York: Free Press, 1995.

Fund, John. "Hayek's Heirs Contemplate Greener Pastures." *Wall Street Journal*, September 19, 1991.

Ganz, John. "The Forgotten Man." *The Baffler*, December 15, 2017. https://thebaffler.com/latest/the-forgotten-man-ganz.

———. *When the Clock Broke: Con Men, Conspiracists, and How America Cracked up in the Early 1990s*. New York: Farrar, Straus and Giroux, 2024.

———. "The Year the Clock Broke." *The Baffler*, November 2018. https://thebaffler.com/salvos/the-year-the-clock-broke-ganz.

Gayre, Robert. "Review: Traitors End by Nathaniel Weyl." *Mankind Quarterly*, October 1971, pp. 119–20.

Geary, Daniel, Camilla Schofield, and Jennifer Sutton, eds. *Global White Nationalism: From Apartheid to Trump*. Manchester: Manchester University Press, 2020.

"Germany—2024 State Election Results." *Politico*, July 2024, https://www.politico.eu/europe-poll-of-polls/germany/.

"Giant at 65, A." *Ron Paul Survival Report*, March 15, 1994.

Gibson, William. *Neuromancer*. New York: Ace Science Fiction, 1984.

Gigot, Paul A. "Potomac Watch: Pat Buchanan Puts Conservatism Back in a Pup Tent." *Wall Street Journal*, December 13, 1991.

Gilman, Sander. "Thilo Sarrazin and the Politics of Race in the Twenty-First Century." *New German Critique* 39, no. 3 (Fall 2012): pp. 47–59.

Giroux, Henry A. "Neoliberal Fascism as the Endpoint of Casino Capitalism." *Fast Capitalism* 16, no. 1 (2019): pp. 7–23.

Giroux, Henry A., and Susan Searls. "Race Talk and the Bell Curve Debate: The Crisis of Democratic Vision." *Cultural Critique* 34 (Fall 1996): pp. 5–26.

Gordon, David. "Hermeneutics versus Austrian Economics (1986)." Mises Institute, April 9, 2015. https://mises.org/library/hermeneutics-versus-austrian-economics.

———. "'Lost in the Move?:' Review of Austrian Economics in America: The

Migration of a Tradition, by Karen Vaughn." *Mises Review* 1, no. 3 (Fall 1995). https://mises.org/mises-review/austrian-economics-america-migration-tradition-karen-vaughn.

———. "'What Should Anti-Economists Do?' Review of the Market Process: Essays in Contemporary Austrian Economics, by Peter Boettke and David Prychitko." *Mises Review* 1, no. 1 (Spring 1995). https://mises.org/mises-review/market-process-essays-contemporary-austrian-economics-peter-boettke-and-david-prychitko.

Gordon, Robert. "SES Versus IQ in the Race-IQ-Delinquency Model." *International Journal of Sociology and Social Policy* 7, no. 3 (1987): pp. 30–96.

Gottfredson, Linda. "Egalitarian Fiction and Collective Fraud." *Society* 31, no. 3 (March–April 1994): pp. 53–59.

———. "The Practical Significance of Black-White Differences in Intelligence." *Behavioral and Brain Sciences* 10, no. 3 (1987): pp. 510–12.

Gottfried, Paul. "The Decline and Rise of the Alternative Right." *American Renaissance*, November 21, 2008. https://www.amren.com/news/2016/08/the-decline-and-rise-of-the-alternative-right/.

———. "Toward a New Fusionism?" *Policy Review* 42 (Fall 1987): pp. 64–70.

Gould, Stephen Jay. *The Mismeasure of Man*, rev. ed. New York: W. W. Norton, 1996.

"Government by Emergency." *Ron Paul Investment Letter*, February 15, 1992.

Graf, Rüdiger. "Human Behavior as a Limit to and a Means of State Intervention: Günter Schmölders and Behavioral Social Science." In *Nine Lives of Neoliberalism*, eds. Dieter Plehwe, Quinn Slobodian, and Philip Mirowski, pp. 143–65. London: Verso, 2020.

Granville, Joseph. *The Warning: The Coming Great Crash in the Stock Market.* New York: FreundlichPress, 1985.

Gutiérrez, David G., and Pierrette Hondagneu-Sotelo. "Introduction: Nation and Migration." *American Quarterly* 60, no. 3 (September 2008): pp. 503–21.

"Haitians for Clinton." *Ron Paul Survival Report*, January 15, 1993.

Hall, Allan. "The European Commission Is. . . ." *Times* (London), July 12, 2011.

Hall, Stuart. "Cultural Studies and the Centre: Some Problematics and Problems." In *Culture, Media, Language: Working Papers in Cultural Studies,*

1972–79, eds. Stuart Hall, Dorothy Hobson, Andrew Lowe and Paul Willis, pp. 2–35. London: Routledge, 1980.

Halpern, Orit. "The Future Will Not Be Calculated: Neural Nets, Neoliberalism, and Reactionary Politics." *Critical Inquiry* 48, no. 2 (Winter 2022): pp. 334–59.

Hammond, Margo. "Race Issue Sours a Needed Debate on Immigration." *Tampa Bay Times*, April 23, 1995.

Hanania, Richard. "A Psychological Theory of the Culture War." *Richard Hanania's Newsletter.* October 22, 2022. https://www.richardhanania.com/p/a-psychological-theory-of-the-culture.

Hardin, Garrett. "Lifeboat Ethics: The Case against Helping the Poor." *Psychology Today*, September 1974.

Harper, F. A. "Liberty: A Path to Its Recovery (1949)." In *The Writings of F. A. Harper*, pp. 205–336. Menlo Park, CA: Institute for Humane Studies, 1978.

Harris, Joshua Lee. "Gadamer, Lavoie, and Their Critics: The Hermeneutics Debate Revisited." *Journal of Markets & Morality* 19, no. 1 (Spring 2016): pp. 61–78.

Harris, Malcolm. *Palo Alto: A History of California, Capitalism, and the World.* New York: Little, Brown, 2023.

Harris, Sam. "Episode 73: Forbidden Knowledge: A Conversation with Charles Murray." *Sam Harris Podcast*, April 22, 2017. https://www.samharris.org/podcasts/making-sense-episodes/73-forbidden-knowledge.

Harrison, Ben. "Reconciliation on the Right." *The Free Market* 8, no. 4 (April 1990): p. 7.

Hawley, George. *Making Sense of the Alt-Right.* New York: Columbia University Press, 2017.

_____. *Right-Wing Critics of American Conservatism.* Lawrence: University Press of Kansas, 2016.

Hayek, F. A. "The Atavism of Social Justice (1976)." In *New Studies in Philosophy, Politics, Economics and the History of Ideas*, ed. F. A. Hayek, pp. 57–68. Chicago: University of Chicago Press, 1978.

_____. *The Constitution of Liberty.* Chicago: University of Chicago Press, 2011.

———. *The Fatal Conceit: The Errors of Socialism*. Chicago: University of Chicago Press, 1988.

———. *The Mirage of Social Justice*. London: Routledge & Kegan Paul, 1976.

———. "Nature v. Nurture Once Again (1971)." In *New Studies in Philosophy, Politics, Economics and the History of Ideas*, ed. F. A. Hayek, pp. 290–94. Chicago: University of Chicago Press, 1978.

———. *Our Moral Heritage*. Washington, DC: Heritage Foundation, 1983.

———. "The Politics of Race and Immigration." *Times* (London), February 11, 1978.

———. "Professor Friedrich Hayek's Closing Speech." March 3, 1984. Speech to Mont Pelerin Society. Margaret Thatcher Foundation Archive, Hayek MSS (Hoover Institution) Box 109,, http://www.margaretthatcher.org/document/117193.

———. *Rules and Order: A New Statement of the Liberal Principles of Justice and Political Economy*. London: Routledge & Kegan Paul, 1973.

Heckman, James J. "Lessons from the Bell Curve." *Journal of Political Economy* 103, no. 5 (October 1995): pp. 1091–120.

Heer, Jeet. "Why Does This Racist Keep Getting Silicon Valley Money?" *The Nation*, August 11, 2023.

Hemmer, Nicole. *Messengers of the Right: Conservative Media and the Transformation of American Politics*. Philadelphia: University of Pennsylvania Press, 2016.

———. *Partisans: The Conservative Revolutionaries Who Remade American Politics in the 1990s*. New York: Basic Books, 2022.

Herbert, Bob. "Throwing a Curve." *New York Times*, October 26, 1994.

Hermansson, Patrik, David Lawrence, Joe Mulhall, and Simon Murdoch. *The International Alt-Right: Fascism for the 21st Century?* New York: Routledge, 2020.

Herrnstein, Richard J., "I.Q." *Atlantic* Monthly, September 1971.

———. *IQ in the Meritocracy*. Boston: Little, Brown, 1974.

Herrnstein, Richard J., and Charles Murray. *The Bell Curve: Intelligence and Class Structure in American Life*. New York: Free Press, 1994.

Holmes, Frank. "Germans Have Quietly Become the World's Biggest Buyers of Gold." *Forbes*, October 11, 2017.

Hoppe, Hans-Hermann. *Demokratie: Der Gott, der keiner ist*. Leipzig: Manuscriptum, 2003.

———. "Demokratie—Der Gott, der keiner ist." *Sezession* 4 (January 2004): pp. 20–23.

———. "Der Staat und die Zuwanderung." *Eigentümlich Frei* 58 (2005–2006): pp. 16–20.

———. "The Economic and Political Rationale for European Secessionism." In *Secession, State and Liberty*, ed. David Gordon, pp. 191–224. New Brunswick, NJ: Transaction Publishers, 1998.

———. "The European Central Bank and the Coming World State." *Ron Paul Investment Letter*, November 15, 1988.

———. "Free Immigration or Forced Integration?" *Chronicles*, July 1995.

———. *Handeln und Erkennen: Zur Kritik des Empirismus am Beispiel der Philosophie David Humes*. Bern: Peter Lang, 1976.

———. "In Defense of Extreme Rationalism: Thoughts on Donald McCloskey's *The Rhetoric of Economics*." *Review of Austrian Economics* 3, no. 1 (Winter 1989): pp. 179–214.

———. *Kritik der kausalwissenschaftlichen Sozialforschung*. Opladen: Westdeutscher Verlag, 1983.

———. "Libertarianism and the Alt-Right: In Search of a Libertarian Strategy for Social Change." Ludwig von Mises Centre (UK), October 20, 2017. https://misesuk.org/2017/10/20/libertarianism-and-the-alt-right-hoppe-speech-2017/.

———. "Nationalism and Secession." *Chronicles*, November 1993, pp. 23–25.

———. "Natural Order, the State, and the Immigration Problem." *Journal of Libertarian Studies* 16, no. 1 (Winter 2002): pp. 75–97.

———. "The Property and Freedom Society—Reflections after Five Years." *The Libertarian Standard*, June 10, 2010. http://libertarianstandard.com/articles/hans-hermann-hoppe/the-property-and-freedom-society-reflections-after-5-years.

———. "Sezessionsbestrebungen als Chance für die Freiheit." *Eigentümlich Frei* 21 (2002): pp. 4–5.

———. *A Short History of Man: Progress and Decline.* Auburn, AL: Mises Institute, 2015.

———. *A Theory of Socialism and Capitalism: Economics, Politics, and Ethics.* Boston: Kluwer, 1989.

———. "Time Preference, Government, and the Process of De-Civilization: From Monarchy to Democracy." *Journal des économistes et des études humaines* 5, nos. 2-3 (June–September 1994): pp. 319–51.

———. "Vom Konzept der Wohlfahrtsmessung der Theorie der Gerechtigkeit—Zur Begründung einer analytischen Theorie der sozialen Wohlfahrt." *Zeitschrift für Politik* 29, no. 4 (November 1982): pp. 403–28.

———. "Von der Unmöglichkeit des Sozialismus." *Junge Freiheit,* October 17, 2003.

———. "Wacht auf, Etatisten!" *Junge Freiheit,* May 27, 2005.

"How to Store Your Gold at Home." *Ron Paul Investment Letter,* March 15, 1988.

HoSang, Daniel Martinez, and Joseph E. Lowndes. *Producers, Parasites, Patriots: Race and the New Right-Wing Politics of Precarity.* Minneapolis: University of Minnesota Press, 2019.

Huf, Ben, Glenda Sluga, and Sabine Selchow. "Business and the Planetary History of International Environmental Governance in the 1970s." *Contemporary European History* 31, no. 4 (November 2022): pp. 553–69.

Hülsmann, Jörg Guido. "Ein unorthodoxer Weg zur Knechtschaft." *Ludwig von Mises Institut Deutschland,* October 5, 2012. http://www.misesde.org/?p=2982.

———. "Fiat-Geld zerstört die Marktwirtschaft." *Ludwig von Mises Institut Deutschland,* December 19, 2012. http://www.misesde.org/?p=3844.

———. "Lagebericht vom Schlachtfeld der Ideen." *Eigentümlich Frei* 87 (2008): pp. 20–25.

———. "Liberale Währungreform: Ein Entwurf." *Eigentümlich Frei* 4 (1998): pp. 111–15.

———. "Wirtschaft und Ethik: Ein unorthodoxer Weg zur Knechtschaft." *Eigentümlich Frei* 115 (2011): p. 56.

Huntington, John S. *Far-Right Vanguard: The Radical Roots of Modern Conservatism*. Philadelphia: University of Pennsylvania Press, 2021.

"In Praise of Huddled Masses." *Wall Street Journal*, July 3, 1984.

"Inflation, Gold, and Gold Shares." *Ron Paul Investment Letter*, January 15, 1988.

"Interview with Javier Milei, An." *The Economist*, September 7, 2023.

Irwin, Ryan M. "Apartheid on Trial: South West Africa and the International Court of Justice, 1960–66." International History Review 32, no. 4 (2010): pp. 619–42.

Jackson, John P. "Baldy Harper and the Racist Right." *Fardels Bear: A History of the Alt-Right*, October 4, 2017. https://altrightorigins.com/2017/10/04/harper-racist-right/.

———. *Science for Segregation: Race, Law, and the Case against Brown v. Board of Education*. New York: New York University Press, 2005.

Jacoby, Russell, Naomi Glauberman, and Richard J. Herrnstein. *The Bell Curve Debate: History, Documents, Opinions*. New York: Times Books, 1995.

Jardina, Ashley. *White Identity Politics*. Cambridge: Cambridge University Press, 2019.

Jikhareva, Anna, January Jirát, and Kaspar Surber. "Eine schrecklich rechte Familie." *Die Wochenzeitung*, November 29, 2018.

Jones, Claire. "How Germany Got Its Gold Back." *Financial Times*, November 10, 2017.

Jones, Garrett. *Hive Mind: How Your Nation's IQ Matters So Much More Than Your Own*. Stanford, CA: Stanford University Press, 2015.

Kamin, Leon. "Scientific American Debunks." *Scientific American* 272, no. 2 (February 1995): pp. 99–103.

Kenny, Michael G. "John R. Baker on Eugenics, Race, and the Public Role of the Scientist." *Isis* 95 (2004): pp. 394–419.

Kiely, Ray. "Assessing Conservative Populism: A New Double Movement or Neoliberal Populism?" *Development and Change* 51, no. 2 (2020): pp. 398–417.

Kincheloe, Joe L., Shirley R. Steinberg, and Aaron David Gresson. *Measured Lies: The Bell Curve Examined*. New York: St. Martin's Press, 1996.

Kinsella, N. Stephan. "History and Principles." Property and Freedom Society, July 20, 2009. http://propertyandfreedom.org/about/.

Kirchik, James. "Angry White Man." *New Republic*, January 7, 2008.

Klausen, Jimmy Casas, and Paulo Chamon. "Neoliberalism out of Place: The Rise of Brazilian Ultraliberalism." In *Market Civilizations: Neoliberals East and South*, eds. Quinn Slobodian and Dieter Plehwe, pp. 221–48. New York: Zone Books, 2022.

Klein, Naomi. *The Shock Doctrine: The Rise of Disaster Capitalism*. New York: Metropolitan Books, 2007.

Kling, Arnold. "Garett Jones on Ultramasculine Economics." EconLog, April 12, 2011. https://www.econlib.org/archives/2011/04/garett_jones_on.html.

Knapp, Peter, Jane C. Kronick, R. William Marks, and Miriam G. Vosburgh. *The Assault on Equality*. Westport, CT: Praeger, 1996.

Konkin III, Samuel Edward. Afterword in J. Neil Shulman, *Alongside Night*, 30th anniversary edition. Pahrump, NV: Pulpless, 2009.

"Koalitionsverhandlungen: Cluster-Sprecher stehen fest." *kurier.at*, October 28, 2017. https://kurier.at/politik/inland/schwarz-blaue-koalition-cluster sprecher-fuer-verhandlungen-festgelegt/294.827.977.

Korfmacher, Carsten. "Die Stunde der Crash-Propheten." *Nordkurier*, May 21, 2020.

Krall, Markus. "'Corona wird zu einem Ende des Euro führen': Markus Krall im Interview." Interview by Martin Müller-Mertens for CompactTV, March 21, 2020. YouTube. https://www.youtube.com/watch?v=80VQCCE1F8E &feature=youtu.be.

———. "Gedanken zur Krise." *Atlas-Initiative.de*. April 4, 2020.

———. *Der Draghi Crash: Warum uns die entfesselte Geldpolitik in die finanzielle Katastrophe führt*. Munich: Finanzbuch Verlag, 2017.

———. *Die bürgerliche Revolution: Wie wir unsere Freiheit und unseren Wohlstand erhalten*. Stuttgart: Langenmüller, 2020.

———. "Politik als Pandemie: Großangriff auf die Freiheit." *Eigentümlich Frei* 202 (2020), pp. 24–27.

———. *Verzockte Freiheit: Wehrt euch! Politiker und Finanz-Eliten setzen unsere Zukunft aufs Spiel*. Munich: Finanzbuch Verlag, 2014.

Krimsky, Sheldon, and Kathleen Sloan, eds. *Race and the Genetic Revolution: Science, Myth, and Culture*. New York: Columbia University Press, 2011.

Kühl, Stefan. *For the Betterment of the Race: The Rise and Fall of the International Movement for Eugenics and Racial Hygiene*. New York: Palgrave Macmillan, 2013.

Lachmann, Ludwig M. "Austrian Economics: A Hermeneutic Approach." In *Economics and Hermeneutics*, ed. Don Lavoie, pp. 132–44. London: Routledge, 1990.

Laclau, Ernesto, and Chantal Mouffe. *Hegemony and Socialist Strategy: Towards a Radical Democratic Politics*. New York: Verso, 1985.

Lagerfeld, Steven. "The Revenge of the Nerds." *Wilson Quarterly*, Summer 2004, pp. 28–34.

Lane, Charles. "The Tainted Sources of 'the Bell Curve.'" *New York Review of Books*, December 1, 1994, pp. 14–19.

Lasch, Christopher. *Revolt of the Elites: And the Betrayal of Democracy*. New York: W. W. Norton, 1994.

Lavin, Talia. *Culture Warlords: My Journey into the Dark Web of White Supremacy*. New York: Hachette, 2020.

Lavoie, Don. "Austrian Models?: Possibilities of Evolutionary Computation." In *The Elgar Companion to Austrian Economics*, ed. Peter J. Boettke, pp. 549–55. Aldershot, UK: Edward Elgar, 1994.

———. "The Market as a Procedure for Discovery and Conveyance of Inarticulate Knowledge." *Comparative Economic Studies* 28 (Spring 1986): pp. 1–19.

Lemann, Nicholas. "Too Many Foreigners." *New York Times*, April 16, 1995.

Levin, Michael. "Why Race Matters: A Preview." *Journal of Libertarian Studies* 12, no. 2 (Fall 1996): pp. 295–321.

"Liberale Gründen deutsches Mises-Institut." *Junge Freiheit*, October 26, 2012.

Lichtschlag, André F. "Autorengespräch: Der Antidemokrat Interview mit Hans-Hermann Hoppe." *Eigentümlich Frei* 41 (2004): pp. 38–43.

———. "Die '17. Libertarian World Convention' in Berlin." *Eigentümlich Frei* 4 (1998): pp. 135–36.

———. "Die Libertären und der 'Libertarianism.'" *Eigentümlich Frei* 1 (1998): pp. 16–17.

———. "Editorial." *Eigentümlich Frei* 69 (2007): p. 4.

———. "Entzieht den Nettostaatsprofiteuren das Wahlrecht!" *Die Welt*, September 19, 2006.
———. "Für die libertär-konservative Sezession." *Sezession* 3 (October 2003): pp. 36–40.
———. "Hilfe—die Libertären kommen!" *Eigentümlich Frei* 10 (2000): p. 35.
Littler, Jo. "Normcore Plutocrats in Gold Elevators." *Cultural Politics* 15, no. 1 (2019): pp. 15–28.
Louvet, Jean-Pierre. *The Coming Investment War—How to Win It*. Gainesville, GA: New Classics Library, 1989.
"Low Arousal Makes British Poor, Professor Says." *Times* (London), September 9, 1969.
Lynn, Richard. *The Chosen People: A Study of Jewish Intelligence and Achievement*. Augusta, GA: Washington Summit Publishers, 2011.
———. *Dysgenics: Genetic Deterioration in Modern Populations*. Westport, CT: Praeger, 1996.
———. *Eugenics: A Reassessment*. Westport, CT: Praeger, 2001.
———. "The Evolution of Racial Differences in Intelligence." *Mankind Quarterly* 32, no. 1 (Fall 1991): pp. 99–121.
———. "Genetic Implications of the Brain Drain." *New Scientist*, March 20, 1969, pp. 622–24.
———. *The Global Bell Curve: Race, IQ, and Inequality Worldwide*. Augusta, GA: Washington Summit Publishers, 2008.
———. "National Planning and Industrial Frustration." In *Growth through Industry*, eds. John Jewkes et al., pp. 143–57. London: Institute of Economic Affairs, 1967.
———. "On Human Diversity: The Global Bell Curve—Updates and Critical Replies." Property and Freedom Society, June 3–7, 2010. Posted by Alt Right Media, August 2, 2013, YouTube, https://www.youtube.com/watch?v=4EWBvUuioSk.
———. *Race Differences in Intelligence: An Evolutionary Analysis*. Augusta, GA: Washington Summit Publishers, 2006.
———. "Race Differences in Intelligence: A Global Perspective." *Mankind Quarterly* 31, no. 3 (Spring 1991): pp. 255–96.

———. Lynn, Richard. Review of Jared Taylor, *White Identity: Racial Consciousness in the 21st Century*. Oakton, VA: New Century Books, 2011. https://store.amren.com/product/white-identity.

———. "Streaming: Standards or Equality?." *Critical Survey* 5, no. 1 (Winter 1970): pp. 26–29.

———. "Self-Control: The Family as the Source of 'Conscience.'" In *The Loss of Virtue: Moral Confusion and Social Disorder in Britain and America*, ed. Digby Anderson. London: Social Affairs Unit, 1992.

Lynn, Richard, ed. *The Entrepreneur: Eight Case Studies*. London: George Allen & Unwin, 1974.

Lynn, Richard, and Tatu Vanhanen. *IQ and Global Inequality*. Augusta, GA: Washington Summit Publishers, 2006.

Machlup, Fritz. *The Production and Distribution of Knowledge in the United States*. Princeton, NJ: Princeton University Press, 1962.

Maddocks, Melvin. "Fathoming Inflation's an Impossible Feat." *Baltimore Sun*, July 14, 1974.

Main, Thomas J. *The Rise of the Alt-Right*. Washington, DC: Brookings Institution Press, 2018.

Marantz, Andrew. *Antisocial: How Online Extremists Broke America*. New York: Viking, 2019.

"Markus Krall im JF-Interview: 'Corona ist der erste Dominostein zur Depression.'" *Junge Freiheit*, March 20, 2020. https://jungefreiheit.de/pressemitteilung/2020/markus-krall-im-jf-interview-corona-ist-der-erste-dominostein-zur-depression/.

Mathias, Christopher. "Richard Hanania, Rising Right-Wing Star, Wrote for White Supremacist Sites under Pseudonym." *Huffpost*, August 4, 2023. https://www.huffpost.com/entry/richard-hanania-white-supremacist-pseudonym-richard-hoste_n_64c93928e4b021e2f295e817.

Mathias, Philip. "Just What Is an Anglo-Saxon?" *Financial Post*, May 11, 1989.

Mayer, Jane. *Dark Money: The Hidden History of the Billionaires Behind the Rise of the Radical Right*. New York: Doubleday, 2016.

McGurn, William. "Let 'Em In: The Argument for Immigrants." *Wall Street Journal*, November 10, 1989.

McIntosh, Matt. "10 Questions for Charles Murray." *Gene Expression*, July 25, 2006. http://www.gnxp.com/blog/2006/07/10-questions-for-charles-murray.php.

Mencimer, Stephanie. "Glenn Beck's Gold Gurus Charged with Fraud." *Mother Jones*, May 19, 2010. https://www.motherjones.com/politics/2010/05/glenn-beck-goldline-weiner/.

Meng, Michael. "Silences about Sarrazin's Racism in Contemporary Germany." *Journal of Modern History* 87 (March 2015): pp. 102–35.

Miller, Jennifer M. "Neoconservatives and Neo-Confucians: East Asian Growth and the Celebration of Tradition." *Modern Intellectual History* 18, no. 3 (September 2021): pp. 806–32.

Milmo, Cahal. "Multi-Millionaire Backers of Climate Change Denial Think-Tank Revealed." *The Independent*, September 2, 2014.

Mirowski, Philip, and Edward Nik-Khah. *The Knowledge We Have Lost in Information: The History of Information in Modern Economics*. Oxford: Oxford University Press, 2017.

Mirowski, Philip, and Dieter Plehwe, eds. *The Road from Mont Pèlerin: The Making of the Neoliberal Thought Collective*. Cambridge, MA: Harvard University Press, 2009.

Mises, Ludwig. *Die Gemeinwirtschaft*. Jena: Fischer, 1922.

———. *Human Action: A Treatise on Economics*. Auburn, AL: Ludwig Von Mises Institute, 1998.

———. *Nation, State, and Economy*. New York: New York University Press, 1983.

———. *Nationalökonomie: Theorie des Handelns und Wirtschaftens*. Geneva: Editions Union Genf, 1940.

———. *Omnipotent Government: The Rise of the Total State and Total War*. New Haven, CT: Yale University Press, 1944.

———. *Socialism: An Economic and Sociological Analysis*. Indianapolis, IN: Liberty Fund, 1981.

———. "Vom Ziel der Handelspolitik." *Archiv für Sozialwissenschaft und Sozialpolitik* 42, no. 2 (1916): pp. 561–85.

Mudde, Cas. *The Far Right Today*. Cambridge: Polity, 2019.

Muller, Christopher. "The Institute of Economic Affairs: Undermining the

Post-War Consensus." In *Ideas and Think Tanks in Contemporary Britain*, eds. Michael David Kandiah and Anthony Seldon, pp. 88–110. London: Frank Cass, 1996.

Murray, Charles. "2006 Atlas Freedom Dinner Keynote Address." *Atlas Highlights*, Winter 2006–2007, pp. 14–25.

———. "Changes over Time in the Black-White Difference on Mental Tests: Evidence from the Children of the 1979 Cohort of the National Longitudinal Survey of Youth." *Intelligence* 34 (2006): pp. 527–40.

———. *Charles Murray and the Underclass: The Developing Debate*. London: IEA, 1996.

———. "Deeper into the Brain." *National Review*, January 24, 2000.

———. *The Emerging British Underclass*. London: IEA Health and Welfare Unit, 1990.

———. *Human Accomplishment: The Pursuit of Excellence in the Arts and Sciences, 800 B.C. to 1950*. New York: Harper Perennial, 2004.

———. *Human Diversity: The Biology of Gender, Race, and Class*. New York: Twelve, 2020.

———. *Income Inequality and IQ*. Washington, DC: AEI Press, 1998.

———. "Investment and Tithing in Thai Villages: A Behavioral Study of Rural Modernization." PhD diss., Massachusetts Institute of Technology, 1974.

———. *Losing Ground: American Social Policy 1950–1980*. New York: Basic Books, 1984.

———. "The Magnitude and Components of Change in the Black-White IQ Difference from 1920 to 1991: A Birth Cohort Analysis of the Woodcock-Johnson Standardizations." *Intelligence* 35 (2007): pp. 305–18.

———. "The Rediscovery of Human Nature and Human Diversity." Mont Pelerin Society Special Meeting, Galapagos Islands, Ecuador, June 22–29, 2013. http://darwinianconservatism.blogspot.com/2013/07/.

———. "Right Questions and Wrong Answers." AEI Lecture, January 8, 2018. YouTube. https://www.youtube.com/watch?v=DDSWxumrGAY&t=1s.

———. *Safety Nets and the Truly Needy: Rethinking the Social Welfare System*. Washington, DC: Heritage Foundation, 1982.

———. "Underclass: A Disaster in the Making." *Sunday Times Magazine*, November 26, 1989.

———. "Underclass: The Crisis Deepens." *Sunday Times*, May 29, 1994.

———. *Underclass: The Crisis Deepens*. London: IEA Health and Welfare Unit, 1994.

———. *What It Means to Be a Libertarian: A Personal Interpretation*. New York: Broadway Books, 1996.

Nadal, Paul. "How Neoliberalism Remade the Model Minority Myth." *Representations* 163 (2023): pp. 79–99.

Nagle, Angela. *Kill All Normies: The Online Culture Wars from Tumblr and 4chan to the Alt-Right and Trump*. Winchester, UK: Zero Books, 2017.

Nash, George H. *The Conservative Intellectual Movement in America since 1945*. Wilmington, DE: ISI Books, 2006.

Neisser, Ulric, et al. "Intelligence: Knowns and Unknowns." *American Psychologist* 51, no. 2 (February 1996): pp. 77–101.

Neiwert, David. *Alt-America: The Rise of the Radical Right in the Age of Trump*. New York: Verso, 2017.

Nelson, Alondra. *The Social Life of DNA: Race, Reparations, and Reconciliation after the Genome*. Boston: Beacon Press, 2016.

New Republic, October 31, 1994.

"No me pises: Argentina's Libertarians." *The Economist*, October 9, 2021.

North, Gary. North, Gary. *How You Can Profit from the Coming Price Controls*. Durham, NC: American Bureau of Economic Research, 1978.

———."It All Began with Fred Schwarz." In *I Chose Liberty: Autobiographies of Contemporary Libertarians*, ed. Walter Block, pp. 239–47. Auburn, AL: Ludwig von Mises Institute, 2010.

O'Sullivan, John. "V-Dare." *National Review*, April 17, 2012.

Olsen, Jon Anstein. "Neo-Darwinian Conservatism in the United States." PhD diss., University of Oslo, 2013.

Olsen, Niklas. *The Sovereign Consumer: A New Intellectual History of Neoliberalism*. Cham, Switzerland: Palgrave Macmillan, 2019.

Olsen, Niklas, and Quinn Slobodian. "Locating Ludwig Von Mises: Introduction." *Journal of the History of Ideas* 83, no. 2 (April 2022): pp. 257–67.

Pavlik, Gregory. P. "Review of Peter Brimelow, Alien Nation." *The Freeman*, December 1995, p. 794.

Pellack, Mathias. "Markus Krall: 'Der Euro wird nicht mehr akzeptiert werden.'" *Junge Freiheit*, November 9, 2020. https://jungefreiheit.de/debatte/interview/2020/der-euro-wird-nicht-mehr-akzeptiert-werden/.

Pemberton, Jo-Anne. *Global Metaphors: Modernity and the Quest for One World.* London: Pluto Press, 2001.

Penner, Mack. "Modes of Influence: The Making of the Calgary School." PhD diss., McMaster University, 2024.

Perlstein, Rick. *Reaganland: America's Right Turn, 1976–1980*. New York: Simon & Schuster, 2020.

"PFP051 | Hoppe, Spencer, Bassani, Gottfried, Lynn, Discussion, Q&A (PFS 2010)." Property and Freedom Society Meeting 2010. Posted Feburary 21, 2018 by Property and Freedom Society, YouTube, https://www.youtube.com/watch?v=upr_FtwWYq8.

"PFP184 | Dürr, Hoppe, Daniels, Kinsella, Discussion, Q&A (PFS 2017)." 2017 Annual Meeting of the Property and Freedom Society, Bodrum, Turkey, 14–19 September, 2017. Posted November 1, 2017, by Property and Freedom Society. YouTube. https://www.youtube.com/watch?v=T4-negu-EoE.

Phillips-Fein, Kim. "Conservatism: A State of the Field." *Journal of American History* 98, no. 3 (December 2011): pp. 723-43.

Pick, Daniel. *Faces of Degeneration: A European Disorder, c. 1848–c. 1918.* New York: Cambridge University Press, 1989.

Plant, Raymond. *The Neo-Liberal State.* Oxford: Oxford University Press, 2010.

Plehwe, Dieter. "Schumpeter Revival?: How Neoliberals Revised the Image of the Entrepreneur." In *Nine Lives of Neoliberalism*, edited by Dieter Plehwe, Quinn Slobodian, and Phillip Mirowski, pp. 120–42. New York: Verso, 2020.

Plehwe, Dieter, Max Goldenbaum, Archana Ramanujam, Ruth McKie, Jose Moreno, Kristoffer Ekberg, Galen Hall, et al. "The Mises Network and Climate Policy." Policy Briefing, Climate Social Science Network, July 2021. https://cssn.org/wp-content/uploads/2021/07/CSSN-Mises-Research-Report.pdf.

Plehwe, Dieter, Quinn Slobodian, and Philip Mirowski, eds. *Nine Lives of Neoliberalism*. New York: Verso, 2020.

Polleit, Thorsten. "Die Geldschöpfung 'Aus dem nichts' führt in die Krise." Ludwig von Mises Institut Deutschland, September 24, 2012. http://www.misesde.org/?p=2925.

———. "Einblick: Weltvirus Sozialismus." *Eigentümlich Frei* 202 (2020): p. 44.

———. "Fiat-Geld zerstört die Marktwirtschaft." Ludwig von Mises Institut Deutschland, December 19, 2012. http://www.misesde.org/?p=3844.

———. "Großer Staat entsteht—großer Staat vergeht." Mises.de, November 10, 2017. https://www.misesde.org/2017/11/groser-staat-entsteht-groser-staat-vergeht/.

———. "Inflation voraus: Die Botschaft der 'Kreditkrise.'" *Eigentümlich Frei* 103 (2010): pp. 34-36.

Poulantzas, Nicos. "The Problem of the Capitalist State." *New Left Review*, November–December 1969.

Pournelle, Jerry. *The Mercenary*. New York: Pocket Books, 1977.

Powell, James B. "How to Protect Yourself Against Urban Violence." *Ron Paul Strategy Guide* (1993), p. 2.

Putnam, Robert D. "Bowling Alone: America's Declining Social Capital." *Journal of Democracy* 6, no. 1 (1995): pp. 223–34.

Rabinbach, Anson. *The Human Motor: Energy, Fatigue, and the Origins of Modernity*. New York: Basic Books, 1990.

"Race Trouble." *Ron Paul Survival Report*, May 15, 1993.

Rachels, Chase. *White, Right, and Libertarian*. Seattle: Createspace, 2018.

"Racial Central Planning." *Ron Paul Survival Report*, October 15, 1993.

Radnitzky, Gerard. "'Demokratie': Eine Begriffsanalyse." *Eigentümlich Frei* 3 (1998): pp. 72-77.

———. "An Economic Theory of the Rise of Civilization and Its Policy Implications: Hayek's Account Generalized." *Ordo* 38 (1987): pp. 47-90.

———. "Requiem für die D-Mark." Eigentümlich Frei 20 (2001): pp. 18–21.

———. "Towards a Europe of Free Societies: Evolutionary Competition or Constructivistic Design." *Ordo* 42 (1991): pp. 139-69.

Ramsey, Bruce. "Don't Default on Me." *Liberty*, October 2010, pp. 24, 38.

Raspail, Jean. *The Camp of the Saints.* Petosky, MI: Social Contract Press, 1994.
"Real Racism." *Ron Paul Survival Report,* March 15, 1993.
Reich, Robert B. "Secession of the Successful." *New York Times,* January 20, 1991.
"Rekindled Flame, The." *Wall Street Journal,* July 3, 1986.
"Rekindled Flame, The." *Wall Street Journal,* July 3, 1989.
"Rekindled Flame, The." *Wall Street Journal,* July 3, 1990.
Restuccia, Andrew. "Trump Fixates on IQ as a Measure of Self-Worth." *Politico,* May 30, 2019. https://www.politico.com/story/2019/05/30/donald-trump-iq-intelligence-1347149.
"Return of the Gold Standard, The." *Ron Paul Survival Report,* September 15, 1996.
Ribeiro, Rafael. "Brazil Pivots toward Economic Freedom." Foundation for Economic Education, May 10, 2019. https://fee.org/articles/brazil-pivotstoward-economic-freedom/.
Richards, Graham. *"Race," Racism and Psychology: Towards a Reflexive History.* London: Routledge, 1997.
Rindermann, Heiner, Oasis Kodila-Tedika, and Gregory Christainsen. "Cognitive Capital, Good Governance, and the Wealth of Nations." *Intelligence* 51 (2015): pp. 98–108.
Robbins, James, and Patrick Buchanan. "The Liberty Interview: Patrick J. Buchanan." *Liberty,* March 1992, pp. 17–20.
Roberts, Paul Craig. "Alien Future." *Chronicles,* July 1995.
———. "I Resign from the Mont Pelerin Society." LewRockwell.com, August 21, 2008.
———. "Sandy Hook Puzzles." paulcraigroberts.org, March 1, 2016. https://www.paulcraigroberts.org/2016/03/01/sandy-hook-puzzles/.
———. "Orlando Shooting—Paul Craig Roberts." paulcraigroberts.org, June 13, 2016. https://www.paulcraigroberts.org/2016/06/13/orlando-shooting-paul-craig-roberts/.
Robertson, Wilmot. *The Ethnostate.* Cape Canaveral, FL: Howard Allen, 1993.
Rockwell, Llewellyn H. "The Case for Paleo-Libertarianism." *Liberty* 3, no. 3 (January 1990): pp. 34–38.

———. "Liberty, Property, and the Austrian School of Economics: Ten Years of the Ludwig Von Mises Institute." Auburn, AL: Ludwig von Mises Institute, 1992.

"Ron Paul Strategy Guide, The." *Ron Paul Survival Report*, February 15, 1993.

Rose, Steven. "The Rise of Neurogenetic Determinism." *Nature* 373 (February 2, 1995): pp. 380–82.

Rossetti, Joshua F. "The Fraser Institute: British Columbia, Canada, and the Neoliberal Thought Collective." MA thesis, Freie Universität Berlin, 2024.

Roston, Aram, and Joel Anderson. "This Man Used His Inherited Fortune to Fund the Racist Right." *Buzzfeed News*, July 23, 2017. https://www.buzzfeednews.com/article/aramroston/hes-spent-almost-20-years-funding-the-racist-right-it.

Rothbard, Murray N. "1996! The Morning Line." *Rothbard-Rockwell Report*, February 1995, pp. 1–12.

———. *Das Schein-Geld-System*. Gräfelfing: Resch Verlag, 2000.

———. "Deflation or More Inflation?" *Inflation Survival Letter*, June 17, 1974, p. 49.

———. *Die Ethik der Freiheit*. Sankt Augustin: Academia Verlag, 1999.

———. "Egalitarianism as a Revolt against Nature." In *Egalitarianism as a Revolt against Nature*, ed. Murray N. Rothbard, pp. 1–20. Auburn, AL: Ludwig von Mises Institute, 2000.

———. *Eine neue Freiheit: Das libertäre Manifest*. Berlin: Stefan P. Kopp Verlag, 1999.

———. "Freedom, Inequality, Primitivism, and the Division of Labor." In Rothbard, *Egalitarianism as a Revolt against Nature*, pp. 247–304.

———. "The Hermeneutical Invasion of Philosophy and Economics." *Review of Austrian Economics* 3, no. 1 (Winter 1989): pp. 45–60.

———. "Inflation: Its Cause and Cure." *Inflation Survival Letter*, May 19, 1976, pp. 148, 57.

———. "Inflation or Deflation." *Inflation Survival Letter*, June 4, 1975, pp. 87–89.

———. "The Nationalities Question (August 1990)." In *The Irrepressible Rothbard*, ed. Llewellyn H. Rockwell, pp. 225–35. Burlingame, CA: Center for Libertarian Studies, 2000.

———. "Nations by Consent: Decomposing the Nation-State." *Journal of Libertarian Studies* 11, no. 1 (Fall 1994): pp. 1–10.

———. "The 'New Fusionism': A Movement for Our Time." *Rothbard-Rockwell Report* 2, no. 1 (January 1991): pp. 1–10.

———. "Race! That Murray Book." *Rothbard-Rockwell Report* 5, no. 12 (December 1994): pp. 1–10.

———. "Right-Wing Populism: A Strategy for the Paleo Movement." *Rothbard-Rockwell Report* 3, no. 1 (January 1992): pp. 5–14.

———. "A Strategy for the Right." *Rothbard-Rockwell Report* 3, no. 3 (March 1992): pp. 1–16.

———. "Toward a Strategy for Libertarian Social Change." Unpublished manuscript (April 1977). https://archive.org/details/Rothbard1977TowardAStrategyForLibertarianSocialChange.

———. "The Vital Importance of Separation." *Rothbard-Rockwell Report* 5, no. 4 (April 1994): pp. 1–10.

Rothbard, Murray N., and Llewellyn H. Rockwell. "For President: Pat Buchanan." *Rothbard-Rockwell Report* 3, no. 1 (January 1992): pp. 1–5.

Rougier, Louis. "Philosophical Origins of the Idea of Natural Equality." *Modern Age* 18, no. 1 (Winter 1974): pp. 29–38.

Ruff, Howard. *How to Prosper during the Coming Bad Years.* New York: Harper & Row, 1979.

Sailer, Steve. "Snow Crash and the Camp of the Saints." *iSteve,* May 27, 2006. https://isteve.blogspot.com/2006/05/snow-crash-and-camp-of-saints.html.

Saini, Angela. *Superior: The Return of Race Science.* Boston: Beacon Press, 2019.

Samorodnitsky, Dan et al. "Journals That Published Richard Lynn's Racist 'Research' Articles Should Retract Them." Stat, June 20, 2024. https://www.statnews.com/2024/06/20/richard-lynn-racist-research-articles-journals-retractions/.

Sanchez, Julian, and David Weigel. "Who Wrote Ron Paul's Newsletters?" *Reason,* January 16, 2008.

Sanderson, Henry. "Gold Bars in Short Supply Due to Coronavirus Disruption." *Financial Times,* March 23, 2020.

Sarrazin, Thilo. *Deutschland schafft sich ab*. Munich: Deutsche Verlags Anstalt, 2010.

———. *Feindliche Übernahme: Wie der Islam den Fortschritt behindert und die Gesellschaft bedroht*. Munich: Finanzbuch Verlag, 2018.

Saul, John Ralston. *Voltaire's Bastards: The Dictatorship of Reason in the West*. New York: Vintage Books, 1993.

Saull, Richard. "Racism and Far Right Imaginaries within Neo-Liberal Political Economy." *New Political Economy* 23, no. 5 (2018): pp. 588–608.

Sautman, Barry. "Theories of East Asian Intellectual and Behavioral Superiority and Discourses on 'Race Differences.'" *positions* 4, no. 3 (Winter 1996): pp. 519–67.

Saxon, Wolfgang. "Stefan T. Possony, 82, a Scholar of International Security Affairs." *New York Times*, May 2, 1995.

"Say Yes to Gary Allen." *Ron Paul Investment Letter*, September 15, 1988.

Schirrmacher, Frank. "Thilo Sarrazin im Streitgespräch." *Frankfurter Allgemeine Zeitung*, October 1, 2010.

Schmelzer, Matthias. *Freiheit für Wechselkurse und Kapital: Die Ursprünge neoliberaler Währungspolitik und die Mont Pèlerin Society*. Marburg: Metropolis, 2010.

Schulman, J. Neil. *Alongside Night*. New York: Avon, 1987.

Schultz, Harry. *Panics & Crashes and How You Can Make Money out of Them*. New Rochelle, NY: Arlington House, 1972.

Schwab, Klaus, and Thierry Malleret. *Covid-19: The Great Reset*. Davos: World Economic Forum, 2020.

Schwartz, Pedro. "The Market and the Metamarket: A Review of the Contributions of the Economic Theory of Property Rights." In *Socialism: Institutional, Philosophical and Economic Issues*, ed. Svetozar Pejovich, pp. 11–32. Dordrecht: Kluwer Academic, 1987.

Seligman, Daniel. "Foretelling the Bell Curve." *National Review*, December 19, 1994.

———. "A Substantial Inheritance." *National Review*, October 10, 1994.

Seligman, Daniel, and William Sheeline. "Brainstorms." *Fortune*, August 3, 1987.

Semán, Ernesto. "Argentina: Into the Abyss." *New York Review of Books*, March 15, 2024.

Sessions, David. "Man, Machines, and Modernity: Inventing 'Industrial Society' in French Social Science, 1930–1975." PhD diss., Boston College, 2021.

Shammas, Victor L. "Burying Mont Pèlerin: Milton Friedman and Neoliberal Vanguardism." *Constellations* 25, no. 1 (March 2018): pp. 117–3. https://onlinelibrary.wiley.com/doi/10.1111/1467-8675.12322.

Shenfield, Arthur. "Equality before the Law." *Modern Age* 17, no. 2 (Spring 1973): pp. 114–24.

———. "The Ideological War against Western Society." *Modern Age* 14, no. 2 (Spring 1970): pp. 158–73.

Shilliam, Robbie. "Enoch Powell: Britain's First Neoliberal Politician." *New Political Economy* 26, no. 2 (2021): pp. 239–49.

Shortell, David. "Why a Brazilian UFC Star is Championing a Dead Austrian Economist." *CNN*, April 28, 2024. https://www.cnn.com/2024/04/28/americas/analysis-mises-ufc-moicano-economy-intl-latam/index.html.

Shriver, Lionel. *The Mandibles: A Family, 2029–2047*. New York: Harper Perennial, 2016.

———. *Mania*. New York: HarperCollins, 2024.

Siegel, Jacob. "The Alt-Right's Jewish Godfather." *Tablet*, November 29, 2016. http://www.tabletmag.com/jewish-news-and-politics/218712/spencer-gottfried-alt-right/.

———. "The Red-Pill Prince." *Tablet*, March 30, 2022. https://www.tabletmag.com/sections/news/articles/red-pill-prince-curtis-yarvin.

Simon, Julian. *The Economic Consequences of Immigration into the United States* (1989). http://www.juliansimon.com/writings/Immigration/.

———. *The Ultimate Resource*. Princeton, NJ: Princeton University Press, 1981.

Singerman, David Roth. "Keynesian Eugenics and the Goodness of the World." *Journal of British Studies* 55 (July 2016): pp. 538–65.

"Simpson-Volstead-Mazzoli." *Wall Street Journal*, July 3, 1987

Skousen, Mark. "Murray Rothbard as Investment Advisor." In *Man, Economy, and Liberty: Essays in Honor of Murray N. Rothbard*, edited by Walter Block

and Llewellyn H. Rockwell. Auburn, AL: Ludwig von Mises Institute, 1988.
Slobodian, Quinn. "Anti-68ers and the Racist-Libertarian Alliance: How a Schism among Austrian School Neoliberals Helped Spawn the Alt Right." *Cultural Politics* 15, no. 3 (2019): pp. 372–86.
——. "The Backlash against Neoliberal Globalization from Above: Elite Origins of the Crisis of the New Constitutionalism." *Theory, Culture & Society* 38, no. 6 (2021): pp. 51–69.
——. *Crack-up Capitalism: Market Radicals and the Dream of a World without Democracy*. New York: Metropolitan Books, 2023.
——. *Globalists: The End of Empire and the Birth of Neoliberalism*. Cambridge, MA: Harvard University Press, 2018.
——. "How the 'Great Reset' of Capitalism Became an Anti-Lockdown Conspiracy." *Guardian*, December 4, 2020.
——. "The Law of the Sea of Ignorance: F. A. Hayek, Fritz Machlup, and Other Neoliberals Confront the Intellectual Property Problem." In *Nine Lives of Neoliberalism*, eds. Dieter Plehwe, Quinn Slobodian and Philip Mirowski, pp. 70–92. New York: Verso, 2019.
——. "Monster of the Mainstream." *New Statesman*, November 20, 2023.
——. "The World Economy and the Color Line: Wilhelm Röpke, Apartheid, and the White Atlantic." *German Historical Institute Bulletin Supplement* 10 (2014): pp. 61–87.
——. "World Maps for the Debt Paradigm: Risk Ranking the Poorer Nations in the 1970s." *Critical Historical Studies* 8, no. 1 (Spring 2021): pp. 1–22.
Slobodian, Quinn, and Dieter Plehwe. "Neoliberals against Europe." In *Mutant Neoliberalism: Market Rule and Political Ruptures*, eds. William Callison and Zachary Manfredi, pp. 89–111. New York: Fordham University Press, 2019.
Snyder, Timothy. *The Road to Unfreedom: Russia, Europe, America*. New York: Tim Duggan Books, 2018.
"Somalian Question, The." *Ron Paul Survival Report*, January 15, 1993.
"Soviets' 500 Day Plan Debated at Cato Round Table." *Cato Policy Report* 1 (1991): p. 4.
Sowell, Thomas. "Ethnicity and IQ." *The American Spectator*, February 1995.

"Speakers." The Mont Pelerin Society Special Meeting June 22 to 29, 2013, University of San Francisco de Quito. https://www.usfq.edu.ec/en/events/mont-pelerin-society-special-meeting-june-22-29-2013.

Spencer, Richard. "The 'Alternative Right' in America." Lecture, Property and Freedom Society meeting 2010. Posted February 21, 2018, by Property and Freedom Society. YouTube. https://www.youtube.com/watch?v=XgPNVNE8C6M.

Starzmann, Paul. "Goldrausch bei der neuen Rechten." *Zeit Online*, February 8, 2016. https://blog.zeit.de/stoerungsmelder/2016/02/08/goldrausch-bei-der-neuen-rechten_21218.

Stephenson, Neal. *Snow Crash*. New York: Del Rey, 1992.

Sterling, Bruce. *A Good Old-Fashioned Future*. New York: Bantam Spectra, 1999.

———. *Islands in the Net*. New York: Ace Books, 1988.

Stern, Alexander Minna. *Proud Boys and the White Ethnostate: How the Alt-Right Is Warping the American Imagination*. Boston: Beacon Press, 2019.

"Steve Bannon's Full Speech in France." *Washington Post*, March 23, 2018.

Stiebler, Reinhard. "'1. Berliner Kolleg' des Instituts für Staatspolitik." *Eigentümlich Frei* 12 (2000): pp. 416–17.

"Surviving the 1990s." *Ron Paul Survival Report*, September 15, 1993.

Tanton, John. "The Camp of the Saints Revisited." *The Social Contract*, Winter 1994–95, p. 83.

Taylor, Charles. "The Politics of Recognition." In *Multiculturalism and the Politics of Recognition*, ed. Amy Gutmann, pp. 25–74. Princeton, NJ: Princeton University Press, 1992.

Taylor, Jared. "Fairest Things Have Fleetest Endings." *American Renaissance*, June 1995. https://www.amren.com/news/2017/03/camp-of-the-saints-jean-raspail-muslim-immigration-european-suicide/.

Teitelbaum, Benjamin R. *War for Eternity: Inside Bannon's Far-Right Circle of Global Power Brokers*. New York: Dey Street Books, 2020.

"Thank you!" *Ron Paul Survival Report*, December 15, 1996.

Tichy, Roland, and Markus Krall. "Die bürgerliche Revolution: Notwendige Reform unserer Gesellschaft." *Tichys Einblick*, March 22, 2020. https://

www.tichyseinblick.de/feuilleton/buecher/die-buergerliche-revolution-notwendige-reform-unserer-gesellschaft/.

Tischauser Jeff, and Kevin Musgrave. "Far-Right Media as Imitated Counter-publicity: A Discourse Analysis on Racial Meaning and Identity on Vdare.com." *Howard Journal of Communications* 31, no. 3 (2020): pp. 282–96.

Todd Jr., Jesse E. "The Horror of Immigration." *Daily Press* (Newport News, VA), July 9, 1995.

Tucker, William H. *The Cattell Controversy: Race, Science, and Ideology.* Urbana: University of Illinois Press, 2009.

———. *The Funding of Scientific Racism: Wickliffe Draper and the Pioneer Fund.* Urbana: University of Illinois Press, 2002.

Turk, James. "Gold as Natural Money." Mises Institute, October 4, 2022. https://mises.org/wire/gold-natural-money.

Tyler, C. K. "'Disadvantaged' May Pay New Tax." *Washington Times,* July 18, 1993.

"Using Gold During Chaos." *Ron Paul Survival Report,* September 15, 1994.

Velasco, Gustavo R. "On Equality and Egalitarianism." *Modern Age,* Winter 1974, pp. 21–28.

Ventresca, Roberto. "Neoliberal Thinkers and European Integration in the 1980s and the Early 1990s." *Contemporary European History* 31, no. 1 (2022): pp. 31–47.

Vettese, Troy. "Limits and Cornucopianism: A History of Neo-Liberal Environmental Thought, 1920–2007." PhD diss., New York University, 2019.

Vials, Christopher. "Empire after Liberalism: The Transatlantic Right and Identitarian War." *Journal of American Studies* 56, no. 1 (2022): pp. 87–112.

Wainer, Howard, and Daniel H. Robinson. "Profiles in Research: Linda S. Gottfredson." *Journal of Educational and Behavioral Statistics* 34, no. 3 (September 2009): pp. 395–427.

Walker, Martin. "Dark Dreamer of Star Wars." *Guardian,* May 5, 1995.

Walker, Michael A., ed. *Freedom, Democracy and Economic Welfare: Proceedings of an International Symposium.* Vancouver: Fraser Institute, 1988.

Walpen, Bernhard. *Die offenen Feinde und ihre Gesellschaft: Eine hegemonie-theoretische Studie zur Mont Pelerin Society.* Hamburg: VSA-Verlag, 2004.

Walsh, David Austin. *Taking America Back: The Conservative Movement and the Far Right.* New Haven, CT: Yale University Press, 2024.

Wasserman, Janek. *Marginal Revolutionaries: How Austrian Economics Fought the War of Ideas.* New Haven, CT: Yale University Press, 2019.

Wattenberg, Ben J. *The First Universal Nation: Leading Indicators and Ideas about the Surge of America in the 1990s.* New York: Free Press, 1992.

Weede, Erich. "Mass Immigration: Cost or Benefit?" *Hungarian Review* 6 (June 2015): pp. 8–17.

———. "Ungleichheit als Schicksal und Notwendigkeit." In *Soziologie der sozialen Ungleichheit*, ed. Bernhard Giesen and Hans Haferkamp, pp. 189–220. Opladen: Westdeutscher Verlag, 1987.

———. "Vertragen die alternden europäischen Sozialstaaten die Massenzuwanderung, die wir haben?" *Orientierungen zur Wirtschafts- und Gesellschaftspolitik* 143 (June 2016): pp. 54–66.

———. "Welche Art der Einwanderung braucht unser Land?" Forum Freiheit 2017 "Die Zukunft der Freiheit," November 7, 2017. https://hayek.de/wp-content/uploads/2017/10/Weede-Welche-Einwandg.-braucht-unser-Land.pdf.

"We Will Survive, and Prosper!." Ron Paul Investment Letter, December 15, 1992.

Weede, Erich, and Sebastian Kämpf. "The Impact of Intelligence and Institutional Improvements on Economic Growth." *Kyklos* 55, no. 3 (2002): pp. 361–80.

Weiss, Bari. "Meet the Renegades of the Intellectual Dark Web." *New York Times*, May 8, 2018.

Weiß, Volker. *Die autoritäre Revolte: Die neue Rechte und der Untergang des Abendlandes.* Stuttgart: Klett-Cotta, 2017.

"Welcome Back, Peter." *Financial Post*, March 11, 1978.

Wendling, Mike. *Alt-Right: From 4chan to the White House.* London: Pluto Press, 2018.

Weyl, Nathaniel. "Envy and Aristocide in Underdeveloped Countries." *Modern Age* 18, no. 1 (Winter 1974): pp. 39–52.

———. *Traitors' End: The Rise and Fall of the Communist Movement in Southern Africa.* New Rochelle, NY: Arlington House, 1970.

Weyl, Nathaniel, and Stefan Possony. *The Geography of Intellect*. Chicago: Henry Regnery, 1963.

"What to Expect from the 1990s." *Ron Paul Investment Letter*, December 15, 1989.

Wheatley, Natasha. *The Life and Death of States: Central Europe and the Transformation of Modern Sovereignty*. Princeton, NJ: Princeton University Press, 2023.

"Who Speaks for Us?" *American Renaissance* 1, no. 1 (November 1990). https://www.amren.com/archives/back-issues/november-1990/#cover.

Whyte, Jessica. *The Morals of the Market: Human Rights and the Rise of Neoliberalism*. New York: Verso, 2019.

Wicherts, Jelte M. et al. "Another Failure to Replicate Lynn's Estimate of the Average IQ of Sub-Saharan Africans." *Learning and Individual Differences* 20, no. 3 (June 2010): pp. 155–57.

Williams, Thomas D. "Exclusive Interview with German Populist AfD Leader Beatrix Von Storch." Breitbart News Network, September 29, 2017. http://www.breitbart.com/london/2017/09/29/exclusive-interview-german-populist-afd-leader-beatrix-von-storch/.

Williamson, John. "What Washington Means by Policy Reform." In *Latin American Adjustment: How Much Has Happened?*, ed. John Williamson, pp. 7–20. Washington, DC: Institute for International Economics, 1990.

Wilson, E. O. *Sociobiology: The New Synthesis*. Cambridge, MA: Belknap Press of Harvard University Press, 1975.

Winston, Andrew S. "Neoliberalism and IQ: Naturalizing Economic and Racial Inequality." *Theory & Psychology* 28, no. 5 (2018): pp. 600–18.

Witt, Ulrich. "Evolutionary Economics." In *The Elgar Companion to Austrian Economics*, ed. Peter J. Boettke, pp. 541–48. Aldershot, UK: Edward Elgar, 1994.

Wolfe, Tom. "1988 Wriston Lecture: Fact and Fiction in the New York of the Eighties." Manhattan Institute. https://www.manhattan-institute.org/html/1988-wriston-lecture-fact-and-fiction-new-york-eighties-6392.html.

Wolpoff, Milford H., and Rachel Caspari, *Race and Human Evolution*. New York: Simon & Schuster, 1997.

Wood, Tony. "Javier Milei's Agenda." *London Review of Books*, December 14, 2023.

Yarvin, Curtis, "Patchwork: A Political System for the 21st Century (Chapter Two: Profit Strategies for Our New Corporate Overlords)." *Unqualified Reservations*, November 13, 2008. https://www.unqualified-reservations.org/2008/11/patchwork-2-profit-strategies-for-our/.

———. "South Africa: The Solution." *Unqualified Reservations*, October 21, 2009. https://www.unqualified-reservations.org/2009/10/south-africa-solution/.

———. "Why I Am Not a White Nationalist." *Unqualified Reservations*, November 22, 2007. https://www.unqualified-reservations.org/2007/11/why-i-am-not-white-nationalist/.

Young, Michael. *The Rise of the Meritocracy, 1870–2033*. London: Penguin Books, 1958.

———. *The Rise of the Meritocracy, 1870–2033*. 2nd ed. New Brunswick, NJ: Transaction Publishers, 1994.

Zolberg, Aristide R. *A Nation by Design: Immigration Policy in the Fashioning of America*. Cambridge, MA: Harvard University Press, 2008.

Zuckerberg, Donna. *Not All Dead White Men: Classics and Misogyny in the Digital Age*. Cambridge, MA: Harvard University Press, 2018.

Index

Near Futures series design by Julie Fry
Typesetting by Meighan Gale
Printed and bound by Maple Press